# Banking and Economic Rent in Asia

A stable and sound financial system plays a critical role in mediating funds from surplus units to investors, making it a prerequisite for economic development. Financial intermediaries have been vulnerable to adverse changes in the local and global economy and experienced frequent bubble-and-bust episodes historically. Analyses of financial crises reveal that the incentive created by neo-liberal financial principles is inconsistent with stable financial systems, and viable solutions require structuring institutions in a way that incentives are well aligned with the fundamental principles of financial systems.

By drawing on the theoretical framework of the financial restraint model, this book analyses financial sectors' rents or bank rents and their effects on banks' performance and stability, and presents evidence on the relationship between rent and incentive through case studies of both developed and developing countries.

**Yasushi Suzuki** is Professor at Ritsumeikan Asia Pacific University, Japan.

**Mohammad Dulal Miah** is Assistant Professor at the University of Nizwa, Oman.

**Manjula K. Wanniarachchige** is a Senior Lecturer at the University of Ruhuna, Sri Lanka.

**S. M. Sohrab Uddin** is Professor at the University of Chittagong, Bangladesh.

# Routledge International Studies in Money and Banking

For a full list of titles in this series, please visit www.routledge.com/series/SE0403.

82 **The Global Financial Crisis and the New Monetary Consensus**
*Marc Pilkington*

83 **A New Measure of Competition in the Financial Industry**
The Performance-Conduct-structure indicator
*Edited by Jacob A. Bikker and Michiel van Leuvensteijn*

84 **Money, Valuation and Growth**
Conceptualizations and Contradictions of the Money Economy
*Hasse Ekstedt*

85 **European Banking Union**
Prospects and Challenges
*Edited by Juan E. Castañeda, David G. Mayes, and Geoffrey Wood*

86 **Wages, Bonuses and Appropriation of Profit in the Financial Industry**
The Working Rich
*Olivier Godechot*

87 **Banking and Monetary Policies in a Changing Financial Environment**
A Regulatory Approach
*Wassim Shahin and Elias El-Achkar*

88 **Modern Monetary Theory and European Macroeconomics**
*Dirk H. Ehnts*

89 **Capital Flows, Financial Markets and Banking Crises**
*Chia-Ying Chang*

90 **Banking and Economic Rent in Asia**
Rent Effects, Financial Fragility, and Economic Development
*Edited by Yasushi Suzuki, Mohammad Dulal Miah, Manjula K. Wanniarachchige, and S. M. Sohrab Uddin*

# Banking and Economic Rent in Asia

Rent Effects, Financial Fragility, and Economic Development

**Edited by
Yasushi Suzuki, Mohammad Dulal
Miah, Manjula K. Wanniarachchige,
and S. M. Sohrab Uddin**

Routledge
Taylor & Francis Group

LONDON AND NEW YORK

First published 2017
by Routledge

2 Park Square, Milton Park, Abingdon, Oxfordshire OX14 4RN
52 Vanderbilt Avenue, New York, NY 10017

*Routledge is an imprint of the Taylor & Francis Group, an informa business*

First issued in paperback 2019

*British Library Cataloguing-in-Publication Data*
A catalogue record for this book is available from the British Library

*Library of Congress Cataloging-in-Publication Data*
A catalog record for this book has been requested

ISBN: 978-1-138-67532-2 (hbk)
ISBN: 978-0-367-35056-7 (pbk)

Typeset in Galliard
by Apex CoVantage, LLC

# Contents

*List of figures*                                                     vii
*List of tables*                                                       ix
*List of contributors*                                                  x
*Preface*                                                              xi
*Acknowledgements*                                                    xii

**Introduction**                                                        1

**PART I**
**Theoretical framework for empirical analyses**                       11

1   **Overview of theories of financial sector rent and bank
    rent opportunities: a critical view**                              13
    YASUSHI SUZUKI, MOHAMMAD DULAL MIAH, AND
    MANJULA K. WANNIARACHCHIGE

2   **Banks as financial intermediaries and their roles in
    economic development**                                             26
    MANJULA K. WANNIARACHCHIGE, MOHAMMAD DULAL MIAH,
    AND YASUSHI SUZUKI

3   **Creating bank rent in developing countries:
    an integrated model**                                              38
    MANJULA K. WANNIARACHCHIGE

4   **A new conceptualization of Islamic bank rent**                   58
    YASUSHI SUZUKI AND S. M. SOHRAB UDDIN

**PART II**
## Empirical studies

69

5 China's non-performing bank loan crisis: the role
of economic rents 71
YASUSHI SUZUKI AND MOHAMMAD DULAL MIAH

6 Bank rent, bank performance, and financial stability
in Sri Lanka 86
MANJULA K. WANNIARACHCHIGE

7 Islamic bank rent: comparison among Bangladesh,
Indonesia, Malaysia, and Pakistan 121
YASUSHI SUZUKI, S. M. SOHRAB UDDIN, SIGIT PRAMONO,
AND SHOAIB KHAN

8 Financial sector rents in GCC countries: are Islamic
banks different? 138
YASUSHI SUZUKI AND MOHAMMAD DULAL MIAH

9 Japan's quantitative easing policy: implications
for bank rents 156
YASUSHI SUZUKI AND MOHAMMAD DULAL MIAH

Conclusion 181

*References* 187
*Index* 200

# Figures

| | | |
|---|---|---|
| 1.1 | Financial sector rents as incentive for portfolio monitoring | 15 |
| 1.2 | Creation of rent | 17 |
| 1.3 | Rent and expected return | 18 |
| 2.1 | Functions and components of a financial system | 30 |
| 3.1 | Extended bank rent model | 47 |
| 3.2 | Bank rent cube | 54 |
| 5.1 | Financial deepening in post-1978 China | 74 |
| 5.2 | Interest rate spread 1978–2001 | 79 |
| 6.1 | Size of banking systems relative to GDP in India and Sri Lanka | 91 |
| 6.2 | Interest rates and credit in Sri Lanka during 1990–2010 | 93 |
| 6.3 | Interest rates, and time and savings deposits in Sri Lanka during 1990–2010 | 93 |
| 6.4 | Inflation in Sri Lanka and selected nearby countries (1961–2009) | 107 |
| 6.5 | Volatility of inflation and bank interest spreads | 108 |
| 6.6 | Intensity of civil war and bank interest spread | 111 |
| 6.7 | Intensity of civil war and credit growth | 113 |
| 6.8 | War intensity and branch network expansion | 115 |
| 6.9 | Performance of equity market in Sri Lanka (January 1993–June 2009) | 116 |
| 8.1 | GDP growth rate (annual percentage) | 140 |
| 8.2 | Domestic credit to private sectors (percentage of GDP) | 141 |
| 8.3 | Number of listed companies (left axis) and market capitalization (right axis), 2015 | 143 |
| 8.4 | NIM of five GCC countries | 152 |
| 9.1 | Uncollateralized overnight rate (in percentage) | 161 |
| 9.2 | Annual changes in CPI (in percentage) | 161 |
| 9.3 | Current account balance of BoJ (in trillion yen) | 162 |
| 9.4 | Outright purchase of a Japanese government bond (in trillion yen) | 163 |
| 9.5 | Changes in the bank's asset | 169 |
| 9.6 | Changes in interest income (left axis) and trading income from securities (right axis) as a percentage of total income | 169 |
| 9.7 | Interest rate spread (as a percentage of total loans) | 170 |

viii  *Figures*

9.8   Business condition survey (large enterprise/manufacturing)    172
9.9   Changes (year-on-year basis) in gross capital stock    173
9.10  Borrowing by corporations from the banking system
      (percentage of total assets)    174
9.11  Currency swap    176
9.12  Currency swap pricing upon the interest rate parity    177
9.13  Currency swap pricing upon the interest rate parity plus
      Japan premium    177

# Tables

4.1   The averages of ROA and NPL of Islamic banks                                    63
4.2   Income from *murabaha* (in percentage) of different Islamic banks               64
4.3   Cost to income ratio in *riba*-based banking and Islamic banking
      of conventional banks                                                           65
4.4   Ratio of operating expenses to income in *riba*-based banking
      and Islamic banking of conventional banks                                       66
5.1   Non-performing loans (NPLs) in the state-owned
      commercial banks                                                                72
5.2   Breakdown of the ratio of non-performing loans among the
      big four banks (as of December 2003)                                            72
5.3   A synopsis of interest rate spread and reform characteristics                   78
5.4   Contributions to industrial growth (industry value added)                       82
6.1   Banking system in Sri Lanka, 2013                                               89
6.2   Interest rates, inflation, banking system and equity market
      in Sri Lanka                                                                    90
6.3   Descriptive statistics                                                          95
6.4   Regression results                                                              97
6.5   ANOVA results on revenue efficiency and ROA                                    104
7.1   Comparative position of the Islamic banking sector in
      Bangladesh, Indonesia, and Malaysia by the end of December
      2012, and in Pakistan by the end of December 2014                              126
7.2   The averages of ROA and NPL of Islamic banks in Bangladesh,
      Indonesia, Malaysia, and Pakistan                                              128
7.3   Income from *murabaha* (as a percentage) of different Islamic
      Banks in Bangladesh, Indonesia, Malaysia, and Pakistan                         130
7.4   Cost to income ratio in *riba*-based banking and Islamic banking
      of conventional banks                                                          132
7.5   Ratio of operating expenses to income in *riba*-based banking
      and Islamic banking of conventional banks                                      135
8.1   Selected macroeconomic indicators, 2015                                        140
8.2   Descriptive statistics (average 2005–2014; in million US$)                     145
8.3   Year-wise aggregate data of PLL, ROAA, and NIM                                 146
8.4   Country-wise data of PLL, ROAA, and NIM                                        150
9.1   Composition of revenue of the three largest banks in Japan                     171

# Contributors

**Yasushi Suzuki** is Professor at Ritsumeikan Asia Pacific University, Japan.

**Mohammad Dulal Miah** is Assistant Professor at University of Nizwa, Oman.

**Manjula K. Wanniarachchige** is Senior Lecturer at University of Ruhuna, Sri Lanka.

**S. M. Sohrab Uddin** is Professor at University of Chittagong, Bangladesh.

**Sigit Pramono** is Chairman at SEBI School of Islamic Economics, and Lecturer at University of Indonesia, Indonesia.

**Shoaib Khan** is Assistant Professor at University of Haripur, Pakistan.

# Preface

A coherent analysis of 'rent' dedicated to the banking sector is missing in the contemporary literature. Only a few scholars argue on 'financial sector rent' or 'bank rent' but their models mostly set the baseline for empirical analyses. Various types of rent including monopoly rent, natural resource-rent, Schumpeterian rent for innovation, monitoring rent etc. have been theoretically discussed. However, empirical analysis does not sufficiently complement the theory. This book contributes to the extant literature by accumulating empirical studies on the role of financial sector rent in Asian developing economies – including several economies that have adopted the mode of Islamic finance – and by proposing the steps toward framing a general theory of financial sector rent.

Almost thirteen consecutive years of teaching of Financial Economics Master/ Doctoral courses at Ritsumeikan Asia Pacific University (APU) gave me the arguments in this book. The arguments, I believe, incubated Dr. Mohammad Dulal Miah, Dr. Manjula K. Wanniarachchige and Dr. S. M. Sohrab Uddin. I am very proud that I have edited this book together with them. This book, we believe, provides a platform for further academic discussion and debate toward reaching a pragmatic solution for a very critical area of an economy, the financial system.

Yasushi Suzuki
Professor, APU
December 2016
(In Singapore)

# Acknowledgements

The editors would like to thank Routledge/Taylor & Francis Asia Pacific for their guidance and support toward the publication of this book. *Yasushi* would like to acknowledge that his work was supported by JSPS Grant-in-Aid for Scientific Research (C), Grant Number 24530212; 15K03374. He would like to thank Akiko Suzuki for her constant support, and Kenji Yokoyama, Toshitsugu Otake, A. Mani, Mohammad Hashim Kamali, Tan Chin Tiong, Ryoichi Hayakawa, and Ritsumeikan Asia Pacific University (APU), for providing him with a pleasant research environment for completing this work. *Dulal* would like to thank Ahmed Masoud Al Kindi, Said Eid Younes, Lohani Ashraf Ali Khan, Syed Mahbubur Rahman, Shamsudheen Arumathadathil, Mir Ferdousi, and the co-editors for their persistent support and encouragement. *Manjula* would like to acknowledge the immense support extended by the chief-editor in completing this work. Further he wishes to thank Thanuja K. Ranasinghe, Zhang Wei-Bin, Moriki Hosoe, A. Mani, Eades Jeremy, Nishantha Giguruwa, and Chandana Pushpakumara for their encouragement and support. *Sohrab* would like to convey heartiest gratitude to the chief editor for allowing him to work as a research fellow. He remains grateful to his parents and also to his wife, Habiba Jainab Farhana, for their endless inspiration and support.

# Introduction

A sound financial system is a prerequisite for economic development. It plays a critical role in mediating funds from surplus units to deficit units. Corporate sectors are usually the deficit units in an economy and are considered an engine of economic growth. They make investments in an effort to generate profits, based on their rational judgments. However, investment requires funding. Corporate sectors, as net demanders, have to procure funds at a reasonable cost from surplus units. Households are assumed as the net savers or surplus units. These two sectors interact through the financial system. Thus an efficient financial system that can successfully mediate funds from savers to investors is considered an essential precondition for economic growth. Historical accounts of most developed countries support this hypothesis (Gerschenkron, 1962; Levine, 1997; North and Weingast, 1989).

Despite their widespread importance, financial systems are not well developed particularly in developing countries. According to the World Development Indicators (WDI), domestic credit provided by banks of least developed countries (LDCs) to private sectors accounted for only 25 per cent of GDP in 2014, compared to 146 per cent in OECD countries. The scenario is same for lower middle income countries, where the respective estimate constituted only 40 per cent of GDP. Relevant statistics from the capital market also provide a similar picture. For instance, market capitalization as a percentage of GDP accounted for only 18.6 per cent (average of 2008–2010) for low income countries and 56.7 per cent for lower middle income countries. The respective statistics for the developed economies is found to be 151 per cent.[1] Based on these data and other related statistics, it can be concluded that the access of people to the formal financial system, particularly in the developing countries, is miniscule.

On the other hand, the existing financial systems are rarely stable and efficient. History is replete with examples that financial intermediaries in both developed and developing economies are mostly vulnerable to local and international financial shocks. Frequent bubble-and-bust episodes in the financial market, including the current worldwide sub-prime meltdown (2007–2009), which is just another tally to the record book of the financial crisis, bear a clear manifestation that crises in the financial markets are systemic. Caprio and Klingebiel (2002) identify 113 systemic banking crises in 93 countries and 50 borderline crises in 44 countries since the late 1970s (as of 1999). They show that more than 130 of 180 IMF countries have either experienced a crisis or faced serious banking problems. Another interesting study by Calomiris and Haber (2014) analyzes the history of financial crisis for a sample of 117 countries and finds that only 34 countries (29 per cent) were crisis free from 1970 to 2010, whereas 62 countries experienced one, 19 countries suffered from two, one country underwent three, and the other one faced no less than four crises. The study further estimates that 18 per cent of the countries in the world are preternaturally crisis prone. These statistics prove that banking crises are 'an equal opportunity menace' (Reinhart and Rogoff, 2013).

A significant volume of research has attempted to explain the reasons why financial crisis are frequent and systemic (Kindleberger, 2005; Reinhart and Rogoff, 2011; Rochet, 2013; Shiller, 2000; Wolf, 2014). Although each crisis is different in terms of origin, magnitude, and effect, some commonalities are striking among them. For example, most waves of financial crisis can be explained by the excessive risk-taking of lenders. Stiglitz (2012) argues that in the post-Glass–Steagall era some banks have transformed into mega-banks believing on the presumption that they are 'too big to fail'. This ideology has indeed led them to shoulder the amount of risk they are practically unable to absorb. In the same token, Calomiris and Haber (2014) show that in the post–Second World War period banks in the worlds' most developed economies became excessively leveraged and maintained smaller amounts of low-risk assets.

Banks as financial intermediaries have to deal with borrowers' credit risk. But in view of the neo-liberal perfect market, estimation of credit risk is fairly easy. Banks can assess the creditworthiness of each borrower applying some objective measures of risk assessment tools (expected default frequency, for example). In so doing, they can determine the level of credit at a point where marginal cost is equal to marginal revenue, a state of equilibrium at which profit is maximized. In reality, this neo-classical perception creates wrong incentive to the lenders by motivating them toward excessive risk-taking (Crotty, 2009). Contrary to the neo-classical ideology of perfect market, credit markets are frequently crippled by asymmetry of information and positive transaction cost. Moreover, lenders have to undertake prudential monitoring activities to alleviate the problems of adverse selection and moral hazard. A competitive equilibrium, in which marginal cost is equal to marginal revenue, might create an incentive toward excessive risk-taking in an attempt of lender's search for excess profit.

If financial fragility is the result of excessive risk-taking as stated previously, strategies to avoid recurrent financial crisis should focus on how to curb the risk-taking propensity of lenders. This obviously calls for designing institutions such that lenders (financial intermediaries in this particular regard) are provided with right incentives in commensuration with the principles of a stable financial system.

Different schools of thoughts have emerged to prescribe some policy prescriptions toward this direction. New Institutional Economics (NIE) is one of such schools, advocating for setting up right institutions. Contrasting itself from the neo-classical free market doctrine, the NIE advocates for creating and maintaining sufficient 'rent' for banks. 'Rent' is defined as excess income which does not exist in a new classical competitive market. Excess income is supposed to work as incentive for undertaking prudential screening and monitoring so that credit risk can be socialized. Furthermore, rent will create an incentive for banks to increase financial infrastructure and thereby tap unbanked population to the formal financial system, which in turn is expected to facilitate financial deepening. As such, the concept of 'rent' has been developed as an analytical tool to examine its effects on the performance of financial intermediaries as well as financial development.

Theoretical literature has advanced well in extending the analysis of rents to different branches of economics. However, empirical literature placing a micro-focus on real world cases to unveil the applicability and strengths of the model has not advanced as much as the model deserves. In addition, the question as to whether the existing model can be universally applicable (regardless of a country's level of economic development) is still unresolved. This book, therefore, is an attempt to fill this gap. It particularly aims to (1) elaborate the concept of rent for financial intermediaries, (2) examine the distinctive characteristics of bank rent model and its role to the development of financial system, (3) outline the weaknesses inherent with the existing model of rent, (4) check the applicability of the model to new and emerging economic phenomena, and (v) extend the model to Islamic banks. In so doing, this book first critically analyzes the existing definition of rent as 'excess income' and identifies drawbacks for which the model may have selectively applied. The book then links the effects of rent to performance of financial intermediaries in terms of their stability. In this pursuit, it brings different dimensions and evidence, analyzing a wide range of cases which include developed, rapid progressing, and developing economies. This book is, we believe, the first attempt to bring many issues pertaining to rent together in a coherent manner.

Besides applying the existing model of rent to examine its impact on financial intermediaries of different countries, the book advances the traditional model of rent to analyze the Islamic banking system, which can be considered a significant contribution of this book. Although the history of Islamic banking is not completely new, the literature of financial sector rent remains silent on the issue. This ignorance can possibly be attributed to the fact that the literature either takes it for granted that Islamic banks are different from conventional banks in operations or the traditional rent model cannot be applied to the Islamic banking upon the prohibition of interest (*riba*). While the first presumption is realistic, the second conjecture however, demands further research.

Islamic banks have to assume risks directly involved with profit-and-loss sharing (PLS) contracts, which is different from the predetermined-rate lending of conventional banks. Moreover, the former should comply with *Shari'ah* principles (Islamic norms and commercial laws). If so, Islamic banks need to earn more profits as incentives to absorb borrowers' credit risk upon the PLS contract and to maintain their reputation as *Shari'ah*-compliant lenders. In this pursuit, the book offers a definition of 'Islamic bank rent' as a buffer to absorb the unique risk and uncertainty faced by Islamic banks. The definition is believed to provide a new tool for analyzing rent effects of Islamic banks and how the case of Islamic bank differs from that of conventional banks. As Islamic banking is expanding on a global scale, it becomes important to discuss if rents, necessary for their operations, practically exist.

Needless to say, the field of institutional economics is expanding significantly due to its relevance to the development issues of countries across the world. Although a vast array of literature exists that focuses on different aspects of NIE, a complete body of work on financial sector rent or bank rent is still absent. It is to be noted that the contemporary literature discusses rents in general without any particular reference to financial sector. Although a few scholars argue on financial sector rent, their models mostly set the baseline for empirical analysis. For instance, various types of 'rent', including monopoly rent, natural resource-rent, Schumpeterian rent, monitoring rent, and so on, have been theoretically discussed (Khan, 2000, for example). However, empirical analysis does not sufficiently complement the theory. The book thus contributes to the extant literature by accumulating the empirical studies on the role of financial sector rent in Asian developing economies and by proposing the steps toward the general theory of financial sector rent.

To achieve the aforementioned objectives, this book is divided into two parts. In the first part, we sketch the theoretical framework for our empirical analysis. Part I is composed of four chapters. Chapter 1 offers a detailed analysis on the concept of rent and its role in the development of financial systems. In so doing, it first summarizes the basic ideas put forth by the financial restraint model. It is argued that rent is an essential element that provides incentive to managers for undertaking prudential monitoring activities. If so, financial sector rent is compatible to the managerial incentive model discussed in the economic literature. For instance, in the Marxian tradition, the analysis of banking credit and interest is undertaken on the basis such that *stagnant* or *idle* money is systematically generated in the course of industrial accumulation, transformed into interest-bearing capital by the credit system, and returned to accumulation to receive a share of surplus value. The money capital accumulated through the sale of commodity capital and the hoarding of temporarily idle money are collected and centralized in the financial institutions, and transformed into potential money capital available to industrial capital. A share of surplus value would be necessary to attract the idle money so that money capital available to industrial capital contributes to the capital accumulation for the society. Hence surplus or profit works as incentive for capitalists. Also, in the modern analysis of the 'theory of firm', profit is mentioned as a means to resolve the monitoring problem stemming from the asymmetry of information and transaction cost. This chapter links these concepts to the broader framework of managerial incentive models.

In Chapter 2 the authors analyze the linkage between financial development and economic growth, delving into the rich stock of financial literature. Even if the burgeoning literature is not completely in accord with the proposition that financial development precedes economic growth, the positive association between them is, however, endorsed. The reality is that the degree of their association may vary from country to country, depending on other socio-economic supporting and complementary institutions, but the finance-growth nexus is ostensible. Thus instead of asking whether finance causes economic growth, this chapter considers it more practical to answer what are those socio-economic conditions under which finance can function as a critical growth driver. With this view, the chapter describes a typical financial system which consists mainly of direct financing (capital market) and indirect financing (financial intermediaries) routes. Also, the comparative advantages of these routes are highlighted.

Chapter 2 further highlights the role of banks as financial intermediaries. It is recognized in the literature that financial institutions may emerge to ameliorate the problems created by information asymmetry and transaction cost. In this view, how these problems are mitigated by financial intermediaries is discussed in detail. Financial restraint models that forward the concept of rent resemble other contemporary theories that describe the existence of financial intermediaries especially in respect to their basis of analysis. For instance, financial restraint model assumes that the credit market is predominantly characterized by the asymmetry of information and high transaction costs. These frictions in the market may lead to adverse selection and moral hazard problems. Based on these assumptions, the model argues that the competitive equilibrium may fail to provide necessary incentive for banks to undertake prudential monitoring activities. Thus sufficient rent has to be created and maintained through regulatory process so that borrowers are effectively screened and tightly monitored by lenders to minimize the possible adverse selection and moral hazard problems. Rent thus created will motivate intermediaries to increase their financial infrastructure and other related facilities.

While this book recognizes and relies on the contribution of the literature of rent, it also expresses some reservations about the assumptions required by the traditional rent model to be suitable as policy option for developing countries. These issues have been addressed in Chapter 3. The author here discusses the existing models and then highlights their inherent weaknesses. It is argued that the conventional bank rent-based studies have failed to provide credible explanations as to why some developing countries have failed to attain expected level of financial development, even if sizable interest spreads prevailed in their banking systems. In an attempt to explain this paradox, Chapter 3 offers a new model dissecting the total rent into three sub-categories such as price rent, operating rent, and macroeconomic rent. The chapter emphasizes the fact that the idea of rent in the traditional model narrows down the focus, but says nothing from the inside. In this sense, the breakdown of the whole will undoubtedly provide new dimensions for analyzing rent and its effects. Moreover, the micro issues brought about by the model will certainly help policymakers identify the real problem and thereby find customized solutions. The chapter finally concludes by stating that banks would be able to enjoy sufficient rent only when all three types of rent opportunities contribute positively on a net basis.

One among many weaknesses of the traditional rent model is that the model remains silent on the question as to whether the model can be applied for the case of Islamic bank. As mentioned earlier, Islamic banks are functionally different from conventional banks. Therefore the system deserves an extra attention. The authors in this chapter shed an analytical light on how the concept of rent for Islamic bank can be different from the concept of rent applicable to conventional banks. The primary difference, which has to be accounted for as far the analysis of bank rent is concerned, is the cost incurred by Islamic banks for compliance with *Shari'ah* principles. This additional component of cost for Islamic bank is definitely affecting their rent opportunity. From this analytical perspective, the authors have developed a model to analyze 'Islamic bank rent'. The distinctiveness of the model is that it bisects the traditional rent into 'risk premium' and 'Islamic bank rent'. While risk premium is applicable to both categories of bank, Islamic bank rent, however, is required for Islamic banks to comply with the Islamic commercial laws.

These four chapters lay the basic foundation for the empirical analysis presented in Part II of the book. The first chapter of Part II discusses the case of China, a country which has been growing at an impressive pace for the last couple of decades. GDP growth rate averaged 9.9 per cent from 1978 to 2010. Total GDP amounted to USD10.36 trillion (in 2014 price), which has earned it a middle income rank with USD7,595 per capita GDP in 2014. Its unprecedented economic growth for such a long period has accompanied lots of questions and paradoxes. The central paradox lies in the fact that the state-owned commercial banks, which share a substantial portion of total financing activities in China, are saddled with huge accumulation of non-performing loans. Despite this fact, China has been able to achieve miraculous growth, keeping its formal banking system grossly underdeveloped. To unfold this paradox, the authors first discuss why the banking sector in China remained underdeveloped. They analyze data for the period of 1977 to 2005 and find that in the early years, banks' net rent was negative, which means that they were financially repressed by the government, perhaps to achieve other important socio-political objectives. However, with the gradual easing of financial repression, banks performed comparatively better. Based in this analysis, the authors argue that bank rent matters as potential incentive to undertake sound screening and monitoring activities.

The authors then explain the finance-growth paradox. Analyzing various macroeconomic data and facts, they show that the formal financial system during the rapid growth period of China was superseded by the informal one, especially for financing private enterprises which play a crucial role for accelerating Chinese economic growth. As a consequence, banks' poor performances could not have excessive debilitating effects on economic progress. However, the authors warn, there is a limit of the elasticity of informal financing. Unless prompt and rigorous actions from the Chinese government to redress the ongoing banking mess are in place, the tempo of its current economic growth may be halted in the near future.

Chapter 6 examines the effects of bank rent on Sri Lankan financial system. The banking system in Sri Lanka indeed challenges the traditional bank rent model. For instance, the stability of the political system facilitated by the resolution of the endemic civil war has stabilized the financial system of the country. The effects of this stability are reflected in many socio-economic indicators, including lower rates for lending and borrowing. Of course, a lower lending rate has squeezed the level of banks' nominal spread. A paradox arises here: despite a thinner slice of nominal interest rate, banks' profitability remains stable and upward trending. In explaining this anomaly, the author argues that the rent in the traditional sense comprises only the price. However, the traditional rent model neglects two components of the package: operating rent and macroeconomic rent. As a consequence, price rent opportunities alone can unlikely explain this anomaly. This is a critical inconsistency of the conventional model. In contrast, the author shows that although the nominal spread declines in the aggregate, the macroeconomic rent has increased, which can be attributed to the gradual reform of the financial sector. Moreover, development of the banking infrastructure facilitates banks to reap the benefits of economies of scale. Their combined positive effects have outweighed the erosion of price rent. Therefore banks have been able to maintain and enhance their profitability, even in a state of declining price rent.

Chapter 7 analyzes the effects of rent on Islamic banks. The authors examine the composition of balance sheets of Islamic banks in four Muslim dominant countries: Bangladesh, Pakistan, Indonesia, and Malaysia. Like dual banking systems in other countries, Islamic finance contributes a significant portion to meet the total financing needs in these four countries. Although Islamic principles encourage *Shari'ah*-based financial institutions toward PLS-based financing, the reality, however, is different. For instance, the current financing pattern of Islamic banks in the sample countries shows that the pure PLS mode of financing, including *musharaka* and *mudharaba*, combine only a tiny percentage of the total assets of Islamic banks. Rather, assets of these banks are highly concentrated on *murabaha* schemes. Despite the fact that Islamic banks in Indonesia and Malaysia contribute with *musharaka* modes of investment – a joint partnership where two or more persons combine either their capital or labor – this mode of financing is seriously skewed toward real estate financing (diminishing *musharaka*), which cannot be considered as pure PLS investment. Based on these facts and other evidences, the authors argue that the asset-based financing, including consumer financing – the *quasi-murabaha* syndrome – in Islamic banks can be attributed to banks' tendency to capture rent opportunities for protecting their 'franchise value' as *Shari'ah*-compliant lenders, while hesitating to be engaged with the participatory financing. From this vantage point, the chapter concludes stating that the *murabaha* syndrome can be ironically justifiable and will continue so long as Islamic banks can capture an endurable level of rent from this mode of financing.

Like Chapter 7, Chapter 8 concentrates on examining the rent effects on banks in the Gulf Cooperative Council (GCC) countries. Almost all countries in the GCC follow a dual banking system (the Sultanate of Oman is relatively new to this version). As a result, the region has become a hotbed for comparative studies between Islamic and conventional banks. Following this tradition, Chapter 8 examines the bank rent opportunity for banks in the GCC region. It was mentioned earlier that Islamic banks require additional cost for *Shari'ah* compliance to mitigate the displaced commercial risk and a cushion against uncertainty involved with the PLS financing. Thus the spread margin for Islamic banks should be higher than the conventional banks. Analyzing historical data from a handful number of Islamic and conventional banks, the authors find that Islamic banks indeed enjoy higher spread margins in three of the five countries included in this study. The supposed anomaly to the Islamic bank rent model put forth by the remaining two countries is logically explained in this chapter. One point to note is that not all Islamic banks are following pure PLS financing, but rather the *murabaha* or mark-up-based financing dominates the assets. Where the mode of financing for Islamic banks is substantially akin to conventional banks, the difference between Islamic and conventional banks in terms of capturing rent is not so pronounced. Hence no existence of extra spread makes sense.

The final chapter of the empirical analysis applies the bank rent model to a rather new branch of the subject. Quantitative easing (QE) has been an interesting topic in recent times, owing to the fact that some developed economies have initiated even negative interest rates as part of the QE mechanism. Japan has been experiencing financial and economic slowdown for a long period of time. The country has adopted several policy measures to reinvigorate the ailing economy. One of such policy measures was the implementation of quantitative easing policy, a change in the composition of a central bank's balance sheet that is designed to ease liquidity and/or credit conditions. The basic tenet of the policy is that by purchasing or selling risk assets from the national economy, the central bank adjusts the money supply so that the target level of inflation is achieved. During a depressed economic condition, banks would increase the money supply so that the interest rate falls, which in turn stimulates credit expansion. However, many economies have failed to achieve this objective. For instance, Japanese banks, instead of expanding credit to much needed sectors, have capitalized huge rent under the Abenomics,[2] mainly by trading the Japanese government bonds (treasury bonds). While the burgeoning literature attributes the reasons for failure of QE to several factors, including communication gap, early or late exit from the QE policy, and so on, the literature overlooks the rent effect of QE policy. This chapter takes this view into account. It shows an upward trend of return of assets captured by the Japanese banks under the Abenomics, achieved simply through trading treasury bills during the time of QE.

The book then concludes summarizing the major findings and offering a general theory of the financial sector rent. As mentioned earlier, a coherent analysis of rent dedicated to the banking sector is missing in the contemporary literature. This book therefore provides a platform for further academic discussion and debate toward reaching a pragmatic solution for a very critical area of an economy, the financial system.

# Notes

1 According to the WDI classification, low-income economies are defined as those with a GNI per capita, calculated using the World Bank Atlas method, of $1,025 or less in 2015; lower middle-income economies are those with a GNI per capita between $1,026 and $4,035; upper middle-income economies are those with a GNI per capita between $4,036 and $12,475; high-income economies are those with a GNI per capita of $12,476 or more.
2 The term refers to the economic policies advocated by Shinzō Abe, the Prime Minister of Japan elected in December 2012. Abenomics is based upon three basic principles: fiscal stimulus, monetary easing, and structural reforms.

# Part I

# Theoretical framework for empirical analyses

# 1 Overview of theories of financial sector rent and bank rent opportunities

## A critical view

*Yasushi Suzuki, Mohammad Dulal Miah, and Manjula K. Wanniarachchige*

## 1. Introduction

The concept of financial sector rent as a distinct tool of institutional analysis is comparatively new. It has attracted renewed interest from both academicians and policymakers, especially after the Asian financial crisis in 1997. The reason to attach financial sector rent to that specific crisis is that rent in the financial sector was widespread during the period of rapid industrialization of some East Asian economies. On the other hand, their financial sectors were at the center of the crisis. International Monetary Fund (IMF) has pointed out that the primary responsibility to the shortcomings of the crisis rests on East Asian capitalism – in particular, the East Asian financial markets (Radelet et al., 1998). This has prompted scholars and policymakers with particular interest in the East Asian growth miracle to assess the role of institutions in promoting and stabilizing the financial system. To this endeavor, the theory of financial sector rent has provided a new analytical tool to explain the effects of rent in financial development. It has been argued that the rent for financial institutions (referred to, in this book, as *financial sector rent* or *bank rent* if it is captured particularly by banks) can be welfare-enhancing if they induce efficient monitoring of their credit portfolio (Hellmann, Murdock, and Stiglitz, 1997; Stiglitz and Weiss, 1981). Since monitoring is inherently linked to the incentive provided to agents, the management incentive model is the starting point for the analysis of financial sector rents (Khan, 2000).

*Rents*, in the economic literature, refer to 'excess income' which, in the neo-classical equilibrium model, should not exist. However, as argued later, the widely known 'financial restraint' regulation which creates bank rent opportunity as an incentive for private banks to become prudent monitors and fund-providers is important because it challenges the neo-classical argument that a no-rent competitive equilibrium in the financial market is possible and efficient. Needless to say, the neo-classical equilibrium in the financial market is simply a utopia because such ideology is preoccupied by the assumptions that information is symmetric between and among the agents in the financial markets and the transaction is costless. But in reality, neither of these assumptions is true. Markets are frequently crippled by the presence of asymmetry of information and high transaction cost, which results in adverse selection, moral hazard, and ultimately the market failure (see Chapter 2 for the details). Avoiding such possible market failure requires prudential screening and monitoring. Screening has two facets, the demand side and the supply side. From the demand side perspective, a sufficient number of creditworthy borrowers must be present in the credit market to screen and choose from. Market competitive interest rate may not be low enough to attract *credential* borrowers in the credit market. This necessitates the interest rate to be set low enough so that *creditable* borrowers are encouraged to join the formal borrowing market. The process may help avoid a possible adverse selection problem. From the supply side perspective, lenders should undertake a prudential monitoring which requires costly skills and efforts. Unless sufficient incentive is created for lenders, it is unlikely that necessary screening and monitoring efforts will be put in place. Based on this argument, the bank rent model advocates for regulated deposit and/or lending rates such that the bank rent opportunity (the spread margin between deposit and lending rates) as incentive is maintained for the banks to become prudent monitors, while the lending rate remains still attractive for creditable borrowers.

In this chapter we aim to offer an overview on the concept of bank rent. To achieve this objective, we first elaborate the concept of bank rent. Although the concept of bank rent was intrinsically enumerated in the institutional economics literature long before the invention of the financial restraint model, the latter can be credited with formalizing the concept as a distinct policy development tool. However, the merit of the bank rent model has been under-emphasized in the existing literature. We show that the logic of rent as incentive mechanism can be derived from the very notion of 'residual income' or the Marxian concept of 'surplus', which is often prescribed to overcome the monitoring problem involved with high transaction cost. Secondly, we look at certain prerequisites (and limitations) required in the Hellmann et al. (1997) financial restraint model that must be met for bank rent to be effective. This overview thus sets the baseline for the empirical analysis included in Part II of this book.

## 2.   The concept of bank rent and its roles

The Stiglitz and Weiss (1981) model is important because it shows that credit is intrinsically rationed due to asymmetric information problem. Since lenders cannot perfectly and without cost select the right borrowers *ex ante* and monitor the behavior of borrowers *ex post*, the price mechanism does not always clear the excess demand for funds. For instance, even when a borrower, deemed by a bank to be uncreditworthy, offers to pay higher interest rates, the bank may decline the loan application, because this offer is interpreted as a signal of higher default risk. Hellmann et al. (1997) expand this theory by arguing that the government can boost the incentives for banks by enhancing bank rents so that they actively monitor their loan portfolios. If the government imposes a ceiling on the deposit rate below the market-clearing rate, rent opportunities may emerge in the form

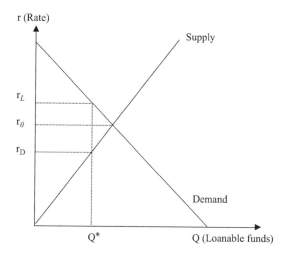

*Figure 1.1* Financial sector rents as incentive for portfolio monitoring

of a significant gap between deposit and lending rates that will give banks strong incentives to monitor their portfolio more carefully.

In the typical form of indirect financing (see Chapter 2), the household sector is the net supplier of funds and the corporate sector is the net borrower of funds, whereas banks act as financial intermediaries. Figure 1.1 shows the market equilibrium at interest rate $r_0$ as the intersection of a supply curve of household funds and a corporate demand curve for funds. If the government intervenes in the financial sector by regulating the deposit rate, financial intermediaries can capture rents. The lending rate will be determined in accordance with the demand curve indicating the relationship between availability of loanable funds and rate (price) at $r_L$; and the gap between the regulated deposit rate, $r_D$, and the market lending rate, $r_L$, is the source of the rent. The rent will continue to be available for banks, more precisely for owners of banks, only if the banks' portfolio of assets and liabilities is managed sufficiently well to keep the portfolio solvent (Khan, 2000, p. 58).

The model also argues that while savings may respond favorably to higher interest rates, this elasticity is likely to be very low (Hellmann et al., 1997, p. 168). On the other hand, the model assumes that the amount of savings depends on the available infrastructure for deposit collection, in particular on the extent of the bank branch network and the efficiency of services. The model thereby claims that when the return to intermediation is high, banks have strong incentives to increase their own deposit base. The model considers the possibility that the 'rent effect' on saving is large – that is, there is increased savings due to greater deposit security and/or increased investments in improving the deposit infrastructure, which ultimately facilitates greater access to the formal financial sector. This will shift the supply curve rightward in Figure 1.1. If the rent effect is large relative to the interest elasticity of savings, it is possible that the total volume of funds intermediated through the formal financial sector will be larger with the financial restraint policy than with the competitive market forces (Hellmann et al., 1997).

Although the net benefit to society is not always consistent with that for individuals, the important role of bank rent is to create incentives for individual banks particularly private banks to operate as long-run agents that monitor borrowers effectively. The prospective benefits from monitoring efforts in the financial restraint mode include the rent that a bank earns if it can preserve its 'franchise value' (Hellmann et al., 1997, pp. 171–174) and its 'reputation' (Stiglitz, 1994, p. 223). On the other hand, the threat of losing these rent opportunities prevents banks from shirking their monitoring function (Aoki, 1994).

The analysis of rent is inherently linked with the origin of profit, because the concept of *rent* has been catalyzed in the literature as an 'excess income' or surplus. Here we wish to elaborate on the unique character of bank rent from typical type of rent, which is understated in the existing literature.

From the view of Marxian and classical economists, profit is considered as a surplus or residual income which remains as leftover after factors of production, particularly labor, are paid off (Khan, 2000). For Marx, as the capitalist hires labors, the produce coming out from their effort belongs to the capitalist. A part of that produce is paid as wages minimum being the amount required to maintain the subsistence level. Capitalists enjoy the remaining as surplus. This surplus in the Marxian term is called 'profit', which depends critically on the degree to which the capitalist could control the labor process in the factory.[1] In contrast, profit in the neo-classical model is determined by the value of the marginal product of capital (the value of output produced by the last unit of capital). Here the capitalist plays no role in determining profits since the value of the marginal product of capital depends only on technology, the number of workers working the capital stock, and the price at which the product can be sold.

The neo-classical welfare-economics framework distinguishes excess income from normal income as producers' surplus. Let us illustrate this by looking at the case of a monopoly (Figure 1.2), where a monopolist is given the power to determine the level of output in that market. The restriction of supply, say to $OQ_2$, raises the price to $OP_2$, while the marginal cost of producing the smaller output ($OQ_2$) is OB. As a result, the last unit produced by the producer now costs less than its price. The difference gives the producer an above-normal profit of CD on the last unit, which is technically a rent because the producer earns a return higher than could have been earned in its next-best alternative (which is the rate of return in a no-rent market). Since this above-normal profit is earned on each of the $OQ_2$ units produced, the total rent earned by the producer is shown by the rectangle $BCDP_2$. The level of output $OQ_2$ is determined by the monopolist to maximize the size of this rent.

Now we should ask: what does it mean by normal profit as producer's surplus for banks? It is not practical to assume a sharply increasing marginal cost curve in the banking sector. Due to ample loanable funds in the interbank money market (or under the financial regulation of setting up the ceiling of deposit rate), the

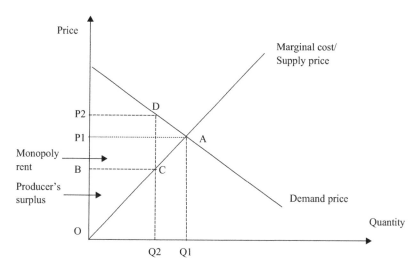

*Figure 1.2* Creation of rent

sharp difference in the cost (variable cost for banks) between funding the last unit and funding the smaller unit is not assumed, so far as the fund taker is adequately credible. Rather, in general, since the banking industry needs huge *sunk costs* in the form of fixed investment for building up branch network and computer systems for operation, the magnitude of economies of scale, as the diminishing average fixed cost for lending to be captured by banks, are considered very large. Therefore we can draw a flat marginal cost curve for banks (see Figure 1.3), though the marginal cost can be still diminishing. In a static analysis under a particular financial environment of ample loanable funds and under a particular condition of sunk fixed costs, it is reasonable to assume that there is no significant difference in the marginal cost between funding the last unit and the smaller unit. In this context, in our view, it is less meaningful to distinguish excess profit from normal profit like the producer's surplus, as far as the analysis of financial sector rent is concerned.

Here we wish to elaborate on the unique role of bank rent as incentives for bank managers to become prudent monitors and managers. The previously mentioned 'marginal product of capital as profit' view is seriously criticized by Alchian and Demsetz (1972). They recognize that the profit rate is not determined in this way because the marginal product of capital is impossible to measure independently of how well the production team as a whole is working. Instead, they argue that profits must be a residual after workers and suppliers have been paid (Khan, 2000). The question is why this leftover or residual is required if factors of productions have already been paid.

The logic of residual return stems from the asymmetry of information problem. Resource owners (labor and capital) increase productivity through cooperative

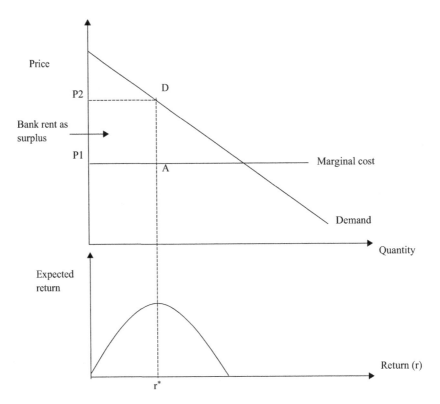

*Figure 1.3* Rent and expected return

specialization, and this leads to the demand for economic organization, or what we call a 'firm'. In team production, marginal products of cooperative team members are not so directly observable. Clues to each input's productivity can be secured by observing behavior of individual inputs. If detecting such behavior was costless, members would have no incentive to shirk, because they cannot impose the cost of shirking on others. Since costs must be incurred to monitor each other, each input owner will have more incentive to shirk when he works as part of a team than if he did not work as a team.

One way to reduce shirking of agents is to select someone with specialized knowledge to check the input performance of team members. If owners of cooperating inputs agree with the monitor that he is to receive any residual product above prescribed amounts, the monitor will have an added incentive not to shirk as a monitor. The specialist who receives the residual rewards will be the monitor of the members of the team. The monitor earns his residual through the reduction in shirking that he brings about by observing and direct-ing the actions or uses of these inputs. In this sense, profit as residual plays a critical function as a reward for good management. The role of management is to carry out this observation or monitoring, and the profit which owners and managers earn as a residual after paying all direct costs is their reward for monitoring.

Figure 1.3 shows the relationship between the expected return and the nominal lending rate. After a critical rate of r*, the expected return starts falling down due to the so-called adverse selection effect (too many bad risks are attracted at higher rates of interest) and 'moral hazard effect' (even good borrowers may be forced to act in riskier way than the bank would like at higher rates of interest). The optimal rate of interest at individual banks is not necessarily the market-clearing rate which might be the optimal rate of interest at the macro-perspective. However, it makes sense for the individual bank to seek the individually optimal rate of r* to maximize the expected return as incentives enough to become prudent monitors and managers.

Marx also had pointed out that the capitalists' search for profit created incentives for managing the labor process but, more importantly, it drove technical innovation (Khan, 2000). An important difference between Marx, and Alchian and Demsetz is that for the latter, the role of management is entirely defined by the problem of asymmetric information. Workers can hide information about the effort they have put in, and uncovering this information requires effort by management. In contrast, Marx's analysis suggests that the labor process is involved with more serious conflicts, in particular distributive conflicts over wages, and worker resistance to technologies, which dehumanizes work. Thus, in both of these traditions, management plays a role in disciplining the labor process. In both perspectives, management has an incentive to manage because its rewards are based on the surplus, which depends on how well they manage. Clearly, there are close analytical links between the role of rents in creating incentives for managing the work process, and the role of rents in generating information or innovations (Khan, 2000).

On the other hand, as another unique character of bank rent, we should note that the profit earned by banks is still subject to the default risk of borrowers. Some scholars attempt to seek for the reasonability of pricing upon the statistical and objectifiable expected default frequency (EDF) of each borrower. However, we should note that different from ordinary goods trade in cash, the expected return from lending should cover a risk premium to respond to the default risk of borrowers and fundamental uncertainty.[2] In our view, the bank rent as the spread determined by banks is reflected in the subjective EDF and a risk premium to cover unspecified adverse events; nevertheless the subjective EDF is to some extent reflected in the statistical or objectifiable EDF. As a complete set of risk markets is necessarily absent, it is impossible in theory to determine a definite value of the EDF without risk of error, even using all available data sets. In this sense, it is less meaningful to distinguish excess profit from normal profit in the concept of bank rent. We presume that the rent opportunity is reflected in the expected return including a risk premium to cover unspecified adverse events. In this context, the role of bank rent as a buffer or cushion in responding to unexpected losses can be argued.

## 3. An overview of financial restraint policy

To what extent does the bank rent incentive model contribute to our understanding on the role of financial rents in financial intermediations? The outcomes of monitoring rents depend on various factors. For instance, the incentive to monitor can be significantly diluted if the bank does not face a credible threat of bankruptcy. This may result in a moral hazard problem, since bank managers and owners know that their bank will not normally be allowed to go bust. In such a case, rent may fail to produce the desired outcome such as good management of banks (Khan, 2000). Also, even if bank managers have the incentive for monitoring to maintain their rents, unless banks have an effective power to monitor and discipline borrowers, the outcomes would be unproductive. This implies that there are certain prerequisites that must be met for bank rent to be effective. We now turn to review these conditions (and limitations of the model), which are discussed in the Hellmann et al. (1997) financial restraint model.

The essence of *financial restraint* is that the government creates rent opportunities in the private sector through a set of financial policies. Hellmann et al. (1997) argue that where the banking sector is weak, government regulations create rents for banks, which in turn strengthen their incentives to monitor the borrowers. The availability of these rents makes banks more valuable to their owners, as the rent opportunity provides them with what the authors of the model call the 'franchise value'. If the protection of this value requires good portfolio management, the rent sustaining franchise value needs to be created for better monitoring (Khan, 2000). Rents are created by setting the deposit rate below the competitive equilibrium level. Moreover, to preserve rents in the financial sector, the government must regulate entry and sometimes direct competition. The control of deposit rates may be compensated by a set of controls on lending rates. Such controls serve to affect the distribution of rents between the financial and production sectors. Hellmann et al. (1997) argue that rents in the financial and production sectors can play a positive role in reducing information-related problems that hamper perfectly competitive markets. In particular, these rents induce private-sector agents to increase the supply of goods and services, such as the monitoring of investments or the provision of deposit collection which might be underprovided in a purely competitive market. Needless to say, it is necessary to accumulate the empirical evidence to see if their argument is held.

Financial restraint is a fundamentally different policy from financial repression. Financial repression refers to a condition in which the government extracts rents from the private sector by keeping the nominal interest rates below the rate of inflation. In contrast, no rents are extracted by the government under financial restraint regime. Rather, deposit rate controls create rents that are captured by financial intermediaries and by firms, if additional lending rate controls are applied (Hellmann et al., 1997). Thus a number of preconditions must be met in order for financial restraint policy to operate effectively. The preconditions include a stable macro environment, low and predictable inflation, and positive real interest rates. Heavy taxation (direct or indirect taxation such that government can ask banks for high reserves requirement or can force banks to buy government bonds at a suppressed interest rate) on the financial sector is incompatible with financial restraint. We should critically assess the applicability of the financial restraint model to developing countries, because most of developing countries face difficulties in controlling these preconditions. Wanniarachchige argues on this issue in Chapter 3.

Hellmann et al. (1997) consider two broad categories of rent effects. First, giving rents to financial intermediaries and production firms will increase their own equity stakes and make these institutions behave in a more proprietary way. Second, the authors often think of rents not so much as the transfer of wealth, but as opportunities to create wealth. Rent opportunities thus link actions of agents to the receipt of the resources. Hellmann et al. (1997, p. 164) further note that the government creates rent opportunities to induce economically efficient actions which private markets would not undertake because of the divergence between private and social returns. The optimal interest rate for maximizing the expected private returns in individual banks does not necessarily lead the society to the equilibrium where any imbalance between demand and supply would be cleared in aggregate level, due partly to information asymmetries and divergence in uncertainties between banks and borrowers. We agree to their view that information asymmetries and divergence in uncertainties between banks and borrowers are intrinsic in causing various types of market failure. In addition, we are concerned about information asymmetries and divergence in uncertainties between the regulator and the regulated banks, which may cause various types of state failures of omission and commission.

The Hellmann et al. (1997) model identifies a number of ways in which financial restraint can foster financial deepening. They argue that rents create 'franchise value' for banks that induces them to become more stable institutions with better incentives to monitor the firms they finance and manage the risk of the loan portfolio. Rents create incentives for banks to expand their deposit base and increase the extent of formal intermediation in the economy. In addition, the government can sometimes target rents for specific bank activities to compensate for market deficiencies, such as the lack of long-term lending. When financial restraint passes some rents to the production sector through lending rate controls, there can be further beneficial effects. Lower lending rates reduce the agency problems in lending markets (Hellmann et al., 1997, pp. 165–166). It is to be noted that the financial restraint policy is basically prescribed for economies with low state of financial development. However, it is also suggestive for banks, as prominent monitors, even in matured economies to preserve 'franchise value'. It is also necessary to accumulate the empirical data to see if the rent effect is large or marginal.

Hellmann et al. (1997) insist that financial restraint is not a static policy instrument. Rather, the set of policies envisioned herein should be adjusted as the economy matures (Hellmann et al., 1997, p. 166). As financial depth increases, and in particular as the capital base of the financial sector strengthens, state interventions including government-created ceilings on the deposit rate below the market-clearing rate may be progressively relaxed, and the economy may make the transition to a more classic free market paradigm. Thus the policy choice presented here is not simply a static contrast between laissez-faire and financial restraint, but a dynamic decision governing the order of financial market development (Hellmann et al., 1997, p. 166). This view is agreeable. However, how a matured economy can transit to a financially liberalized paradigm is another issue. Suzuki (2011) argues about Japan's transition failure from the bank rent-based financial mode to another alternative, where Japan finally failed to respond to intensifying uncertainty as the economy matured and was globalized.

As hinted previously, the financial restraint model argues that a reduction in savings rate from the market equilibrium rate is not believed to trouble deposit mobilization to a significant extent. This argument depends on the assumption that interest elasticity of savings is low. There has been a considerable debate about the interest-elasticity of savings, because theory cannot accurately predict the reaction of savings to the change in interest rate due largely to the offsetting wealth and substitution effects. In the model, it is expected that savings are likely to be more responsive to other factors important to households than merely the interest rate. For instance, households are typically risk averse, and they place greater emphasis on the security of deposits. Second, household savings depend crucially on the availability of convenient deposit infrastructure – in particular, on the extent of the bank branch network and the efficiency of services provided to the local communities. We basically follow the assumption that interest elasticity of savings is low. However, we should note that the supply of loanable fund has a limit typically in developing countries, because the availability of saving money is fundamentally limited.

Hellmann et al. (1997) is aware that capital requirement is the appropriate instrument to fight moral hazard in banking. If banks are poorly capitalized, they may have an incentive to 'gamble on their resurrection' by accepting high credit risk, an act that may destabilize the financial system. Therefore a remedy to financial instability is to increase the capital base of financial intermediaries. On the other hand, the model insists that deposit rate control can be expected to be more effective than capital requirements, especially in the context of developing economies. In the latter case, fewer funds will be available to private loan markets, leading to a rise in the cost of funds, particularly in developing countries where private lending activity needs to be developed rather than restricted (Hellmann et al., 1997, p. 172). As a result, financial restraint can be considered appropriate policy option compared to the capital requirement in the question of financial deepening particularly in developing countries. This book does not cover this issue.

Hellmann et al. (1997) further assume that new rural branches require significant capital to open and these branches make economic losses during their first few years of operations as a new market is being developed. Consequently, investments in rural branches will negatively affect the equity of the bank (Hellmann et al., 1997, p. 174). Second, banks are shy in providing long-term funding under the condition of free market competition, because on top of the usual agency problem, long-term financing is involved with inflation risk as well as liquidity risk. Reliable prediction of these risks involving the future is infeasible. The combined effect is that commercial banks in most developing economies are typically reluctant to engage in long-term lending. Given the underdeveloped bond and equity markets in these economies, entrepreneurs may not be able to access to long-term financing. Of course, governments in many countries have attempted to overcome this obstacle by establishing and operating development banks that provide long-term capital. When government engages in direct lending, if it suffers from agency problems of its own, the danger that 'government failure' might outweigh the market failure is apparent (Hellmann et al., 1997, pp. 176–177). Nevertheless, bank rent can be an effective tool to motivate banks toward catering the long-term financing needs of entrepreneurs. Yet it is necessary to accumulate the empirical cases to clarify the reality of financial deepening.

However, rent creation is not enough on its own. Rent has to be maintained for some period of time. Restriction on competition is required in this regard. To regulate competitive behavior in the banking industry, the government needs to control the new entry to the industry. This does not mean that the government prevents all entry, but it means that new entry does not erode the rents that are necessary to induce banks to value their franchise. Or in other words, too much entry would prevent most competitors from achieving an efficient scale, thus lowering their ability and desire to invest in better information and monitoring capabilities and worsening the overall quality of intermediation (Hellmann et al., 1997, p. 178). From this perspective, the financial restraint model points out the need to place restrictions on this competition in order to prevent socially wasteful duplication of activity. However, the investments that banks make can have one of two effects on how they gather increased deposits – bring new depositors into the formal financial sector or compete for the shares of other banks. The first is socially beneficial, while the second is socially wasteful. Moreover, countries with low financial depth offer a greater potential for deposit creation, and a greater mix of the former should result from the increased competitive pressures generated by rents. Consequently, concerns of 'excessive competition' remain secondary in the early stages of financial deepening (Hellmann et al., 1997, pp. 178–179). This issue is partly related to the rent for learning and incubating. It is also necessary to accumulate the empirical evidence to see if the rent for learning is large or growth-retarding.

When financial restraint creates rent for intermediaries, it is not that the supplier of funds enjoys the rent alone. A part of the rent is transferred to the borrowers. Theoretically, a higher lending rate determined in the absence of financial restraint keeps the good borrowers out of the market. The average quality of the applicant pool falls as higher-risk projects continue to apply, which may lead a bank to adverse selection. Also, moral hazard arises because higher lending rates encourage firms to divert funds to higher-risk activities. Finally, there is an even more direct and simpler effect; even without altering actions, at a higher lending rate there is a higher probability of creditors defaulting on their loans. If bankruptcy costs are positive, the social surplus from investment is reduced (Hellmann et al., 1997, p. 181). At a regulated loan rate, which could be lower in accordance with financial deepening under the ceiling of deposit rate, borrowers can capture a portion of the created rents. This rent facilitates the easy access of creditworthy borrowers to the formal financial system. Moreover, when the lending rate falls, agency costs are reduced as a result. A lower lending rate increases the quality of the pool of applicants, decreases the convexity of the return function for the firm, and reduces the probability of bankruptcy. We basically agree with this view. However, we note that it is difficult to estimate how much of the rent created for the financial sector is transferred to the corporate sector.

Of course, the benefit of reduced agency costs must be weighed against other costs associated with the interest rate ceiling (Hellmann et al., 1997, p. 183). The model further warns that the financial restraint may turn into financial repression (Hellmann et al., 1997, p. 196). Hellmann et al. argue that financial restraint, like any other powerful economic intervention, creates opportunities for politicians and bureaucrats to misuse the policy for their special interests. Therefore the effects of the model rest on how successfully an economy can check the loopholes of the policy. If properly executed, bank rent is expected to contribute positively to the development of financial system. We agree with their view. The empirical study on Japan's quantitative easing and negative rate regime in Chapter 9 may contribute to this argument.

## 4.  Conclusion

There are some sectors in the economy where the resources are underprovided in the absence of government intervention. The financial sector is one among them, where the market has repeatedly failed to provide socially optimum levels of services. Moreover, the financial market is pretty sensitive to any local and international shocks. Perhaps because of its fragile nature, the financial sector is one of the strictly regulated industries in many economies regardless of their level of economic development. In line with this tradition, the financial restraint model advocates for government intervention in the financial market aiming at stabilizing the financial system by providing banks with larger incentives, which is presumably more than that of competitive equilibrium. The basic assumption of the model, as discussed previously, is that neo-classical equilibrium profit is insufficient to ensure socially optimal level of infrastructure for financial services. As a result, many participants remain outside of the formal financial system. To tap this financially excluded population, private financial service providers should be encouraged by providing them with some extra profit or what is called 'rent'. This rent basically comes from the suppressed deposit rate, which will remain below the market clearing rate. Of course, such a policy would hurt depositors and may turn into a welfare loss. However, the debilitating effect of the policy on deposit rate can be avoided if the real interest rate remains above zero. If so, the negative reaction from the depositors due to reduced rate will be very limited. Also, the asset substitution effect (the possibility that the depositors can invest their money in alternative sources, including depositing in foreign banks, or invest in real assets such as gold or real estate) will not be high. From this perspective, it is expected that the benefits received will outweigh the welfare loss to the society.

Of course, the financial restraint model is not without limitations. There are certain economic conditions which have to be ensured in order to reap the pre-scribed benefits from the model. For instance, the real interest rate should be positive (i.e., the inflation should be low). The elasticity of deposit to interest rate should be low. Furthermore, the rent opportunity is not considered a permanent feature of the financial system but rather a transitory solution. Once the expected level of financial development is achieved, rent from the financial sector should be dissipated. Although economically it seems fairly easy, politically it might be tough. We consider these issues in the coming chapters, especially Chapters 2 and 3.

## Notes

1 Although the formal analysis of 'surplus value' is due to Marx, the discussion begins in Adam Smith's *Wealth of Nations*, where he develops the theory of value. See Smith (1776, p. 265). Marx recognized Adam Smith's contribution and contends 'Adam Smith conceives of *surplus-value* as the *general category*, of which profit in the strict sense and rent of land are merely branches'. Stark (1944) argues that the Marxian analysis of surplus-value was a strictly logical development of the Smithian doctrine of value.

2 We adopt the Knightian definition of uncertainty as the subjective assessment of the likelihood of events whose objective probability is not susceptible to measurement. Subjective probability can be distinguished from statistical or objective probability in the sense that uncertainty cannot be reduced to measurable risks. See Chapter 2, section 4.3. Uncertainty may be more or less ignored, or alternatively, subjective probabilities may be applied, together with a risk premium to cover unspecified adverse events (Suzuki, 2011).

# 2   Banks as financial intermediaries and their roles in economic development

*Manjula K. Wanniarachchige,*
*Mohammad Dulal Miah, and Yasushi Suzuki*

## 1.   Introduction

The real challenge of economic development hinges on our ability to change the fortunate of nearly four billion people who live at the bottom of the population pyramid (Collier, 2007). They are not only falling behind but sometimes also falling apart. Among many strategies that can be adopted to rescue these bottom billions, financial inclusion or what Prahalad and Hart (2004) call 'inclusive capitalism' is a crucial one. Financial inclusion, in simpler term, means that financial services are to be made accessible to individuals as they strive to improve their standards of living. In this sense, financial development is a critical element required for poverty alleviation and economic progress.

Financial markets affect economies in multifaceted ways, especially by supplying funds to firms that actively seek external financing. A developed financial system ensures depositors' trust toward the financial systems while encouraging lending institutions to disburse sufficient funds to eligible individuals and enterprises. One critical way in which finance helps the real economy to grow is that financial development facilitates socializing credit risk. In other words, the system absorbs the risk associated with socially profitable projects by encouraging investors with diverse risk appetite to participate in the formal financial system. Enterprises, especially small and medium, which do not enjoy easy access to formal finance in a repressed financial system, can finance their projects once the financial system is developed (Rajan and Zingales, 2004). This may have a snowball effect on the total economy. For instance, the increased access to finance for firms results in increased competition in the product and service markets which facilitates the spread of new technologies. Also, competition weeds out inefficient incumbent firms that may survive in a non-competitive market. Moreover, new intermediaries will emerge, responding to the increased needs of finance from new firms. This will create a pressure for competitors in both financial and product markets to enhance their efficiency and innovation, which in turn leads to economic progress. Thus financial systems form an integral part of economic development.

A typical financial system comprises capital markets (bond and equity markets) and financial intermediaries (banks and other such depository corporations). The former is also known as a direct financing route, whereas the latter is labeled as an indirect financing route. Although it is difficult to differentiate countries based on the financing pattern, the common tradition in the financial literature is that the Anglo-Saxon countries are traditionally characterized by market-based financial systems. Here, capital markets are functionally strong and diverse. Shareholders' rights are well protected. In contrast, the Japan-German system is commonly referred to a bank-based system because firms in those countries rely relatively more on banking systems than on the capital market.

In this chapter we analyze the salient characteristics of both direct and indirect financing routes along with their role in mitigating various frictions, including information asymmetry and higher transaction cost in the market. Then we shed an analytical light on the question as to why we do not see one integrated financial market instead of having a capital market separated from the independent financial intermediaries. In other words, why do financial intermediaries exist even though they are redundant in the Arrow-Debreu general equilibrium model? These aspects are widely discussed in the contemporary theories of banking. We critically examine the rationale put forth by these theories on the existence of financial intermediaries.

## 2. An overview of finance-growth nexus

The role of finance in economic growth has been an issue of academic discussion since the time of Adam Smith. Smith emphasized the role of finance as a means of lowering transaction cost and greater specialization (Beck, 2011). Much later, Bagehot (1873) stimulated the discussion articulating that the loanable funds, when channeled effectively through the financial systems, encourage economic activity of some sectors, which in turn facilitates the development of backward and forward linkage industries through its positive spillover effects. Similarly, Schumpeter (1934) argued that financial intermediaries play a pivotal role in economic development because they provide prospective entrepreneurs with the access to necessary finance for technological innovation. However, the role of finance in economic development did not receive adequate attention from academicians and policymakers until the seminal works of Goldsmith (1969), McKinnon (1973), and Shaw (1973). Their hypothesis, commonly known as the Goldsmith-McKinnon-Shaw hypothesis, states that an increase in the stock of money relative to the level of economic activity increases financial intermediation, followed by productivity increases and economic growth. Because of its emphasis on the supply of money as a stimulus to increased economic activities, this school is labeled as the supply-leading hypothesis (Patrick, 1966).

In the tradition of supply-leading hypothesis, empirical literature mostly follows the notable work of King and Levine (1993). Their seminal study establishes that financial development is positively correlated with contemporaneous rates of economic growth, physical capital accumulation, and economic efficiency improvements. Similarly, Beck, Demirguc-Kunt, and Levine (2001), Bencivenga and Smith (1991), Bloch and Tang (2003), Botric and Slijepcevic (2008),

Claessens and Laeven (2005), Greenwood and Jovanovic (1990), Jappelli and Pagano (1994), Jayaratne and Strahan (1996), and Levine (2003) find a forward causality between finance and economic growth. The basic premise behind such evidence is that external financing is a necessary precondition for firms in financing their investment opportunities because the capacity for self-financing is limited, given that most of the investment opportunities are indivisible and discrete. Thus the proponents of this school generally attempt to prescribe financial development as a key precondition for attaining higher economic growth (Berglof and Bolton, 2005). However, it is also argued in the literature that the effect of financial deepening[1] on economic growth is stronger in developing countries than in industrialized economies (Calderón and Liu, 2003).

In contrast to this supply-leading hypothesis, studies such as Botric and Slijep-cevic (2008), Greenwood and Jovanovic (1990), Harrison, Sussman, and Zeira (1999), and Robinson (1952) show a reverse causality from increased economic activity toward the advancement of the financial system. This happens because the increased economic activity creates more investment opportunities, leading to an increase in the demand for financial services. An increased demand makes it feasible to implement costly financial structures (Greenwood and Jovanovic, 1990), which results in the declining cost of financial intermediation (Botric and Slijepcevic, 2008; Harrison et al., 1999) subsequently contributing to financial development.

Some researchers, on the other hand, argue that the relationship is bi-directional (Bloch and Tang, 2003; Demetriades and Hussein, 1996; Greenwood and Jovanovic, 1990) due to the feedback effects (Harrison et al., 1999). Patrick (1966), in his stages of development hypothesis, explains this anomaly, stating that the supply-leading effects dominate in the early stages of economic development, whereas the demand-following effects are more pronounced as an economy approaches toward maturity. Dawson (2008), Lucas (1988), and Tang (2006), however, deny any significant correlation between finance and economic growth.

The differences in the empirical findings can be attributed to the differences in theoretical and methodological approaches, the differences among countries' level of economic development, and the prevailing political and institutional frameworks. For instance, Yilmazkuday (2011) shows that small governments negatively affect the finance-growth nexus in low income countries, whereas big governments adversely affect this relationship in high income countries. Law and Singh (2014) find that there exists a finance threshold in the finance-growth nexus. Below this threshold, finance yields positive effects on economic growth, whereas above this threshold, a negative effect emerges. Similarly, Law, Azman-Saini, and Ibrahim (2013) argue that the development of finance is beneficial only after a certain threshold level of institutional development is attained. Until then, the effect of finance on growth is nonexistent. Further, an inflation threshold is also evidenced in the finance-growth nexus. For instance, Rousseau and Wachtel (2002) find that the effect of finance on growth turns to be positive when inflation falls below a threshold level, while deflation causes strong positive effects of finance on growth. In comparing the effect between transition and market economies, Fink, Haiss, and Mantler (2005) find a weak relationship between finance and growth in market economies, whereas the relationship is strong in transition countries.

Although the effect of finance on growth depends on many complementary macroeconomic elements, the following propositions are widely accepted in the burgeoning literature, which show that finance facilitates economic development by:

1  Enhancing technological change and productivity growth through improving the efficiency of allocating savings and credit (Allen and Gale, 1997; Schumpeter, 1934; Tian and Zhou, 2008)
2  Mobilizing savings and financing of discrete investment opportunities, particularly in advanced technology, leading to higher level of aggregate investments (Goldsmith, 1969; Jappelli and Pagano, 1994; McKinnon, 1973; Shaw, 1973)
3  Reducing the friction in the economy through providing an efficient platform with lower transaction costs for exchanging financial resources between savers and investors (Ahmad and Malik, 2009; Hellmann and Murdock, 1998; Tuuli, 2002)
4  Improving the productivity and quality of investments through fostering capital market discipline and monitoring (Ahmad and Malik, 2009; Diamond, 1984)

Hence the development of a country's financial system is crucial because it can cater the financial requirements of various sectors in the economy. Due to its widespread importance, policymakers and regulators are increasingly focusing on formulating appropriate institutional frameworks for improving the performance and maintaining the resilience of financial systems.

## 3.  Anatomy of a financial system

A financial system transfers financial resources from those who hold excesses to those who experience shortages in financing their operations and investments. Generally, this takes the form of transferring household savings toward investments in the corporate sector. However, in reality, it may also involve transfer of excess funds within the corporate sector or within the household sector. Moreover, this transfer may be facilitated by the market itself or by some specialized intermediaries. Therefore the term *financial system* has a broader meaning and encompasses both direct financing and indirect financing, as illustrated in Figure 2.1.

The entities with an excess may, therefore, consist of both the households and corporate entities endowed with excess financial resources. On the other hand, the entities with a deficit may comprise corporate entities as well as households that have a shortage of resources in financing their investment and consumption. Even though the households can reasonably be ignored as entities with a deficit, for simplicity, because their financial needs are, in general, for consumption purposes, the ignorance of the corporate entities with excess money on the side of

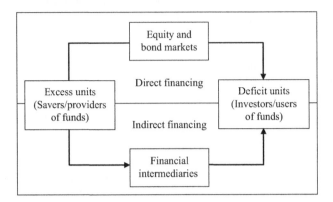

*Figure 2.1* Functions and components of a financial system

savers, together with ignorance of fund transfers among firms, can be regarded as a drawback in most of the textbook models representing the financial system in which finance flows from households to firms.

In the direct financing route, entities with an excess amount of funds directly invest the funds mechanized through capital market. Generally, the equity markets and bond markets constitute direct financing route. Hence the investment processed through the direct financing route usually involves the exchange of such instruments as bonds and equity between the buyers (fund providers) and sellers (fund users). In so doing, the savers are directly exposed to the risks involved with investment projects. Moreover, the fund providers themselves have to screen the projects and monitor the actions of the fund users to avoid possible losses associated with adverse selection and moral hazard problems. Meanwhile, the investments channeled through the direct financing route are relatively long-term in nature. Therefore attempts to liquidate such investments by fund providers in the short-run may result in capital losses. Given this nature of investment in the capital market, risk-loving investors holding long-term financial resources usually prefer to invest their funds through direct financing route. In contrast, under the indirect financing route, fund providers do not directly interact with the users of funds. Instead, they channel their funds for investment through the financial intermediaries, including banks and non-bank financial intermediaries. In such a case, screening and monitoring roles toward borrowers are not performed by the depositors themselves but rather the financial intermediaries involving with lending activities accept borrowers' credit risk. Usually, risk-averse investors prefer this route in investing their savings because the risk associated with direct financing is relatively high.

Regardless of whether the banking or capital market dominates the financial system, the magnitude of the contribution of a well-functioning financial system to a country's economic growth is immense (Ahumada and Fuentes, 2004; Honohan, 2005; Levine, 1997; McKinnon, 1973; Shaw, 1973). The savers in the financial system can earn a return on their excess financial resources, while the investors can finance their fund shortages in making profitable investments. When a society lacks an organized and well-functioning financial system, an efficient flow of funds to the corporate sector cannot be guaranteed. As a consequence, much of the economy's surplus may remain underutilized while, at the same time, leaving a substantial portion of the profitable investment opportunities untapped due mainly to the financial constraints faced by the corporate sector. Concurrently, a lack of financing can negatively affect the adoption of new technologies, and thus the economy gets locked in with obsolete technologies. This situation may lead to a prolonged economic stagnation and thereby may create a wide array of negative consequences to the economy.

The bank rent model advocates for financial development through the indirect financing mode. The logic of doing so relates to the question as to why banks are so important in the financial system. The following section discusses the critical roles of banks that justify their existence as distinct financial intermediaries besides the capital market. Influential theories of financial intermediaries take the view of market imperfection caused by various frictions. Banks help alleviate market frictions and thereby ensure a greater flow of financial assets.

## 4. Banks as financial intermediaries

Banks are a common type of financial intermediary and form an essential part of the indirect mode of finance. Banks are typically defined as financial institutions ". . . whose current operations consist in granting loans and receiving deposits from the public" (Freixas and Rochet, 2008, p. 1). In the conventional banking model, fund providers deposit their funds in the banks for a predetermined rate of return, the interest rate. Banks pool such deposits and subsequently channel toward the fund users, capitalizing on their expertise and scale advantages. However, banks offer a variety of other services in addition to their fundamental role in accepting deposit and granting loans.

Banks usually dominate the financial systems in developing economies mainly because other modes of financing are underdeveloped. It is often argued that the bank-based financial system better serves in mobilizing and allocating capital, and ensures better monitoring (Allen and Gale, 1995; Demirgüç-Kunt and Levine, 1996; Hoshi, Kashyap, and Sharfstein, 1990). Furthermore, firms in their infant stages tend to rely heavily on bank-based financing in addition to self-financing, given the difficulties they face in accessing to capital market financing. Moreover, when fund providers are relatively risk averse, banks become attractive because fund providers hesitate to provide their money directly to the fund users. Hence most developing economies, where majority of the enterprises are in their infant stages and a substantial share of economic activities is carried out through the informal economy, tend to have bank-dominant instead of capital-market dominant financial systems.

The center of the theory of financial intermediation is preoccupied by the concept of market friction, including the asymmetry of information, positive transaction costs, and indivisibilities of investment opportunities.[2] In a perfect market there is no reason for financial intermediaries to exist because the activities performed by banks can be undertaken by fund providers themselves. This justification is quite similar to the argument in which it is commonly claimed that the bilateral transactions between buyers and sellers are not efficient in the markets for goods and services (van Damme, 1994). In the process of financial intermediation, financial intermediaries like banks generally perform four main functions (i.e., facilitation of information collection, economizing transaction costs, absorbing general uncertainty, and maturity transformation and liquidity insurance). Sections 4.1 through 4.4 discuss the nature and importance of these four functions.

### 4.1   Banks facilitate information collection

In the 1970s the information school emerged as an effective approach to analyze the problems pertaining to different branches of economics. The basic tenet of the school relies on the assumption that one of the transacting parties has superior information compared to their counterparts. Or in other words, information regarding the business or project for which financing is required is not symmetrical between the lender and the borrower. The borrowers of funds know well about the riskiness of the project for which funding is required and their repaying capacity as well as the willingness to pay. Moreover, the lenders might think that they cannot make an assessment of the feasibility of the business or project planned by the borrower or the technology possessed by them. In this circumstance, the market value of a project must reflect the average project quality. In case the market places average value greater than the average cost of a project, potential supply of low quality projects may be very large (Leland and Pyle, 1977) because the low returns associated with good projects would yield negative net present values. As a result, at a higher interest rate the owners of good projects would lose incentives to undertake those projects. Therefore they withdraw from the market or divert their borrowed funds toward more risky projects without letting the lender know.

Concurrently, the borrowers with risky projects know that if the project succeeds the higher returns associated with risky project can still yield positive net present values. Of course, the result would be a negative net present value if the project fails. However the bad borrowers do not necessarily intend to repay the loans. In other words, if the project is successful the borrowers benefit, whereas if the project is unsuccessful the lenders suffer. Therefore, even if the interest rates rise the bad borrowers remain in the market. More precisely, at excessively higher interest rates moral hazard or default will be more probable. Thereby the pool of investment projects becomes unfavorable for the lenders and the probability of adverse selection increases (i.e., the probability of selecting a bad project by the lender increases). Since the fund providers in general and non-professional investors in particular are also aware of the adverse selection and moral hazard effect, their readiness to lend decreases when the interest rate increases. Thus, where the degree of information asymmetry is substantial and the supply of bad projects is large relative to the supply of good projects, the financial system may fall short of channeling the required funds from the savers to investors. This entails that information is an economic good.

Information which is not publicly available can be obtained with an expenditure of resources as there is an economic value. General investors at their own initiatives can collect this information, or if there are some economies of scale, firms can gather and sell information about particular classes of assets. Leland and Pyle (1977) suggest two problems for this kind of information gathering and selling. First, the purchasers of information may be able to share or resell their information to others, without diminishing its usefulness to themselves (the problem of appropriability). Second, it may be difficult or impossible for potential users to distinguish good information from the bad information (the problem of reliability). If so, the price of information will reflect its average quality. Again, this can lead to market failure if entry is easy for firms offering poor quality information.

Financial intermediaries, particularly banks, can solve these problems better than any other institutions. In the process of mediating transactions, banks acquire considerable information that might be valuable in loan assessment and monitoring (Stiglitz, 1994). The problem of appropriability will be solved because banks, instead of selling information directly and making it a public good, uses the collected information to boost their return by managing their loan portfolio. While information alone can be resold without diminishing its returns to the reseller, claims to the intermediary's assets cannot be. Thus a return to the bank's information gathering can be captured through the increased value (over cost) of its portfolio. The problem of reliability, on the other hand, can be overcome through a signaling process in which the information producer's willingness to invest in their firm's equity serves as a signal of the quality of the firm's information and the assets selected on the basis of this information. Thus reliability of information can be achieved if the information producers have sufficient stake on the project about which information is produced. This implies that the information producer's initial wealth endowment acts as a constraint on the reliability and as a barrier to entry in the information production industry (Campbell and Kracaw, 1980; Leland and Pyle, 1977). Banks enjoy an advantage in terms of initial endowment of wealth compared to any other form of information producers, individuals or firms. In addition, long-term relationships between the banks and the borrowers ease the future information collection and thereby increase the reliability of information.

## 4.2   Banks economize on transaction cost

While information production is a reason for financial intermediaries to exist, Campbell and Kracaw (1980) argue that intermediaries can do so at a cheaper cost compared to the market. In other words, financial intermediaries can economize on transaction cost in collecting and processing information of borrowers. Transaction costs in economics are described as equivalent to "friction in physics"

(O. E. Williamson, 1985), or "costs for moving an economic system" (Arrow, 1974). These may include ex ante costs associated with searching for suitable transaction partners, negotiation, drafting contracts, and ex post costs associated with monitoring and exercising of rights under the contract, and making a claim, filing a suit, and so on.

Many authors, including Campbell and Kracaw (1980), Gurley and Shaw (1960), and Leland and Pyle (1977) have considered transaction costs as the reasons for the existence of financial intermediaries. Financial intermediaries have an advantage over individuals in collecting information mainly, as they can collect and process information at a relatively cheaper cost because, first, banks possess specialized skills and scale advantages. Long-term relationships between banks and borrowers reduce the probability of moral hazard (Mayer, 1988). Moreover, banks can possess superior screening technology which is infeasible to acquire at the individual level. Given the fixed-cost nature of transaction cost associated with most of the screening technologies, the average cost of screening to a bank decreases as the number of borrower increases (S. D. Williamson, 1986). This makes the information collection of banks more productive and less costly. Moreover, the ability to diversify banks' loan portfolio minimizes the risk while enhancing the return. This return partly may serve as a resource for screening and monitoring effort as well.

Second, financial intermediaries can avoid the duplication of screening and monitoring efforts. These monitoring activities by banks may also generate external benefits. For example, a renewal of a short-term bank loan provides a positive signal to other market participants and hence avoids duplication of information costs (Fama, 1980). As such, banks can save a portion of screening cost as part of the overall transaction cost. For example, if individual fund providers have to assess the creditworthiness of a borrower independently, there would be a sizable duplication of effort where resource utilization is wasteful. If this duplication can be avoided, society gains from saving the transaction costs. On the other hand, a below optimum level of monitoring may result due to the free riding problem, where no lender monitors the borrower because his or her share of the benefit is small (Diamond, 1984). These problems can be avoided if lenders select one among them with the authority to screen and make the investment decision on the other's behalf and divide the transaction cost among them. However, this arrangement is infeasible at the individual level due to various reasons, including the inability to find a person who is trustworthy and possesses required skills and expertise to make the right decision. Moreover, there will be no guarantee that the screening and monitoring effort put forth by the assigned monitor is optimum. For instance, in the absence of sufficient incentives, the monitor might not have sufficient motivation to put sincere effort in screening and monitoring activities.

Obviously, banks as financial intermediaries can overcome these problems on a greater scale. For instance, licensing from the government for banking operations legitimizes banks as long-term financial partners in the society. Moreover, supervision by the regulatory authorities along with the provision of deposit insurance facilitates the banks to build credibility among the depositors. Therefore, as elaborated by Krasa and Villamil (1992), it is optimal that individual lenders delegate the screening and monitoring activity to a financial institution, instead of performing it on their own.

### 4.3 Banks absorb general uncertainty

The new Keynesian or information economists believe that if information is perfectly available at zero transaction cost and given no asymmetry of information among the players in the financial market, the price mechanism would take our economy to the equilibrium, ensuring the optimal allocation of financial resources. However, the lending and investment business is always subject to the associated credit risk and, in particular, general uncertainty. From the post-Keynesian perspective, which pays more attention to the economic behavior under conditions of uncertainty, one of the most important and meaningful roles of banks is to challenge and absorb the credit risk and general uncertainty.

Since the consequences of actions extend into the future, accurate forecasting is essential for making objectively rational choices. But in the real world, most choices take place under conditions of uncertainty. Knight (1921) drew a famous distinction "between 'measurable uncertainty' i.e. 'risk', which may be represented by numerical probabilities and 'unmeasurable uncertainty' which cannot". Numerical probabilities are in turn based on the possibility of repeated observation of an event that allows the calculation of a statistical probability for that event. In contrast, many events in the economic domain are not of this type. For instance, there is no repeated observation that can give us an objective probability for the success of an innovative process. Here the risk involved is a subjective judgment, and this can vary across persons making the judgment based on their experience and knowledge of subtle and unquantifiable aspects of a situation. The formulation of subjective probability judgments is what Knight described as decision-making under uncertainty.

Knightian uncertainty, the same as Keynesian uncertainty, emerges when (a) stochastic variation is not governed by stable probability distributions; (b) agents lack costless information providing insight into the 'true' state of affairs in the economy; (c) agents cannot always determine the extent to which their own actions are responsible for the outcomes they experience; or (d) it is impossible to preclude the possibility of systemic risk, because the economy has no parameters (Dymski, 1993). The fundamental implication of Keynes's uncertainty is that all economically meaningful behavior derives from agents' efforts to protect themselves from uncertainty.

Uncertainty makes the decision processes complex and volatile. In practice, uncertainty may be more or less ignored, or alternatively subjective probabilities may be applied, together with a risk premium to cover unspecified adverse events. Under conditions of uncertainty, banks are still expected to challenge the risk and uncertainty for economic progress and perhaps for alleviation of poverty particularly in developing economies. From this perspective, banks exist as a buffer or cushion to absorb the general uncertainty.

## 4.4   *Asset transformation and liquidity insurance*

Banks are credited with managing liquidity risks better than the individuals. In the case of direct financing, lenders commit their funds to the borrower's project for a certain period of time. For some uncertain events, some members in the coalition may wish to withdraw their funds earlier than the committed time period. In most circumstances, the project cannot be liquidated earlier than the maturity period without losing its value. Of course, early liquidation of the project affects the interest of the members in the coalition who wish to continue with the project. One solution to the problem can be that the members who wish to continue with the project can manage funds to finance those who want to withdraw their funds earlier than the maturity period. Such a solution is infeasible for various reasons. For instance, the existing members might not possess sufficient financial capability to finance the withdrawing partners. In case they seek outside funding, the asymmetry of information and transaction cost will cripple the process. Moreover, the decision of early withdrawal of funds, for whatever reasons, by some partners is likely to shake the confidence of the continuing partners about the success of the project. The aggregate effect is that the lender faced with a need for liquidity might not be able to sell or borrow the full present value of what could be extracted in the future.

This illiquid nature of direct lending is expected to affect the initial terms of loan and lenders' interactions with the entrepreneurs. Since the loan does not repay much when there is a liquidity issue, the lender expects a liquidity premium from the entrepreneur and may incorporate contractual terms that allow the lender to liquidate the entrepreneur's project when the lender is in need of liquidity. Here the lender's need for liquidity creates a liquidity risk for the entrepreneur, and the lender may even refuse to lend if the probability of facing a liquidity need is high. Taking into consideration the uncertainty involved with the future, nobody can accurately predict the probability of liquidity need at an interim stage. Thus an extra level of cautiousness on the part of lenders may stop the flow of funds even to profitable projects.

Banks as financial intermediaries can solve liquidity problems because they can refinance by issuing fresh demand deposits (Pyle, 1971). New depositors will be willing to replace old depositors who withdraw, since the new depositors will be confident that the bank will repay. As argued in Bhattacharya and Thakor (1993), this is possible because of the non-convexity in establishing individual insurance markets for each of the many small risks that impinge on an agent's income, health, and property. The sum of these risks, whose realization affects the agent's demand for withdrawals, is insured by the deposit contract. As a result, bank's deposits are a desirable asset for fund providers who have the need for liquidity and are liquid even though loans made by the bank are illiquid. Moreover, the provision for deposit insurance and reserve requirement provides extra guarantee, besides bank's capability to generate demand deposit, to satisfy the early withdrawals. Thus liquidity insurance provides another reason for financial intermediaries like banks to exist.

## 5.  Conclusion

Despite the long-standing debate, finance makes a substantial contribution in achieving economic growth. Most theories justify the existence of financial intermediaries, particularly banks, through emphasizing their role on reducing market anomalies, which prohibits the flow of expected levels of funds from fund providers to fund users. In so doing, these theories compare a world in which fund providers directly interact with the fund users to a world in which the funds are channeled through the financial intermediaries. Given the various frictions in the financial markets, banks can coordinate the lending activities better than individuals involved with the direct financing route. Banks are able to save a portion of transaction costs due to their scale economies compared to the individuals. Also, they can provide liquidity assurance to the savers in withdrawing their funds. Concurrently banks are capable of converting safety funds into risk funds so that the funds of risk-averse depositors can be used to finance bankable investment projects. These comparative advantages give financial intermediaries like banks raison d'être as distinct financial intermediaries which play an important role in financial development parallel to the capital market.

## Notes

1  Financial deepening in this book refers to an expansion in the amount of bank credit relative to the GDP. In this sense, the total assets, total credit, or total deposits of the banking system relative to GDP tend to reflect financial deepening.
2  The terms 'bank' and 'financial-intermediary' are sometimes used interchangeably on the excuse that banks are predominant in the indirect route.

# 3 Creating bank rent in developing countries

## An integrated model

*Manjula K. Wanniarachchige*

## 1. Introduction

The nature and functions of credit markets are far more complex than the non-financial market. Complex agency relationships and intertemporal credit transactions that characterize a typical banking system create a variety of agency costs. On the other hand, conflicts of interests between agents and principals, under the conditions of high information costs and bounded rationality, increase the probability of adverse selection and moral hazard. This necessitates screening and monitoring, and credible incentives for the players in a financial system to act with due diligence in a mutually beneficial manner.

Banking systems generally dominates the financial systems of developing countries, since capital markets are still in their infant stages. Thus a systematic focus on developing the banking systems is crucial in an attempt to ensure smooth and efficient financial intermediation in those countries. Incentives created in terms of bank rent opportunities, as suggested in the financial restraint model introduced by Hellmann et al. (1997), provides the impetus for banking systems development particularly in developing countries. However, the current bank rent theory does not explicitly state either the exact components of extra incomes or the ways in which extra incomes are to be created when some of its preconditions are absent. For example, the current empirical studies have often defined bank rent opportunities in terms of the extent of interest spreads or net interest margins, while plainly ignoring the effect of other factors that have not been explicitly incorporated into the financial restraint model. Significantly, the effects of these other factors are prominent in developing countries. Consequently, existing debate has failed to explain why most of the developing countries have failed in achieving a sufficient financial development. Therefore the existing bank rent concept and related empirical models need to be expanded further to improve their applicability in developing countries because those economies are characterized with unique conditions.

An attempt is made in this study to expand the current conceptualization of bank rent as an effective mode for banking system development in developing countries by integrating three essential components – namely, price, operating, and macroeconomic rent opportunities. Since the proposed model addresses the strategies to be adopted at various levels in the economic system, its applicability in countries, where the preconditions specified in the conventional bank rent model are absent, remains high.

Discussion in this chapter is organized into seven sections, including this introduction. Section 2 provides an introduction on bank rent and its effects on banking system development. Section 3 discusses the alternative approaches for banking system development and the nature of bank rent-based approaches. Section 4 illustrates the weaknesses associated with existing bank rent-based approaches, whereas section 5 presents a new model of bank rent which addresses those weaknesses. Section 6 states the conclusions derived from the discussions in this chapter, while section 7 provides a set of implications of the proposed model. Further, the discussions in Chapter 6 elaborate the model presented in this chapter with some illustrative empirical evidences.

## 2.   Bank rent and its effects

Existing approaches designed to foster resilience of banks and efficiency of financial intermediation can be grouped into two broad categories (i.e., laissez faire market-based regulations and incentive-based approaches). The laissez faire market-based regulations tend to create external forces and are mainly based on coercion for disciplining the banks through a standardized set of rules like capital regulations, reserve requirements, deposit insurance schemes, lender of last resort services, disclosure requirements, and heavy reliance on external credit assessments suited for arm's length banking. The Basel Committee on Banking Supervision (BCBS) fully embraces this type of framework, which leads the way for Anglo-American type of banking system. Empirical evidences pertaining to these approaches are mixed, and therefore the validity of those approaches has often become the subject of scholarly debate. Moreover, these approaches focus mainly on achieving financial stability rather than on financial deepening and improving the efficiency of financial intermediation.

Owing to inherent limitations associated with the Anglo-American type of banking regulations, incentive-based approaches have attracted widespread attention in recent years as new tools for achieving resilience and efficiency of banking systems. Crucial works by Stiglitz and Weiss (1981) on credit rationing and Hellmann et al. (1997) on financial restraints have laid the foundations for incentive-based approaches, which are often known as bank rent-based approaches or market enhancing approaches. These approaches aim to create a self-enforcing mechanism within the banking system by creating credible incentives for the players in it. In other words, these approaches aim to create opportunities for additional returns, termed as rent opportunities, which can be enjoyed only by pursuing prudent strategies as long-run agents. Significantly, these approaches simultaneously focus on ensuring financial stability as well as on improving the efficiency of financial intermediation when compared with relatively narrower focus of laissez faire market-based regulations. These approaches do not rely solely on the market forces, whereas the implementation of market enhancing interventions is recommended.

The term *rent* in this context, as defined by Khan (2000), refers to 'excess income' or more precisely the excess return or abnormal profit as often termed in economics. More precisely, "a person gets a rent if he or she earns an income higher than the minimum that person would have accepted, the minimum being usually defined as the income in his or her next-best opportunity" (Khan, 2000, p. 21). Thus the usage of the term *rent* here is quite different from the income that accrues to an owner of an inelastically supplied factor of production (e.g., land). In perfectly competitive markets, excess returns disappear in the long-run due to free entry and competition. Hence only normal returns can prevail in such markets. Based on these facts, the bank rent can be defined as the excess returns that are not available to banks on a continuing basis in a competitive market (Hellmann et al., 1997; Khan, 2000).

Bank rent opportunities, if preserved on a continuing basis, enhance the franchise value of banks, as reflected in an increase in the long-run net worth which the bank owners and managers are unable to realize in the short term. If banks pursue strategies which eventually affect the long-run viability of the bank negatively, the opportunities to capture rents eventually disappear. As a result, the franchise value tends to decline. The fear of losing franchise values acts as a credible incentive and eventually motivates the banks to pursue prudent strategies and to manage their risk portfolios effectively through actively involving in screening and monitoring (Aoki, 1994; Hellmann et al., 1997).

Moreover, when a bank earns positive rents, the transactions based on implicit contracts are sustained (Sharpe, 1990) because the bank tends to protect their venture by acting in good faith. Concurrently, extra resources resulting from bank rent facilitate the investment in relationship-specific assets and in screening and monitoring systems which are costly to produce and maintain. As a consequence, when increased transaction costs prevent the formulation of complete contracts and when incomplete contracts discourage risky transactions, the bank rent provides incentives and expands the opportunities for the banks to engage in relationship-based lending while relying on implicit and incomplete contracts. Here, the costs of ex post negotiations can be covered by the bank rent. Relationship-based lending, particularly in less competitive markets, encourages the firms and banks to form mutually beneficial relationships. These closer relationships result in a set of loyal clients who repeatedly transact with a particular bank. Through these relationships, the banks can avoid some of the costs associated with information asymmetry and are able to maximize ex post rents. For example, banks can exploit their information monopolies to charge higher interest rates from informationally captured firms (Schenone, 2009). The firms also, on the other hand, are able to secure a source of guaranteed financing, even if they are informationally opaque.

Moreover, banks can invest part of extra returns in screening and monitoring systems. Therefore the probabilities of adverse selection and moral hazard tend to decrease. Thereby the probabilities of defaults in the loan portfolios tend to decrease. Further, bank rent opportunities provide a cushion for facing unexpected adverse situations through creating healthy reserves within banks. Therefore when the rent opportunities are available, banks tend to have stronger incentives to allocate more funds particularly toward riskier projects involving innovations.

## 3. Creation of bank rent

As explained in the credit rationing model, interest rate does not act as an effective device for clearing imbalances in credit markets compared to price in commodity markets (Stiglitz and Weiss, 1981). The quality of a credit contract largely depends on the credibility of the borrower. Concurrently the borrowers in a credit market are heterogeneous. Therefore the lenders need to properly identify the borrowers before determining a suitable interest rate and terms of credit. However, imperfect information and transaction costs prevent the lenders with bounded rationality from identifying good borrowers from the bad borrowers ex ante when the credit decision is made.

When collecting and processing of information are prohibitively costly, banks tend to charge an average interest rate from all borrowers rather than attempting to comprehensively ascertain the exact risks associated with each borrower. Generally, this average interest rate is higher than the rate that the good borrowers expect to be offered. This results in lower or negative net present values for good borrowers' projects because the discounted values of low returns associated with less risky projects decrease as the interest rate increases. On the other hand, under such average interest rates, the bad borrowers can get loans at interest rates below their expected level, given the high returns associated with their high risk projects. This in turn increases the attractiveness of the loans to bad borrowers while decreasing the attractiveness of the loans to good borrowers. As a result, when the banks increase interest rates, good borrowers usually leave the market because they cannot afford those higher interest rates. But the bad borrowers still tend to remain in the market since the loans are still attractive, given the fact that they do not intend to repay the loans if their projects fail. Thus the quality of the loan applicant pool deteriorates, along with the increase in interest rates particularly beyond a certain threshold level (Hellmann et al., 1997). Concurrently, an increase in the tendency of borrowers to misrepresent information is expected. Therefore the probabilities of adverse selection and moral hazard increase. Thus, despite the existence of an excess demand for credit, banks tend to reject some of the loan applications while keeping the interest rate at an optimal level instead of increasing the interest rate beyond the threshold. This optimal interest rate does not necessarily clear the imbalances between the credit demand and supply, but such interest rate can mitigate the issues associated with adverse selection and moral hazard. Consequently, some seemingly identical borrowers receive credit while others do not receive (Stiglitz and Weiss, 1981). This is commonly known as credit rationing.

Significantly, the level of credit extended by the banks as a whole, under credit rationing, rests below the equilibrium quantity of lending that would have prevailed in a (perfectly) competitive market. Hence in a static sense, credit rationing can increase the financial constraints for firms in the short-run. Nevertheless, banks can minimize the potential losses associated with moral hazard and adverse selection which are otherwise inherent in the system. This, in a way, creates a rent opportunity for banks and eventually leads to an increase in the franchise value of the bank. In the long-run, this causes a right-ward shift in the credit supply curve, expanding the amount of credit available.

In practice, however, credit rationing on its own cannot resolve the information problems in the banking industry, because the credit rationing model does not explicitly discuss the mechanisms that create extra returns to deal with the information costs.[1] For example, credit rationing merely minimizes the possible increases in the issues associated with adverse selection and moral hazard, rather than eliminating them. For example, under the previously listed conditions, the banks still have to arbitrarily select some of the seemingly identical borrowers while rejecting others because banks are not endowed with sufficient resources to actively engage in screening and monitoring of the borrowers to make an objective decision regarding (1) whom the credit should be extended to, and (2) how the borrowers actually invest the borrowed money. The financial restraint model pioneered by Hellmann et al. (1997) argues that the government can intervene in credit markets with market enhancing tools (financial restraints) to create rent opportunities for the banks. These rent opportunities, in turn, allow the banks to deal with the information costs, and to actively screen and monitor their loan portfolios.

The financial restraint model recognizes that excessive competition is quite harmful for the productivity and resilience of financial intermediaries. For example, assume that a bank initially finances a risky project with strong learning effects in which the benefits accrue in later stages on a long-term basis. This initial financing would inevitably be associated with higher interest rates, given the high uncertainty of the outcomes of the project. However, after observing the success of the project, other banks in a competitive market may start to compete by offering lower interest rates. As a consequence, rent opportunities available for the initial bank tend to diminish. Hence, on the one hand, this possibility can induce the initial bank to shirk on screening and monitoring activities in its attempt to cut costs which they may not be able to recover later. On the other hand, it can motivate the initial bank to focus on short-term investment opportunities with front-loaded returns rather than lending to projects with strong learning effects which can be materialized only in the long run (Emran and Stiglitz, 2009). Thus, in such a context, not only the stability of the banks diminishes due to decreasing rent opportunities, but also their long-run productivity declines due to reduced investments in technology and other relationship-specific assets. Therefore the model calls for a set of restraints on free competition to preserve rent opportunities on a continuing basis in such a way that the financial stability of the banks can be enhanced while guaranteeing a higher level of investments for the economy.

Commonly applied financial restraints in practice include deposit rate ceilings, entry barriers, and sometimes controls on the lending rates. The main objective of financial restraints is to maintain a substantial margin between lending and deposit interest rates in real terms through interest rate ceilings. According to the financial restraint model, such an interest spread constitutes the rent opportunities available for the banks. Nevertheless, deposit rate control alone is not sufficient to maintain adequate interest spreads. Entry restrictions for the banks and restrictions on expanding the branch network also can be used as effective financial restraints in maintaining the desired level of interest spreads on a continuing basis. Thus the essence of financial restraints is concerned with controlling the competition within banking systems. The resulting rent opportunities contribute to increase the franchise values. In this sense, the financial restraint model elaborates how the rent opportunities can be created.

The financial restraint model views the market mechanism and the activities of the government as complementary forces rather than substitutes. Further, the financial restraint policies leave the ultimate locus of control in economic activities in the private sector. Hence the government merely facilitates the market mechanism through creating rent opportunities that can be captured by banks only through functioning efficiently and prudently. In contrast, financial repression policies place the locus of control on the government by enforcing a wide range of severe restrictions. Moreover, the bank rent opportunities created through financial restraints have quite different characteristics from transfers of wealth in terms of subsidies. In the latter case, the wealth is often transferred to recipients regardless of their actions. As a result, the recipients of subsidies may enjoy those benefits without making productive investments. But the financial restraints simply create opportunities for additional incomes (rent opportunities) that can only be captured by implementing prudent and efficient strategies. If the banks are involved in inefficient lending, the resulting increased defaults may eventually overrule the profit opportunities created in terms of interest spreads.

In a static sense, when financial restraints are imposed, the total amount of credit extended to the society becomes lower than what would have been extended under the market equilibrium. However, using the resulting rent opportunities, the banks can make more investments to expand their activities, to improve the quality of banking services, and to build their credibility and reputation. Hence the financial restraint policies, by creating rent opportunities, can facilitate the development in the banking system and its technology. As a result, the supply curve shifts to the right in the long run. This can be further justified based on crucial assumptions of the financial restraint model. For example, the model accepts that the extent of savings depends on the extent of the banking infrastructure available for mobilizing deposits and the quality of the banking services offered to bank clients (Hellmann et al., 1997). Moreover, the model is based on the assumption that the responsiveness of the deposits to decreased deposit interest rate is low. Thus the amount of credit extended to the society increases in the long run and may even exceed the amount that would have been available if the competitive equilibrium is preserved.

## 4.   Critique on the financial restraint model

Even though the financial restraint model provides a strong framework for developing banking systems, its applicability in developing countries can be debated on a number of aspects. First, the model assumes that financial and economic deregulation fosters excessive competition which, in turn, reduces or eliminates the rent opportunities available for the banks if the governments do not intervene. But empirical studies do not provide convincing evidences concerning all developing countries that financial deregulation necessarily reduces the profitability of banks (Hanazaki and Horiuchi, 2001). Actually, the levels of competition in some of the developing country banking systems are still not intense enough to erode interest spreads. Hence the comparison of conditions that would have prevailed in perfectly competitive markets with those in developing country banking systems is not justifiable (Demetriades and Luintel, 1997).

Second, under the financial restraint model, rent opportunities are created under a protective framework designed to control the prices (i.e., interest rates). But Hellmann et al. (1997) recognize that the firms in developing countries are "able to capture rents in equilibrium" due to the imperfection of competition. Hence the real necessity of a protective framework (i.e., restraints) in the context of some developing countries is debatable. Further, such a protective framework may aggravate the inefficiency associated with already collusive less-competitive banking systems. On the other hand, given the possibility of political influences, the appropriateness of the protective framework for the economy cannot be guaranteed on a long-term basis.

Third, a stable macroeconomic environment with a relatively low level of inflation is a prerequisite for successfully implementing financial restraint policies. These preconditions necessary for implementing financial restraints cannot be found in most of the developing countries. For example, when inflation is quite high, government may face difficulties in setting a deposit rate ceiling in such a way that the real interest rates still remain positive. If the real interest rates become negative, the public may refrain from savings in monetary assets and may choose non-financial assets instead.

Fourth, banks in developing countries offer a variety of non-financial benefits to attract deposits, even when the deposit rates are lower. In this context, increased costs of providing these non-financial benefits (i.e., the cost of non-price competition) may erode the rent opportunities, even if the interest expenses are lower when the ceiling on deposit rate is imposed. Even though Hellmann et al. (1997) already recognize this possibility, their model is silent on how to curb the non-price competition.

Fifth, the model assumes that the banks voluntarily increase their prudence, and therefore they actively invest in screening and monitoring mechanisms merely due to the availability of rent opportunities. The main premise behind this argument is that when the increased competition erodes rent opportunities, banks tend to shirk their screening and monitoring activities. However, when the banks are rationally managed, the owners and managers may not shirk their monitoring activities merely due to lack of excess incomes, because such behavior may result in further loss of profit opportunities (Hanazaki and Horiuchi, 2001).

Sixth, Hellmann et al. (1997) recognize "poor institutional structure" as "the biggest weakness of many financial systems" in developing countries. Even though rent opportunities may improve the conditions of the banking system its capacity to improve the institutional structure is questionable because banks have little or no control over the fundamental institutions of the economy. Hence the adverse effects associated with the economy-wide factors cannot be eliminated using bank rent.

Seventh, as Hellmann et al. (1997) note, financial restraint policies may also be subject to political rent seeking (in addition to the anomalies, i.e., bribery, that could result from self-interested loan officers acting under the conditions of credit rationing). For example, in the absence of appropriate regulatory monitoring and sanction mechanisms alongside a system of proper corporate governance, banks may use part of the rent for unproductive rent seeking activities rather than making productive investments necessary for the banking system development. Therefore there is no guarantee that the national regulators implement the financial restraint policies for the betterment of the financial system. Sometimes collusions among bankers and national regulators may pave the way for unnecessary rent opportunities which banks can extract as free-riders. For example, banks may confine their expansion to more profitable areas while neglecting the rural areas, but the national regulator is unable to rectify such anomalies due to collusive relationships.

Eighth, the financial restraint model argues that the banks voluntarily lower the lending rate in the long-run such that the quantity of credit extended to the economy becomes larger than the amount expected to be extended in the absence of financial restraints. But given the prevailing constraints on competition, banks in oligopolistic markets[2] may simply extract the available rent opportunities without making investments needed for the advancement of the system. More precisely, highly leveraged banks can free-ride on available rent opportunities and extract as much rent as they can in the short-run because the financial restraint model does not create any credible penalties for inefficient management. In the absence of such penalties, protective regulations may stimulate inefficiency and excessive risk taking.

Finally, the policies of financial repression include regulatory ceilings on interest rates, directed credit, entry restriction (Korosteleva and Lawson, 2010; McKinnon, 1973), and sometimes may include specific taxes on financial institutions, high reserve requirements, requirements to participate in budget financing, and exchange rate regulations as well. These types of unproductive government interventions have been recognized as some of the main causes behind the shallow financial depth and unsatisfactory economic growth in many developing countries (Kang and Sawada, 2000; Korosteleva and Lawson, 2010; McKinnon, 1973). But the financial restraint model embraces some of these strategies as policies of financial restraints and has attempted to distinguish them from the policies of financial repression. Significantly, Stiglitz (1993) uses the term financial repression for this type of policies and argues that "financial repression can be used as the basis of an incentive scheme to encourage higher savings and more efficient allocation of capital" (p. 41), while stressing the magnitude of the repression policies. In this context, the position of Hellmann et al. (1997) is unclear and conflicts with that of McKinnon (1973). As far as the specific conditions prevailing in some of the developing countries are concerned, the arguments of McKinnon (1973) seem to be still more realistic.

Due to these issues, the creation of rent opportunities through implementing financial restraints in developing countries is debatable. As a result, the capacity of studies based on the conventional bank rent models is limited in addressing the issues pertaining to the shallow financial depth and inefficient financial intermediation in developing countries. Therefore this chapter first argues that the rent opportunities created in terms of interest spreads are merely a necessary condition, whereas the mere existence of healthy interest spreads does not necessarily guarantee true rent opportunities for the banks, particularly in developing countries. Second, the creation of rent opportunities according to the model proposed here does not require a specially designed protective framework as suggested in the financial restraint model (e.g., interest rate ceilings and entry barriers). Under a set of standard regulatory measures (such as the Basel framework), the banking systems in developing countries cannot reach an overcrowded situation with excessive competition. Therefore the banks in those countries may enjoy opportunities to earn excess profits, even in the absence of a specifically designed protective framework.

## 5.   An extended bank rent model

Given the inherent issues associated with the existing models and their limited applicability in developing countries, this section proposes a new model that incorporates a broad set of factors that can affect the bank rent opportunities. Since the proposed model does not rely on any preconditions, it is applicable in any context. In other words, any condition that may prevail in a given economy can be categorized under one of the three type of rent opportunities discussed in the proposed model.

Figure 3.1 illustrates the proposed model which decomposes the total rent opportunity into three abstract subcomponents – namely, price rent opportunities, operating rent opportunities, and macroeconomic rent opportunities. The figure also contains an illustrative list of variables that characterize each type of rent opportunity. This type of detailed decomposition facilitates the identification of different types of rent opportunities and enables the exploration of how alternative types of rent opportunities interact with each other to determine the ultimate rent opportunity available for the banks. By doing so, the model helps explain (1) why some of the banking systems with healthy interest spreads have failed to achieve sufficient development; and (2) how financial regulators and economic policymakers can create effective rent opportunities for the banks without excessively focusing on interest rates and mechanisms that affect the

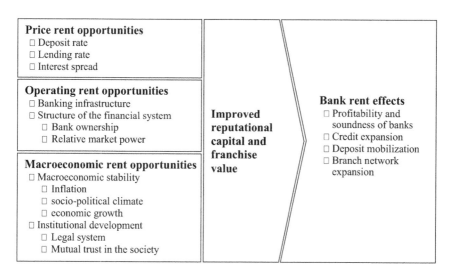

| Price rent opportunities |
| Deposit rate |
| Lending rate |
| Interest spread |

**Price rent opportunities**
☐ Deposit rate
☐ Lending rate
☐ Interest spread

**Operating rent opportunities**
☐ Banking infrastructure
☐ Structure of the financial system
  ☐ Bank ownership
  ☐ Relative market power

**Macroeconomic rent opportunities**
☐ Macroeconomic stability
  ☐ Inflation
  ☐ socio-political climate
  ☐ economic growth
☐ Institutional development
  ☐ Legal system
  ☐ Mutual trust in the society

**Improved reputational capital and franchise value**

**Bank rent effects**
☐ Profitability and soundness of banks
☐ Credit expansion
☐ Deposit mobilization
☐ Branch network expansion

*Figure 3.1* Extended bank rent model

market mechanism. Sections 5.1 through 5.3 discuss the nature of each type of rent opportunity in detail.

## 5.1 Price rent opportunities

The term *price rent opportunities* refers to the rent opportunities resulting from the difference between the cost of deposits and return on loans (i.e., the interest spread). This, to a large extent, is equivalent to the concept of bank rent as used in the financial restraint model and in most of the existing empirical studies. Price rent opportunities allow banks to earn extra profits capitalizing on the lower cost of funds and higher return on loans. In general, higher interest spreads, *ceteris paribus*, entail possibilities for higher rent opportunities. But the proposed model does not consider the entire spread, the difference between deposit interest rate and lending interest rate, as total rent opportunity, because a part of the interest spread inevitably has to be allocated to cover other operating expenses. More precisely, the interest spread is decomposable into its cost and profit components (Randall, 1998). Moreover, nowadays banks earn a sizable amount of non-interest income. Therefore the interest spread alone does not necessarily reflect the degree of rent opportunity available.

Banking systems in developing countries constantly enjoy healthy interest spreads compared to the banks in industrialized countries (Barajas, Steiner, and Salazar, 1999; Mujeri and Younus, 2009). If interest spread represents the available rent opportunity, as argued in the conventional bank rent literature, why is the financial depth shallow in most of the developing countries, despite the healthy interest spreads they have enjoyed on a continuing basis for decades? In fact, the higher spreads in most of those countries are partly a result of the low level of competition. The entry of new banks is implicitly constrained in developing countries due to difficulties in meeting the scale required to be efficient given the limited transaction volumes. State dominance in the banking system acts as another barrier for competition in developing countries. Also, minimum capital requirements and other regulatory conditions necessary for establishing new banks and branches constrain the expansion of banking systems. Hence in developing countries, banks in large number have not emerged despite financial liberalization. Therefore most of such banking systems are characterized with either oligopolistic competition or, at most, monopolistic competition (Guzman, 2000), rather than with excessive competition as presumed in most of the existing bank rent literature. Further, underdeveloped information infrastructures and technologically backward operating systems make access to information more costly in developing countries. Thus, even in the absence of explicit controls on interest rates, there is little tendency for the interest rates to converge with the equilibrium rates through a price competition. Further, higher levels of inefficiencies, higher operating costs, and higher inflation and risk premiums have also contributed to widen the interest spreads in those banking systems. Concurrently, the magnitude of non-interest incomes also contributes substantially to the profitability of the banks. This effect is not captured by the interest spread. When there is a substantial income in terms of non-interest incomes, banks can reduce the interest spreads (Mujeri and Younus, 2009). Nevertheless, the significance of non-interest incomes in developing countries is generally trivial. Therefore this can be another reason for higher interest spreads prevailing in those countries.

Due to inherent possibility of market failures in credit markets, banks and banking regulators cannot maneuver the interest rates solely at their discretion. Imperfect information prevents the lenders from appropriately assessing the creditworthiness of the borrowers and their future intentions. Therefore interest rate alterations may create complex effects on financial intermediation, as also illustrated in the credit rationing model. Despite rigorous research, the relationships between the interest rate and financial development indicators like the amount of deposits or lending and the extent of branch network have not been well established (Dullien, 2009). Hence the role of interest rate as a predictor of financial intermediation is rather weaker than the conventional literature claims.

In fact, interest payments constitute the main return for depositors but are not the only means of attracting deposits. Japanese households, for example, keep a healthy portion of their wealth in bank deposits (Suzuki, 2011, pp. 106–108), though the interest rates are almost zero. Hence there might be some other incentives for them to keep their savings in the form of bank deposits rather than investing them in other types of assets. For example, apart from financial benefits, the banks offer a variety of non-financial benefits in attracting deposits (Spellman, 1980; White, 1976). These non-financial benefits may include the goods and services given as gifts, extended opening hours at bank counters, and a widespread branch network and so on. Also, Hellmann et al. (1997) suggest that the amount of deposits depends on the safety of deposits, on the efficiency of the services provided by the financial intermediaries, and on the extent of infrastructure, such as the bank branch network available for mobilizing deposits. These factors reduce some of the costs for customers (e.g., waiting time and travelling costs) in accessing banking services. Therefore non-financial benefits can replicate the effects of interest rate yields by providing convenience yields. On the other hand, non-financial goods and services can be offered as close substitutes for interest payments. This has been a popular form of non-price competition not only in financial markets but also in other markets.

Hence when the degree of non-price competition increases, price elasticity of deposits tends to decrease rapidly (Hellmann et al., 1997, p. 168). In other words, non-financial benefits like convenience yield and marketing campaigns can largely influence the amount of deposits and hence the amount of lending (Cohen and Kaufman, 1965; Spellman, 1980; White, 1976). For example, McKinnon (1973) emphasizes on the relevance of convenience yield in terms of extended bank branch network on deposits and lending by stating that "without interest rate competition, the banks [in Brazil] were induced to compete for customers by simply setting up branches . . ." (p. 85).

On the other hand, an excessively large interest spread can be detrimental to economic activity because it may discourage both savings and investments leading to a substantial financial disintermediation (Barajas et al., 1999; Khrawish, Al-Abadi, and Hejazi, 2008; Randall, 1998). The credit rationing model and the neo-classical economic literature readily support this argument. Therefore interest spread alone does not portray a good picture of the overall rent opportunity. Significantly, widening of interest spreads should not be the primary target of policymakers and banking regulators. Operating and macroeconomic rent opportunities (or losses), as illustrated in subsequent sections, may augment (or nullify) the price rent opportunities. As a result, despite higher spreads, banks in those countries may not actually enjoy a sizable rent opportunity.

## 5.2 Operating rent opportunities and operating losses

The term *operating rent opportunities* refers to the rent opportunities available to the banks as a result of the favorable operating environment in which the banks operate. More precisely, the banks in a better operating environment are able to lower information costs and other production costs associated with inefficiency, while increasing the opportunities to earn profits by offering a more diversified set of services. If the operating environment is adverse, a variety of additional costs emerge for the banks in terms of increased transaction costs and other production costs. Further, this may curtail the banks' ability to offer a diversified set of services to a broad client base. As a result, some of the potential revenues may also disappear. These adverse effects are termed here as operating losses (i.e., negative operating rent opportunities).

The operating environment, in this context, is composed of the banking system structure and the banking infrastructure. Banking system structure, shaped by the composition of the banking system, encompasses the number of banks and the extent of their branch networks, the relative market power of individual banks, the types of banks, and ownership and governance of banks. These factors collectively determine the level and nature of competition and therefore have a profound effect on the determination of the interest rates which, in turn, affect the extent of price rent opportunities as well. For example, the increased competition may erode some of the price rent opportunities through lowering lending rates and increasing deposit rates. However, appropriate levels of competition contribute to enhancing productivity by encouraging efficient resource utilization (Sabot and Székely, 1998, p. 2) because the banks operating under low levels of competition and under special protective regulations (e.g., state-owned banks) do not have sufficient incentives to be efficient. Moreover, competition stimulates the geographical spread of banking services, leading to an expansion of the client base. Therefore the benefits associated with increased competition, particularly in developing countries, may overrule the losses associated with decreasing interest spreads. Anti-competitive measures like regulatory controls on interest rates and entry barriers, on the other hand, can be detrimental to banking system development, because they can have negative implications for productivity growth. In fact, the competition in developing countries is already constrained due mainly to inherent characteristics such as higher transaction costs, higher risk perceptions, and limited client base, rather than due to explicitly imposed regulations like entry barriers and interest rate controls.[3] Therefore further regulatory barriers tend to create more side-effects than benefits.

Apart from influencing interest rates, the banking system structure can have other implications as well. Bank ownership and size, for example, may have different impacts on the profitability and expansion of the branch network (Chang, Hasan, and Hunter, 1998; Clarke, Cull, Martinez Peria, and Sanchez, 2002; De Young and Nolle, 1996; Lensink and Naaborg, 2007; Sathye, 2003). For example, it may be easy for the government to establish new banks and branches capitalizing on their reputational capital, whereas the new private banks may face difficulties in establishing their businesses at the initial stages due to lack of reputational capital. This implies that banks with different sizes and ownerships may entail different rent opportunities irrespective of the interest spread available in the system.

Banking infrastructure, on the other hand, encompasses a wide range of public goods created by the government or collectively by the participants in the financial system to facilitate a smooth intermediation of funds. Nature and extent of banking regulations also can be considered as a part of the banking infrastructure. Efficient banking infrastructure reduces some of the costs which banks have to incur by themselves in the absence of banking infrastructure. For example, payment and settlement systems, credit information systems, credit insurance and rating agencies, credit guarantee systems, and banking regulations collectively determine the level of transaction costs in the system and the quality of credit contracts through making information widely available and through providing an appropriate institutional framework for contracting parties. As a consequence, the cost of monitoring and screening for the banks as well as the adverse selection and moral hazard issues may decrease. Better information systems, however, may foster competition by creating a level playing field for all banks (Amor-Tapia, Fanjul, and Tascón, 2010). As a consequence, the banks may not be able to capture informationally opaque firms through relationship lending. But the benefits associated with this infrastructure often supersede the losses attributable to dissipating information rent opportunities. Simultaneously, infrastructures like efficient payment and settlement systems can substantially improve the quality and diversity of the services offered to bank clients, and help widen the client base of the banks.

Moreover, banking system structure and infrastructure can create substantial convenience benefits for the bank clients (Lanzillotti and Saving, 1969). Due to increased convenience, savers may increase the amount of money deposited in the banks even when the interest rates remain unchanged. For example, Dullien (2009) states that peoples' propensity to keep their savings in monetary assets tends to increase along with the increased accessibility to banks. Further, Hemachandra (2003) highlights the irrelevance of deposit interest rates in Sri Lanka as a determinant of the level of deposits while emphasizing the significance of extended branch network. Beck, Demirguc-Kunt, and Peria (2007) also report that the extent of branch networks positively affects the number of households with a bank account. Expansion of banking services to areas which were not previously served by banks can attract savings into the banking system from other sectors (Cohen and Kaufman, 1965).

Further, banking structure and infrastructure can enhance the capacity of the banks to lend. Moreover, increased outreach of bank branches can mediate issues of information asymmetry and lower information costs. For example, when the banks are closely located to their clients (due to an extensive branch network), the relationships between them tend to be stronger due to frequent transactions and longer-term relationships. In other words, banks are better able to deal with *soft* information relating to informationally opaque clients when the bank is located close to the client. For example, Beck et al. (2007) state that credit constraints for firms are low in countries where the branch network is widespread. As a result, the quality and quantity of lending increase, leading to a higher level of investments and increased economic activity (Jayaratne and Strahan, 1996).

Operating rent opportunities eventually augment price rent opportunities to give a higher overall rent for the banks. More precisely, if substantial operating rent opportunities are available, *ceteris paribus*, the actual rent opportunity available for the bank can be disproportionately high relative to the interest spread. Otherwise, operating losses (i.e., negative operating rent opportunities) can erode some of the price rent opportunities. Banks, in general, pass their operating costs to clients by setting higher lending rates and lower deposit rates (Barajas et al., 1999; Demirguc-Kunt and Huizinga, 1999; Khrawish et al., 2008; Mujeri and Younus, 2009; Randall, 1998). Thus, when a sizeable number of inefficiencies characterize the operating environment, banks tend to widen the interest spreads merely to compensate for higher overheads and inefficiencies. However, such interest spreads fail to generate rent opportunities.

### 5.3    *Macroeconomic rent opportunities and macroeconomic losses*

The term *macroeconomic rent opportunities*, as used in the proposed model, refer to the decreased losses or costs together with expanded revenue opportunities attributable to the favorable macroeconomic environment. It is worth mentioning that the term *macroeconomics* in this context is used in a broader sense to cover a wide variety of economy-wide factors like social, cultural, economic, political, and legal aspects.

Macroeconomic stability of a country plays a crucial role in capital accumulation, investments, and economic activity (Barro, 1995; Younis, Lin, Sharahili, and Selvarathinam, 2008). Turbulences caused by rapid fluctuations and steady increase in the general price level, and fluctuations in the exchange rate and so on erode the net present value of investment and stimulate the incentives for illegitimate borrowers to misrepresent their aims (Azariadis and Smith, 1996). Concurrently, a society characterized by a high level of mutual trust and appropriate institutional arrangements facilitates contracting by lowering transaction costs. An efficient legal system facilitates the resolution of conflicts faster and at a lower cost. For example, an improvement of creditor rights may make it easier for the lenders (banks) to recover any unpaid loans and thus discourage moral hazard by the borrowers. Similarly, mutual trust minimizes the tendencies for misrepresentation and moral hazard by the borrowers. Moreover, when the firms are bound by well-designed institutions and when the economy is characterized with advanced information infrastructures, like credit information systems and credit rating agencies, borrowers have less room for misrepresentation and moral hazard. Hence the necessity of screening and monitoring declines. In contrast, a society characterized with high opportunism makes the contracting difficult, and thus aggravates the screening and monitoring costs.

Political instability, being a part of the macroeconomic context, intensifies the society's overall level of uncertainty (Rodrik, 1999), and thereby deteriorates business confidence, destroys social relationships, and creates extra challenges for the development of financial markets (Baddeley, 2008; Nagarajan, 1997). Increased uncertainty creates extra burdens on measurement, negotiation, and enforcement activities that make arriving at credible predictions on future contingencies difficult. In other words, the transaction costs tend to rise with socio-economic instability. Moreover, agents may prefer current consumption than savings. These result in decreased savings and prolonged pessimism about future investment opportunities (Nagarajan, 1997). Increased costs, higher default risks, and uncertainty necessitate the banks to maintain higher interest spreads (Suzuki et al., 2010) to compensate for increased costs and default probabilities as well as for unforeseen contingencies and maintaining their resilience. Moreover, during political conflicts and turbulences, the investors (borrowers) may hesitate to make long-term investments. Simultaneously, risk perceptions of the banks may increase along with the political uncertainty. As a result, banks tend to limit their operations into safer and politically stable areas – hence the demand for and supply of financial services offered by banks declines. As a consequence, credit may become increasingly rationed and constrained (Azariadis and Smith, 1996; Huybens and Smith, 1999), and the corporate sectors tend to face severe financial constraints compared to those in stable and peaceful countries (Baddeley, 2008).

In this sense, a sizable amount of operating costs and losses tend to decrease when the convenience of the macroeconomic context increases. Concurrently, an expansion in bank lending can be expected because lending in such a context becomes less risky for banks. Also steady economic growth and rapidly growing industrial and services sectors contribute to expand the client base and demand for banking services. Contrary to the arguments based on the conventional bank rent model, this discussion implies that the higher interest spreads prevailing in an economy characterized by severe political tensions and economic turbulences do not necessarily signal the availability of positive rent opportunities for the banks.

It is evident here that the effect of macroeconomic context can be twofold – that is, it may create either a positive effect or a negative effect. While the positive effect is termed as macroeconomic rent opportunities, the negative effect is termed here as macroeconomic losses (i.e., negative macroeconomic rent opportunities). These macroeconomic losses are composed of increased costs or loss of revenue opportunities attributable to bad macroeconomic context and can, in turn, nullify other rent opportunities (i.e., price and operating rent opportunities).

## 6.   Conclusions

The creation of rent opportunities for the banks in developing countries is a challenging task. Even though larger interest spreads can be created with ease using financial restraints, the ability of those interest spreads to generate adequate profits for the banks depends on a variety of other factors that extends far beyond those specified in the conventional bank rent models. In fact, higher interest spreads may merely indicate higher levels of friction prevailing in the banking system, as well as in the economy as a whole. Moreover, even if the interest spreads are marginal, banks can earn higher profits if the operating and macroeconomic rent opportunities are positive and substantial. Therefore the overall rent opportunities available for the banks are not always proportional to the interest spreads. This has been the primary reason why the existing bank rent models have failed to provide credible explanations as to why some of the banking systems with high interest spreads have failed to achieve sufficient growth, while others have achieved healthy growth despite the narrow interest spreads prevailing in those systems.

The model proposed addresses this dilemma by recognizing three different rent opportunities that constitute the overall rent opportunity. Moreover, a special protective framework is not mandatory in creating rent opportunities under the proposed model. Instead, the regulators need to focus on creating operating and macroeconomic rent opportunities, rather than focusing on already available price rent opportunities. In this sense, the proposed model does not appreciate explicit controls on the market mechanism. But depending on the extent of competition prevailing in the system, such control may be implemented on a short-term basis to reduce the excessive competition. Moreover, the proposed model embraces the advantages associated with standard sets of regulations, as suggested by the BCBS, because under a carefully adopted and implemented standard set of banking regulations, developing country banking systems cannot be characterized with excessive competition.

When all three types of rent opportunities are positive and substantial, the maximum possible rent opportunity is available to the banks. In such a circumstance, banks are able to enjoy a disproportionately higher rent opportunity relative to the interest spread. Otherwise, when operating losses and/or macroeconomic losses are present, they may erode the available price rent opportunities, resulting in a lower overall rent opportunity. In this situation the overall rent opportunity available to the banks would be disproportionately lower relative to the interest spread.

The bank rent cube illustrated in Figure 3.2 further elaborates the proposed model. The sides of the cube reflect the net rent opportunities available in each type of rent. For example, the top layer represents the situations characterized by net macroeconomic rent opportunities, whereas the bottom layer represents situations characterized with macroeconomic losses on a net basis. Similarly, the back layer represents situations which are characterized with net operating rent opportunities, while the front layer represents situations characterized with net operating rent losses. High price rent opportunities, marked on the right side layer of the cube, refer to situations characterized with high interest spreads. Again, there is no straightforward answer as to which level constitutes 'high' and which level constitutes 'low'. But an important characteristic associated with

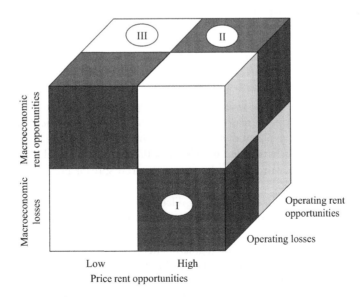

*Figure 3.2* Bank rent cube

the 'high' scenario is that the banks tend to have strong bargaining power when entering into credit contracts. Hence the entire rent opportunity is captured by the banks rather than the corporate sector (i.e., borrowers). Under such a situation, countries may fail to achieve balanced and sustained banking system development due to constrained growth in the non-financial sector. In the 'low' scenario (marked on the left side layer of the cube), either the bank's experience marginal interest spreads or part of the rent opportunities is transferred to the non-financial corporate sector. But in this situation, if operating and macroeconomic rent opportunities are absent, banks may face distress.

Most developing country banking systems stand in the area *I* of the cube where higher price rent opportunities (e.g., higher interest spreads) are dissipated due to operating and macroeconomic losses. Therefore, despite larger interest spreads, banks in those countries fail to generate sufficient profits required for expansion. In contrast, banks in industrialized countries enjoy narrower interest spreads, resulting in fewer price rent opportunities. But a remarkably conducive operating environment, and stable and peaceful macroeconomic context create healthy operating and macroeconomic rent opportunities, locating them in area *III* of the cube. This can be considered as the most socially preferable region for banking systems because the interest spread, in this context, is not excessively high. Therefore the corporate sector can obtain a higher level of financing at a relatively lower cost. In this sense, part of the rent opportunity is transferred to the corporate sector as well, whereas the banks can enjoy sufficient rent opportunities necessary for their advancement and expansion. Banking systems located in area *II* enjoy the highest level of bank rent opportunity (i.e., high price rent opportunities together with positive operating and macroeconomic rent opportunities). A higher level of market concentration can be the reason behind unnecessarily high price rent opportunities. This condition, however, may negatively affect the investment climate of the country, because wider interest spreads may discourage both borrowing and investments due to the high cost of funds. Therefore regulatory failure to continuously monitor the level of rent opportunities may render the banking system economically unproductive.

It should be noted, however, that the three subcomponents of bank rent proposed here are interdependent and mutually nonexclusive. Hence a particular initiative to alter one type of rent opportunity may affect other types of rent opportunities as well. For example, regulatory constraints on competition directly affect the banking system structure (i.e., operating rents) as well as interest spreads (i.e., price rents). Therefore this categorization is rather abstract. Nevertheless, such a detailed analysis sheds light on alternative means for addressing the issues and facilitates the investigation of how the rent opportunities created in terms of interest spreads can be attenuated, particularly in developing countries.

## 7. Implications

The proposed model makes five key implications. First, even though the overall rent opportunity is collectively determined by the extent of the three types of rent opportunities on a net basis, the locus of control in influencing each type of rent opportunities rests at different levels. For example, the price rent opportunities may be created relatively easily at the individual bank level using financial restraint policies. Significantly, the proposed model facilitates the identification of banking systems which are suitable for implementing financial restraint policies and indicates the extent of financial restraints needed based on the nature and extent of other rent opportunities. But individual banks have very limited influence on the market structure and macroeconomic context. The banking regulators, on the other hand, have control over the market structure, and thus the ability to create operating rent opportunities at the industry level. This requires publicly created banking infrastructure, as well as a set of private organizations providing infrastructural facilities to the banking system. The macroeconomic context is the most difficult to control, as it involves not only financial policy but also a variety of other factors. Hence macroeconomic policies are needed to create macroeconomic rent opportunities that are eventually available for all economic entities. Significantly, strategies formulated at each level need to be complementary and consistent.

Second, the magnitude of bank rent opportunities available for different banks is not similar even within the same country, because each bank has diverse operating conditions. For example, state-owned banks and foreign banks may have relatively higher rent opportunities. Large banks may enjoy relatively higher rent opportunities compared to smaller banks. Further, it is likely that the financial regulators may lose traction in the system due to inappropriate and obsolete regulations. This has been the main reason for some banking systems facing occasional distress in recent years. Therefore only a dynamically evolving and customized set of policy initiatives, under continuous supervisory monitoring of the regulators, can stimulate banking system development. For example, in the early stages of financial development, state ownership of banks and attempts to increase competition can be appropriate policy candidates. Further, new and smaller banks can be protected with special policies and regulations. Nevertheless, when the banking system becomes more advanced and is accompanied by an advanced banking infrastructure and a macroeconomic context, a higher degree of liberalization and standardization in the regulations can be accommodated while the government gradually withdraws from the market.

Third, regardless of the magnitude of overall rent opportunity available and the degree of regulatory monitoring, the nature of corporate governance within banks affects the ways in which the captured rent is utilized. In other words, changes in corporate governance may change the level of banking system development, even if the magnitude of rent opportunities and regulatory monitoring remain unchanged. Therefore financial regulators must pay special attention on uplifting the corporate governance in the banking industry to foster the banking system development through improving the productivity of bank rent. Thus proper mechanisms for regulatory supervision and carefully designed penalties for inefficiently managed banks are also essential for ensuring banking system development and financial stability (Hanazaki and Horiuchi, 2001).

Fourth, the behavior and intentions of the players within a banking system are largely affected by the fundamental institutions of that particular country. Those fundamental institutions include not only the formal institutions but also a wide range of informal institutions that have transformed and reshaped those economies over a long period of time. Institutions appropriate for certain contexts can be quite inappropriate in certain other contexts. For example, the failures of developed financial systems like the one in Japan have been widely attributed to the implementation of ill-scheduled and inappropriate institutions (Suzuki, 2011). Therefore an appropriate blend between the internationally available standard set of regulations and those prevailing in particular countries for decades would create more incentives for the players in a banking system.

Finally, there is a possibility that the regulators may abuse their discretionary power over the financial system due to, for example, conflicts of interests. Thus implementation of properly designed standardized regulatory measures, on a complementary basis, is also essential in avoiding unnecessary subjectivity and in maintaining an appropriate level of transparency. This subjectivity that prevailed in Japan's main bank system and in Indonesia's banking system might have substantially contributed to the failure of those banking systems.

## Acknowledgement

The model proposed in this chapter is an outcome of author's doctoral dissertation. The author wishes to acknowledge the valuable comments and inputs made by his doctoral dissertation advisor, Professor Suzuki Yasushi of Ritsumeikan Asia Pacific University, in developing this model.

## Notes

1 Information costs "are in part capital costs" and often "represent an irreversible investment" (Arrow, 1974, p. 39). Thus in the absence of excess incomes, agents may try to avoid incurring such costs.
2 Most of the developing countries have deregulated banking systems with numerous banks. But the market shares are often concentrated in a few large, sometimes state-owned banks. In this sense, the conduct of the banking system in developing countries resembles that of an oligopolistic market rather than monopolistic competition or perfect competition.
3 The regulatory frameworks concerning the financial markets in developing countries are satisfactory (though not outstanding). For example, most of the countries have already adopted the Basel recommendations. Under such regulations, sporadic expansion of banks and bank branches is not possible due to limited transaction volumes and other risk factors prevailing in developing countries. But the study notes the fact that many countries, before implementing contemporary banking regulations, have had banking systems, with an excessive number of small banks leading to excessive competition.

# 4 A new conceptualization of Islamic bank rent[1]

*Yasushi Suzuki and S. M. Sohrab Uddin*

## 1. Introduction

The rise of Islamic banking can be characterized by the dominance of *Shari'ah*-compliant asset-based financing, including *murabaha* (mark-up contract), *bai-muajjal* (variant of *murabaha*), *bai-salam* (forward sale contract), and *ijara* (leasing), rather than by the dominance of profit-and-loss sharing *mudaraba* (trust based contract) and *musharaka* (partnership/equity based contract) that are developed by following the divine rules prescribed in Islamic *Shari'ah* (Çizakça, 2011). The asset-based financing is criticized on the grounds that the markup is determined on the basis of the prevailing market rate of interest, and accordingly, these modes of financing mostly stay between the ultimate form of Islamic banking and conventional banking (Sairally, 2002; Zaher and Hassan, 2001). As was argued in Chapter 1, the analysis of financial sector rents has provided a new tool as an institutional approach to investigating the role of financial institutions. It has been argued that rents for financial institutions may be efficient if they induce efficient monitoring of credit portfolio (Hellmann et al., 1997; Stiglitz and Weiss, 1981). To what extent does the bank rent-incentive model contribute to our understanding of the role of financial rents in Islamic banking?

We assume that Islamic banks must earn profits (surplus) to maintain their 'franchise value' as prudent monitors. This leads us to ask: under the Islamic mode of financial intermediation, how do Islamic banks earn profits to preserve their 'reputation' as prudent *Shari'ah*-compliant (Islamic law–compliant) lenders? Can we observe any unique bank rent opportunity to be captured by Islamic banks? In particular, we are concerned about how the abovementioned so-called *murabaha* syndrome can be explained applying the bank rent approach. Even though El-Gamal (2007) theoretically regards the syndrome as *Shari'ah* arbitrage in a form of rent-seeking, the existing literature still lacks in explaining the syndrome from a practical point of view. Using the bank rent approach and empirical evidence from the banking sector of Bangladesh as a sample, this chapter attempts to analyze the existing pattern of financing of Islamic banking and thus depicts a new way of analyzing the syndrome of asset-based financing, particularly *murabaha*. (We expand the empirical studies on Indonesia, Malaysia, and Pakistan in Chapter 7, and on the GCC countries in Chapter 8.) By doing so, it aims to contribute to the issue of providing necessary incentive for encouraging profit-and-loss sharing modes of financing, which according to Farook and Farooq (2011, pp. 11–12) has been a lacking of the current form of regulation under Islamic banking.

To achieve these objectives, the remaining part of this chapter is organized into three sections. Section 2 proposes a new conceptualization of the bank rent opportunities to be captured by Islamic banks – what we call 'Islamic bank rent'. In so doing, we take the view of incentive mechanism of creating and maintaining the franchise value and reputation for Islamic banks. Such an incentive mechanism is considered one of important institutional settings for determining the efficiency and effectiveness of the mode of banking and financial intermediation. At the same time, we attempt to analyze the logic of the so-called *murabaha* syndrome in the credit portfolio of Islamic banks and to see the positive aspect of the syndrome toward ensuring 'Islamic bank rent' for the banks for keeping their reputation as prudent *Shari'ah*-compliant lenders. Section 3 aims to illustrate our conceptualization of Islamic bank rent by looking at the empirical evidence from the banking sector of Bangladesh as a sample. Bangladesh offers itself as a suitable test case for this particular issue because the country successfully hosts a dual banking system where both Islamic and conventional banks co-exist. The data of Islamic banks and conventional banks that maintain both *riba*-based (interest-based) and *riba*-free windows/branches are analyzed to demonstrate the underlying issues. Finally, section 4 concludes this chapter by raising several policy options for the regulators to design an appropriate regulatory framework for making Islamic banks as prudent financial intermediaries.

## 2.  Conceptualization of Islamic bank rent

As was argued in Chapter 1, under the financial restraint framework, the rent opportunity to be captured by banks as an incentive for prudent monitoring can contribute to keeping the banks' portfolio solvent if the portfolio of assets and liabilities is sufficiently well-managed. The framework also assumes that the amount of savings depends on the available infrastructure for deposit collection, in particular on the extent of the bank branch network and the efficiency of services provided to the local communities. The framework thereby claims that by increasing the returns to intermediation, banks have strong incentives to increase their own deposit bases (see section 1.3 for details). Although net benefits for society are not always consistent with those for individuals, the important role of bank rents is to create incentives for individual banks, particularly private banks, to operate as long-run agents that monitor borrowers effectively. We would then look for explanations for changes in bank commitment to monitoring efforts in accordance with the changes in the bank rent opportunities under this financial restraint system. On the one hand, the prospective benefits from monitoring efforts in the rent-based mode include the rent that a bank earns if it can preserve its 'franchise value' (Hellmann et al., 1997, pp. 171–174) and its 'reputation' (Stiglitz, 1994, p. 223). On the other hand, the threat of losing these rent opportunities prevents banks from shirking in their monitoring function (Aoki, 1994).

The outcomes of bank rents as incentives for prudent monitoring depend on various factors. For instance, the incentive to monitor can be significantly diluted if the bank does not face a credible threat of bankruptcy. This can result in a moral hazard problem, since bank managers and owners know that their bank will not normally be allowed to go bust. If this is the case, rents may not provide a sufficient incentive for the good management of banks (Khan, 2000). Also, even if bank managers did have the incentive to monitor for the purpose of maintaining their rents, unless banks had an effective power to monitor and discipline borrowers, the outcomes would be unproductive. Though we note that the financial restraint model is not adequate on its own (see section 1.3), we wish to propose an expanded concept of those 'Islamic bank rents' that Islamic banks must earn to preserve their franchise value as prudent and *Shari'ah*-compliant monitors and financial intermediaries.

To what extent does the bank rent incentive model contribute to our understanding of the role of financial rents in Islamic banking? Under the prohibition of *riba* (interest or usury), needless to say, it is impossible to simply apply the bank rent opportunities from setting up the ceiling of deposit rate. However, in our view, each Islamic bank has its own schedule of 'the marginal efficiency of capital' *à la* Keynes as the inducement to financing (investment). The marginal efficiency of capital depends on the relation between the supply price of a capital-asset and its prospective yield. We assume here that the former for banks is the rate of profit paid and the latter is the rate of profit received. Benchmarking profit rate in the *murabaha* financing would be easier for Islamic banks to estimate the prospective yield. Even in the process of approving the participatory financing, presumably each Islamic bank tries to estimate the prospective yield for the decision-making in accordance with its own schedule of marginal efficiency of capital.

Islamic banks mobilize deposits on the basis of profit-and-loss sharing agreement and to some extent on the basis of *Wakalah* (agency) against pre-agreed service charges or agency fees. While sharing profit or loss arising on investments, they earn a return on their trading and leasing activities by dint of the risk and liability undertaken and adding value in real business activities (Ayub, 2007, p. 186). On the other hand, the following threat and sanctions mechanisms encourage prudent screening and monitoring. First, *Shari'ah* rules are the cornerstone of Islamic financial products and services. If depositors or customers become aware that the products they have in their portfolios are not *Shari'ah*-compliant, this would seriously undermine customer confidence in the Islamic bank concerned or, on a larger scale, in the Islamic financial services industry as a whole (Bhambra, 2007, pp. 204–205). Second, a prudent or conservative credit screening policy is required to reduce the probability of loss, particularly in the case of *mudaraba-* or *musharaka*-based financing. Third, risk-averse depositors will look for low-risk forms of financing – for instance, *murabaha* and other similar asset-backed financing. In this context, El-Gamal (2006) refers to what Islamic finance practitioners call 'displaced commercial risk'. This may arise if Islamic bank depositors suffer a loss compared to conventional banks' depositors and therefore withdraw their funds from the Islamic bank (El-Gamal, 2006, p. 155). Fourth, strict practice of profit-and-loss sharing principle is a rarity in Islamic banking operations, and in most cases, the return for the depositors is homogenous for all banks irrespective of their scales of profitability (Chong and Liu, 2009, p. 143; Farook and Farooq, 2011, p. 10; Zaher and Hassan, 2001, p. 181). It is highly likely that some Islamic banks are hesitant to share losses with their depositors, maintaining their franchise value as prudent monitors to avoid the displaced commercial risk. Credit risk is similar to conventional banking, but credit risk management and recovery processes are far more complicated in the Islamic banking system than in conventional banking (El Tiby, 2011, p. 44). Unlike conventional banks, Islamic banks have to absorb not only the credit risk but also the risk associated with the compliance of Islamic *Shari'ah* – that is, *Shari'ah* risk. Accordingly, in addition to the difference between the rates of profit received and profit paid (borrowing rate and lending rate respectively in conventional banking), Islamic banks need an extra cushion or buffer to absorb the unexpected loss and the transaction costs associated with the *Shari'ah* compliance to maintain the franchise value.

Here we propose a fairly new conceptualization of 'Islamic bank rent'. It can be defined as the extra profits enough to compensate for the unexpected loss to absorb and the displaced commercial risk to which Islamic banks are facing; in other words, as the excess profits required for maintaining their franchise value and reputation as prudent *Shari'ah*-compliant lenders. The unexpected loss is associated with the difficulty in sharing profit and loss with the fund providers (mainly general depositors) and hence can also be regarded as 'profit-and-loss sharing risk'. As an illustration, the displaced commercial risk and the profit-and-loss sharing risk are associated with the $\alpha$ in the following equation:

*Profits (spread) sought by Islamic banks = Risk-adjusted risk premium + $\alpha$,*

where

*Spread = Rate of profit received – Rate of profit paid.*

We call $\alpha$ as 'Islamic bank rent' (in a narrower sense) in terms of the extra profits to cover the profit-and-loss sharing risk and the transaction cost for the *Shari'ah* compliance in order to maintain the franchise value as prudent *Shari'ah*-compliant lenders. Risk premium in the equation should be reflected in the credit risk of each borrower. Since perfect screening is impossible under conditions of uncertainty, all the commercial banks are expected to earn the surplus by adding the subjective risk premium to cover the unmeasurable risk or uncertainty that the banks are exposed to. Islamic banks also must charge the risk-adjusted risk premium covering the measurable risk plus the associated general uncertainty as the conventional banks charge. In addition to the general uncertainty, Islamic banks are more or less exposed to unique risks. Therefore, beyond the premium, Islamic banks are assumed to earn the extra profits to maintain the franchise value as prudent *Shari'ah*-compliant lenders. It is thus hypothesized that the spread in total sought by Islamic banks should be larger than that by conventional banks.

Linking this *Shari'ah* profit-and-loss sharing risk with the current financing practice of Islamic banks, it is likely that they choose low-risk assets for their portfolio so far as the risk-adjusted return is still satisfactory. Of course, profit-and-loss sharing modes of investments are highly recommended under Islamic *Shari'ah*, even though Zaher and Hassan point out, "Islamic banks are not expected to reduce credit risk by systematically requiring collateral or other guarantee as a pre-requisite for granting profit-and-loss-sharing facilities" (Zaher and Hassan, 2001, p. 176). But from the practical point of view, asset-based modes including *murabaha* are more contributing for protecting their rents compared to fully *Shari'ah*-driven *mudaraba* and *musharaka*, although the asset-based financing, in particular the credit exposure uncovered by the collateral, does not always offset the profit-and-loss sharing risk of Islamic banks. Moreover, in this competitive and liberalized market framework, Islamic banks have to compete with their conventional counterparts in spite of the fact that the risk management tools commonly applied in conventional banking are not applicable to Islamic banking (El-Hawary, Grais, and Iqbal, 2007, p. 779). In other words, the credit risk management tools in Islamic banking still stay behind those used in conventional banking. In addition, unlike conventional banking, the participatory mode of financing requires some other activities, including prior determination of profit-and-loss sharing ratios and frequent monitoring and supervision for ensuring the governance (Sundararajan and Errico, 2002, p. 4). These additional activities may accelerate the transaction costs for Islamic banks, and accordingly the α factor noted earlier, and otherwise encourage them to choose low-risk assets for their portfolio if the risk adjusted return is still satisfactory.

## 3.   An illustration of Islamic bank rent: evidence from the banking sector of Bangladesh

Here we draw the empirical evidence from a country – Bangladesh – where both Islamic and conventional banking co-exist, so as to illustrate our concept of Islamic bank rent. Following the global trend, the Islamic banking sector of Bangladesh has achieved a substantial progress in the recent time. The operation of the first Islamic bank was allowed in 1983 by Bangladesh Bank, the central bank of the country. The total number of banks reached forty-seven by the end of 2011, which includes four state-owned banks, four state-owned developing

*Table 4.1* The averages of ROA and NPL of Islamic banks*

|  | 2006 | 2007 | 2008 | 2009 | 2010 | 2011 |
|---|---|---|---|---|---|---|
| ROA (in %) | 1.41 (1.10) | 1.27 (1.30) | 1.44 (1.40) | 1.67 (1.60) | 2.26 (2.10) | 1.40 (1.60) |
| NPL (in %) | 4.03 (5.98) | 3.38 (5.65) | 2.68 (5.13) | 2.17 (4.42) | 2.33 (5.63) | 2.15 (3.35) |

Source: Constructed by the authors based on the annual report 2011–2012 of Bangladesh Bank and respective banks' annual reports.

Notes: In case of NPL, figures in parentheses represent the averages of twenty-three private banks, excluding Islamic banks. In case of ROA, figures in parentheses represent the averages of thirty private banks, including Islamic banks.

* Six Islamic banks are considered for the computation.

financial institutions (specialized banks), thirty private banks, and nine foreign banks. The Islamic banking sector consisted of seven full-fledged Islamic banks and sixteen conventional banks, including three foreign banks with separate Islamic banking windows/branches. Thus three foreign banks out of nine and twenty private banks out of thirty are engaged in Islamic banking either partly or fully, and all banks involved in Islamic banking are under private or foreign ownership with no state ownership. In aggregate, the market share of the Islamic banking sector reached 18.3 per cent and 20.3 per cent in terms of deposits and credits, respectively, of the overall banking sector at the end of December 2011 (Bangladesh Bank, 2012, p. 43).

Table 4.1 reports return on assets (ROA) and non-performing loans (NPL) of Islamic banks from 2006 to 2011. It shows that the average ROA of Islamic banks represents a steady growth during the period. Most importantly, the average ROA for Islamic banks is higher than that of other private banks throughout the study period. Similarly, NPL also reflects a better picture of the performance of Islamic banks compared to that of private banks. NPL remains lower than the average of all private banks during the whole reported period. To some extent, the upper hand of Islamic banks over conventional counterparts in terms of efficiency and profitability is also reported by Johnes, Izzeldin, and Pappas (2013) and Soylu and Durmaz (2013) by using the sample of eighteen different countries[2] and the Turkish banking sector, respectively.

What is the secret of better performance of Islamic banks compared to other private banks of the banking sector in Bangladesh? To have an idea of this matter, Table 4.2 summarizes the income from *murabaha* of Islamic banks during 2008–2012. It is clear from the table that the majority of their income is derived from the asset-based *murabaha*, whereas the income from equity-based *mudaraba* and *musharaka* is very negligible. Only three banks are involved in the participatory profit-and-loss sharing modes, whereas others have been remained totally hesitant. It is also important to mention that banks with a relatively lower income from *murabaha* reported in the table have been engaged in other asset-based financing, such as *bai-muajjal*, *bai-salam*, and *ijara*, for a majority of their

*Table 4.2* Income from *murabaha* (in percentage) of different Islamic banks

| Name of the bank | Year | | | | |
|---|---|---|---|---|---|
| | *2008* | *2009* | *2010* | *2011* | *2012* |
| Islami Bank Bangladesh Ltd. | 60.00 | 54.82 | 54.25 | 58.20 | 58.68 |
| | (1.70) | (2.58) | (3.63) | (4.13) | (3.78) |
| First Security Islami Bank Ltd. | 77.78 | 81.36 | 79.83 | 75.22 | 75.22 |
| | (0.00) | (0.00) | (0.00) | (0.00) | (0.00) |
| Export Import Bank of Bangladesh Ltd. | 22.82 | 21.48 | 38.98 | 42.51 | 40.09 |
| | (0.00) | (0.00) | (0.00) | (0.00) | (0.00) |
| Shahjalal Islami Bank Ltd. | NA | 20.32 | 15.39 | 15.63 | 17.10 |
| | | (0.00) | (0.00) | (0.00) | (0.00) |
| Social Islami Bank Ltd. | NA | 20.74 | 18.41 | 6.03 | 4.63 |
| | | (0.74) | (0.66) | (0.42) | (0.41) |
| Al-Arafah Islami Bank Ltd. | 34.74 | 29.98 | 35.15 | 25.66 | 15.93 |
| | (0.01) | (0.01) | (0.01) | (0.00) | (0.00) |

Source: Calculated by the authors based on the annual reports of respective banks.

Notes: Figures in parentheses represent the income from profit-and-loss sharing *mudaraba* and *musharaka*. NA stands for not available.

income. Apparently, the contribution of *murabaha* and other asset-based modes of financing provide some form of bank rent opportunities for these Islamic banks to protect their 'franchise value' and 'reputation', as argued in section 2, along with their lower level of NPL. Thus it can be argued that the asset-based modes of financing can bring adequate profits (Islamic bank rent opportunity), while keeping a relatively low level of NPL ratio partly contributing to the financial stability of the Islamic banking sector in Bangladesh.

To demonstrate the Islamic bank rent opportunity captured by Bangladeshi Islamic banks, an analysis of the spread margin in Islamic banking, which is the difference between the rates of profit received and profit paid, ideally generates better picture of the scenario. We spot an analytical light on conventional banks that maintain both Islamic and non-Islamic windows/branches simultaneously. This approach helps us compare the ratio of interest paid to depositors against interest received from borrowers in conventional banking with the ratio of profit paid to depositors against profit received from borrowers in Islamic banking on a non-risk-adjusted basis,[3] and thereby provides an idea of the gross value of any bank rent opportunity. Table 4.3 highlights these ratios of nine sample banks (including 8 private banks and 1 foreign bank) out of 16 available banks during the period 2007 to 2012. In general, it can be argued that the *riba*-free banking practiced by the Islamic banking windows/branches of these banks is associated with a lower ratio than the *riba*-based banking in conventional branches. To be specific, for six of the reported banks, the ratio has remained consistently lower during the whole period under study. It reveals the likelihood of the prevailing higher bank rent opportunity under the

*Table 4.3* Cost to income ratio in *riba*-based banking[a] and Islamic banking[b] of conventional banks

| Name of the bank | Year | | | | | |
|---|---|---|---|---|---|---|
| | 2007 | 2008 | 2009 | 2010 | 2011 | 2012 |
| Prime Bank Ltd. | 75.07 | 80.29 | 80.42 | 64.74 | 75.76 | 76.69 |
| | (62.79) | (65.22) | (59.84) | (53.88) | (64.72) | (65.98) |
| Bank Asia Ltd. | 73.86 | 75.18 | 72.13 | 65.11 | 75.59 | 73.47 |
| | NE | NE | (50.15) | (45.15) | (67.22) | (69.38) |
| The City Bank Ltd. | 78.16 | 68.02 | 63.43 | 49.27 | 52.75 | 61.29 |
| | (54.11) | (57.65) | (81.44) | (81.75) | (104.39) | (73.20) |
| Dhaka Bank Ltd. | NA | 71.05 | 73.58 | 67.14 | 76.06 | 77.90 |
| | NE | (86.78) | (83.45) | (60.07) | (75.20) | (110.93) |
| Jamuna Bank Ltd. | NA | 82.30 | 78.07 | 72.67 | 75.25 | 81.27 |
| | NE | (58.78) | (58.79) | (58.69) | (60.89) | (68.61) |
| Premier Bank Ltd. | 79.68 | 75.50 | 77.30 | 69.48 | 77.52 | 81.09 |
| | (77.93) | (78.97) | (84.95) | (72.43) | (70.31) | (69.18) |
| Southeast Bank Ltd. | 76.51 | 84.04 | 86.55 | 75.09 | 86.81 | 90.11 |
| | (68.88) | (70.30) | (66.97) | (64.32) | (67.85) | (71.95) |
| AB Bank Ltd. | 72.69 | 72.49 | 67.49 | 61.99 | 76.21 | 77.11 |
| | (72.75) | (71.63) | (67.11) | (59.10) | (70.67) | (73.57) |
| HSBC Bank Ltd. | 45.41 | 45.37 | 48.71 | 40.92 | 35.51 | 41.12 |
| | NE | (0.00) | (0.00) | (1.47) | (7.36) | (10.36) |

Source: Calculated by the authors based on the annual reports of respective banks.

Notes: Figures in parentheses represent the ratio from Islamic banking operations. NA and NE stand for not available and not established, respectively.

[a] (Interest paid / Interest received) × 100.
[b] (Profit paid / Profit received) × 100.

asset-based financing in Islamic banking sector, particularly under the dominant *murabaha*.

To have an idea about the importance of the sustainability of 'Islamic bank rent' opportunity, Table 4.4 compares the ratio of operating expenses to interest received from conventional banking with the ratio of operating expenses to profit received from Islamic banking for all of the sample banks reported in Table 4.3. It appears from the table that the ratio is lower in *riba*-free banking than that of *riba*-based banking during the whole period. However, there are still fluctuations in between. Even the foreign sample banks face the periodic ups and downs in the ratio, which may be due to the inability to reduce the profit-and-loss sharing risk by systematically requiring collateral under asset-based financing, as argued by Zaher and Hassan (2001). It appears that higher bank rent is required for responding to the occasional volatility in operating expenses to income ratio of Islamic windows/branches, in spite of the fact that the dominant form of financing in their portfolio is asset-based. This has demonstrated the importance of

*Table 4.4* Ratio of operating expenses to income in *riba*-based banking[a] and Islamic banking[b] of conventional banks

| Name of the bank | Year | | | | | |
|---|---|---|---|---|---|---|
| | 2007 | 2008 | 2009 | 2010 | 2011 | 2012 |
| Prime Bank Ltd. | 25.29 | 24.77 | 31.49 | 33.91 | 28.12 | 24.25 |
| | (6.35) | (6.32) | (5.39) | (6.78) | (5.37) | (5.85) |
| Bank Asia Ltd. | 18.55 | 19.86 | 24.36 | 29.79 | 22.00 | 21.43 |
| | NE | NE | (50.45) | (18.42) | (12.18) | (9.54) |
| The City Bank Ltd. | 32.58 | 38.66 | 37.85 | 45.61 | 39.33 | 34.75 |
| | (12.49) | (13.58) | (8.57) | (28.29) | (30.48) | (6.40) |
| Dhaka Bank Ltd. | NA | 21.08 | 20.82 | 24.44 | 21.21 | 17.01 |
| | NE | (4.48) | (4.45) | (7.03) | (5.27) | (7.60) |
| Jamuna Bank Ltd. | NA | 26.90 | 29.56 | 27.86 | 25.81 | 23.25 |
| | NE | (11.99) | (9.81) | (9.06) | (9.07) | (6.56) |
| Premier Bank Ltd. | 22.54 | 25.04 | 27.50 | 42.82 | 54.43 | 41.19 |
| | (8.91) | (9.40) | (8.25) | (6.03) | (3.30) | (3.29) |
| Southeast Bank Ltd. | 15.71 | 15.40 | 15.68 | 19.00 | 16.87 | 15.22 |
| | (9.32) | (8.56) | (7.80) | (8.31) | (6.85) | (5.32) |
| AB Bank Ltd. | 26.74 | 26.91 | 29.40 | 36.57 | 28.54 | 27.71 |
| | (4.32) | (3.64) | (3.56) | (6.50) | (4.02) | (3.33) |
| HSBC Bank Ltd. | 21.76 | 23.40 | 28.04 | 31.72 | 32.84 | 27.68 |
| | NE | (9.32) | (6.56) | (2247.27) | (39.23) | (15.38) |

Source: Calculated by the authors based on the annual reports of respective banks.

Notes: Figures in parentheses represent the ratio from Islamic banking operations. NA and NE stand for not available and not established, respectively.

[a] (Operating expenses / Interest received) × 100.
[b] (Operating expenses / Profit received) × 100.

preserving a relatively higher bank rent opportunity in Islamic banking, particularly to deal with the associated profit-and-loss sharing risk.

## 4.   Concluding comments

The achievement of a substantial growth and the dominance of the asset-based financing, particularly that of *murabaha*, have been observed complementarily in Islamic banking during the last few decades. Most of the existing studies criticize the *murabaha* syndrome by highlighting its different deviations from the divine rules prescribed in Islamic *Shari'ah*, and accordingly consider it as a mere mean for reducing the risk of Islamic banks. How to enhance fully *Shari'ah* recommended equity-based financing under the current regulatory and governance framework is still regarded as an important but unanswered issue by the existing literature.

This chapter proposes a fairly new conceptualization of 'Islamic bank rent' which should be earned by Islamic banks to compensate the unique risk and/ or cost of Islamic banking as compared to conventional banking. The ratio of borrowing expenses to lending income from regular banking activities in conventional banking is compared with a similar ratio in Islamic banking on a non-risk-adjusted basis. Even upon the comparison, it is found that the spread earned from Islamic banking operations (mainly from *murabaha* with lower credit risk) is generally higher than that from conventional banking. It appears from the findings that Islamic banks use repeated transactions under *murabaha* to seek some form of higher bank rent opportunity for protecting their 'franchise value' and 'reputation' as *Shari'ah*-compliant lenders. However, a few of the sample banks with Islamic banking windows/branches face periodic volatility in transaction costs in spite of this repeated pattern of asset-based financing. If the asset-based financing brings adequate spreads including Islamic bank rent in terms of extra profits to cover the profit-and-loss sharing risk, we would say that the *murabaha* syndrome can be ironically justifiable from the viewpoint of maintaining the financial stability.

Should the Islamic bank rent in the asset-based financing be protected as social costs for maintaining the financial stability, or be squeezed under further competition to seek for the variety of financing as well as to enhance the efficiency in Islamic bank operations? The current profit-and-loss sharing risk provides an idea of the difficulty in assuming the equity-based financing with higher credit risk in practice. Apparently, it is impractical to expect the acceleration of the participatory financing without preserving much higher bank rent for Islamic banks for covering further *Shari'ah*/profit-and-loss sharing risk. The finding of this chapter at least contributes to the expansion of the bank rent theory to the profit-and-loss modes of financing in Islamic banking. However, how long will the syndrome be justified? Islamic scholars and the regulatory authority need to design an appropriate financial architecture which can create different levels of rent opportunities for Islamic banks to avail the benefit from the variety of Islamic financing as declared by Islamic *Shari'ah*. As was argued, the outcomes of monitoring rents depend on various factors. The regulatory authority should design an appropriate architecture which will, to some extent, encourage the competition among Islamic banks not to cause potential moral hazard problems, while strengthening Islamic banks' effective power to monitor and discipline their borrowers so that the monitoring rent opportunity may provide a sufficient incentive for the good management of credit portfolio.

## Notes

1 This chapter is reproduced from Y. Suzuki and S. M. Sohrab Uddin (2014) 'Islamic Bank Rent: A Case Study of Islamic Banking in Bangladesh', *International Journal of Islamic and Middle Eastern Finance and Management*, 7(2), pp. 170–181. We are grateful to Emerald Group Publishing Limited for their consent on our reproduction.

2  The sample countries include Bahrain, Bangladesh, Brunei, Egypt, Indonesia, Jordan, Kuwait, Malaysia, Mauritania, Pakistan, Palestine, Qatar, Saudi Arabia, Sudan, Tunisia, Turkey, United Arab Emirates, and Yemen (Johnes et al., 2013, p. 6).
3  Because the spread is in theory to be reflected in credit risk of each borrower, the bank rent opportunity should be estimated on a risk-adjusted basis. However, the access to details on the associated credit risk undertaken by banks is limited. Our comparative approach is considered the second best to estimate the gross value of bank rent opportunity in Islamic and non-Islamic windows/branches, respectively.

# Part II
# Empirical studies

# 5 China's non-performing bank loan crisis

## The role of economic rents[1]

*Yasushi Suzuki and Mohammad Dulal Miah*

## 1. Introduction

Efficient intermediation of financial resources is considered an engine for economic growth. There is, however, no universal financial system that can serve the purpose of channeling funds from savers to investors equally in all the countries. Different financial systems – bank-based and market-based – must be viewed from their respective country-specific perspectives. For example, Japan and Germany rely mostly on the bank-based system for fulfilling corporate financing needs, whereas corporations in the Anglo-Saxon countries tend to depend more on capital market instruments. In the former case, banks are at the centre of the financial intermediation, whereas capital market is at the core of market-based financial system.

In most developing countries where asymmetry of information is widespread and individual investors have limited capacity to absorb risks and uncertainty involved with investment projects, banks step forward to overcome these problems (see Chapter 2 for the details). These sort of financial institutions possess competitive advantage over individuals for screening and monitoring borrowers, because they have accumulated knowledge and skills through their long involvement with business enterprises that help them discipline the markets. Moreover, banks ensure that the quality borrowers have access to the necessary funds and at a relatively lower cost. If so, a robust banking sector is a precondition for financial development and economic growth, particularly in a bank-oriented financial system.

The Chinese financial system, which can be characterised as a bank-centred system, appears to be incongruent with this view in the sense that the country has been enjoying unprecedented economic growth for the last couple of decades, even if its banking sector remains bedridden. Since 1978, the economy and the financial system have been growing rapidly under the policy of 'reform and opening-up'. Corporations and governments frequently resorted to bank loans, mainly for their funding necessities, because of the lack of sound alternatives like a developed bond or stock markets. According to the Peoples' Bank of China (PBC, 2006), bank loans to non-financial corporations accounted for 66 per cent of their total funding sources – amounting to 1953.29 billion Chinese renminbi

(RMB) – whereas bond financing to those corporations accounted for only 6 per cent at the end of 2005. The so-called big four state-owned banks – China Construction Bank (CCB), Bank of China (BOC), Agricultural Bank of China (ABC), and the Industrial and Commercial Bank of China (ICBC) – disbursed a lion's share of the total banking finance to corporations. According to the statistics released by the China Banking Regulatory Commission, assets of these big four banks amounted to RMB 22.54 trillion as of the end of 2006 and accounted for about 51.3 per cent of the total assets in the banking sector. However, a significant portion of the loan disbursed by these big fours converted into trouble loans, which created a downward pressure on the profitability of these banks (see Tables 5.1 and 5.2).

The success of some bank-centred economies in ensuring sound financial intermediation denies the possibility that the dismal performance of Chinese banks can merely be attributed to the bank-based financial system per se. For example, in Japan, banks played a vital role in the 'rent-based' banking system for fulfilling corporate financing needs, while suffering little from NPLs during its heyday. Rents that were available to banks through various financial policies supposedly

*Table 5.1* Non-performing loans (NPLs) in the state-owned commercial banks

| Year | NPLs (US$ billion) | Total loans (US$ billion) | Ratio of NPLs to total loans (%) | Ratio of NPLs to GDP (%) |
|------|------|------|------|------|
| 1997 | 155 | n.a. | 25 | 17.20 |
| 1998 | 75 | 753 | 10 | 7.90 |
| 1999 | 198 | 793 | 25 | 20.0 |
| 2000 | 196 | 786 | 25 | 18.2 |
| 2001 | 213 | 850 | 25 | 18.4 |
| 2002 | 245 | 968 | 25 | 19.8 |
| 2003 | 232 | 1139 | 20 | 17.0 |

Source: Garcia-Herrero and Santabarbara (2004).

*Table 5.2* Breakdown of the ratio of non-performing loans among the big four banks (as of December 2003)

| Name | Capital adequacy ratio (%) | Ratio of NPLs (%) |
|------|------|------|
| China Construction Bank | 6.51 | 9.12 |
| Industrial and Commercial Bank | 5.52 | 21.24 |
| Bank of China | 6.98 | 16.29 |
| Agricultural Bank of China | n.a. | 30.07 |

Source: Tamaki and Yamazawa (2005).

provided them with an incentive to undertake the roles as prudent intermediaries and monitors.

This successful growth history of China raises several interesting questions: Given the underdevelopment of the formal financial system,[2] how has China been achieving such a high economic growth? How can we explain the contrast between China and Japan? What is responsible for the extreme level of NPLs in the 'big four' while the Chinese economy has expanded rapidly and seemingly so successfully? While the financial-restraint policy worked well during the catching-up period in Japan, can the same framework be applied to Chinese case? This chapter attempts to answer these questions. Here we refer to the Hellmann et al. (1997) financial-restraint model, which provides a theoretical framework for substantiating the efficiency of the rent-based system. In so doing, we analyse the process by which the Chinese bank-centred system has evolved in comparison with the path followed by the Japanese rent-based banking system.

The structure of the chapter is as follows: section 2 briefly discusses the economic realities of China with special focus on the financial deepening as well as the scenario of NPLs in the Chinese banking system. Section 3 describes the aspect of financial restraint policy. Section 4 applies the financial restraint framework in an attempt to explain the reasons of huge accumulation of NPLs. Section 5 explains the paradox as to how China has been growing rapidly even if its formal financial system is overburdened with huge NPLs. The final section concludes the paper, summarizing the major arguments and offers some policy prescriptions.

## 2.  Economic realities in China

The pre-1978 Chinese financial system can be characterised as a mono-banking system similar to that of other centrally planned economies, which put the central bank at the centre for undertaking necessary function of financial intermediation. State budget was the crucial mechanism for accomplishing this task. In other words, state funds were collected through fiscal and other means of revenue collection and these funds were channelled to the state-run corporations. China placed little weight on commercial banking and the capital market as active players for financial intermediation. Moreover, there were few specialised banks, and most functions and authority in the banking system were concentrated in the People's Bank of China (PBC), a central government-owned and controlled bank under the Ministry of Finance.

At the end of 1978, there were only two specialised banks – BOC and the People's Construction Bank of China (PCBC, which was renamed later as CCB) – and an insurance company. Imai (1985) characterises the pre-1978 Chinese financial system as monolithic and hierarchical, with a centralised banking system. Banks' functions as financial intermediaries were constrained by the extraordinarily small bank deposits. However, bank deposits have increased manifold after the reform initiatives paved the way for financial deepening in the modern China.

## 2.1  Financial deepening in the post-reform era

A noteworthy contribution of the reform measures was that saving deposits surged and corporations began relying increasingly on loans from the SOCBs rather than from budgetary allocations. For example, in the early 1980s, government budget accounted for roughly 25 per cent of the state-owned enterprise (SOE) finances. By 1994, that figure declined to about 2 per cent (Lardy, 1998). The percentage of total credit to GDP was a mere 40 per cent in 1977, which rose to 140 per cent in 2006 (Figure 5.1). By this measure, the Chinese banking market is now larger than the bank-based financial system of many countries. In contrast, the share of the stock market in corporate financing is miniscule. In 2004 the stock market mediated only 5 per cent of funds raised by non-financial corporations, whereas bank finance made up more than 80 per cent (see Figure 5.1).[3]

Not only that the Chinese banking system is much larger than the financial system of most bank-based countries with an equivalent level of GDP, the growth of lending has been increasing enormously since the economic reforms in 1978. Annual loan increase now exceeds government revenue. For example, a 1978 government budgetary expenditure of RMB 127 billion was almost seven times the increase in loans; in 1992, the increase in loans of RMB 498 billion surpassed for the first time the annual government expenditure of RMB 439 billion. By 1996 the RMB 1.1 trillion increase in outstanding loans was more than one-third larger than the total government fiscal expenditure of RMB 791 billion (Lardy, 1998). The rate of increase, however, was intense in the first half of this decade. Total domestic credit more than doubled from

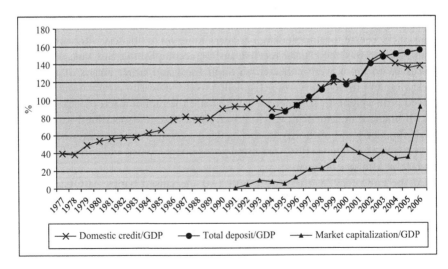

*Figure 5.1* Financial deepening in post-1978 China

Source: World Development Indicators (online version).

2001 to 2006 – equivalent to eight times the total government expenditure and 1.15 times the total GDP in 2005.[4] Whether this dramatic rise in bank lending activities has been the driver of economic growth and sound financial intermediation needs further explanation.

Chinese banking system is dominated by the four largest SOCBs, which have captured approximately 70 per cent of the domestic credit and household deposits. Their assets currently make up almost 55 per cent of total banking-sector assets. Most of the lending activity of the SOCBs has, however, been concentrated on SOEs, which are traditionally the loss making concerns. A high degree of state ownership of financial institutions on the one hand and the SOCBs' tendency to function as government agencies on the other have been accompanied by an emphasis on lending to state-owned or controlled enter-prises. This has resulted in crowding out the non-state sectors. For example, the domestic loan for fixed assets investment by private enterprises was 0 per cent in 1985, which increased merely to 5 per cent in 2000 (OECD, 2005). Similarly, short-term loans to private enterprises and individuals composed only 2.5 per cent of the total short-term loans extended by all financial institutions in 2005 (PBC, 2006).

This conclusion is supported by a World Bank survey in 1999–2000 cover-ing ten thousand firms, the majority of which are privately owned firms operat-ing in eighty-one countries. The survey result showed that 66.3 per cent of the firms surveyed in China ranked the General Financing Constraint, a measure of the perception of the severity of credit constraints, a major constraint on their business. This percentage was the second highest among the surveyed countries, after Moldova with 69.1 per cent response (World Bank, 2000b). In addition, Cull and Xu (2000) report that while domestic bank loans for fixed investment increased from 13 per cent of the total domestic financing in 1981 to 20 per cent in 1990, the average share of bank finance to SOEs increased from 15 per cent to 27 per cent in the same period. Therefore, although direct government budgetary appropriations to the SOEs have seem-ingly been replaced by commercial and other banking activities – which can be seen as structural change – functional changes have not taken place. Massive accumulation of NPL, especially in the SOCBs, reveals this biased portfolio management.

## 2.2   *Extremely high ratio of NPLs in the big four banks*

Despite the dramatic growth of Chinese economy, the level of NPLs in the big four banks is so extreme that the stability and economic prospects of the country could be affected. According to Lardy (1999), the amount of NPLs held by the SOCBs is such that deducting them from the banks' balance sheets would render them insolvent. He further notes that the total net worth of the banks at the end of 1995 – including paid-up capital, reserves, retained profits, and other surpluses – was RMB 269 billion. If we take into account only those parts of bad debts which were due but not repaid from the liquidation proceeds of the bankrupt firms, the net worth of these institutions amounted to RMB 191 billion. These figures, however, do not include RMB 1.394 trillion of bad assets or 20.7 per cent of the total loans outstanding from banks at the end of 1998, which were absorbed by four asset management companies (AMCs). In fact, these AMCs were formed to rescue problem-stricken banks (Ma and Fung, 2002).

Looking at these statistics, it can be said that if the recoverable rate of the remaining NPLs is not substantial, these banks need to show negative net worth in their balance sheets. History shows that the recoverable rate of NPLs is not more than 30 per cent and the deteriorating performance of the SOEs leads to an even more pessimistic prediction. Since the current level of capital is far below the level set by the Basel Committee on Banking Supervision, fulfilling the requirement of capital adequacy in addition to NPL restructuring would cost China 30 per cent of its total GDP (Ma, 2006). Thus NPL is a serious concern as far as the Chinese banking system is concerned. What follows is our attempt to explain the reasons for this problem.

### 2.3   Policy burden of the big four

The explanation that has attracted widespread attention from scholars and policy-makers concerning the NPL problem in China centres on 'policy lending'. Policy loans are given by government on non-market terms, often on the excuse of correcting market failure – a reason used frequently in the case of huge public investments such as infrastructure. In this sense, policy loans are favourable loans either in terms of borrowing rate or state favouritism toward certain sectors. Because of excess state favouritism, these big four banks have been known as 'wholly state-owned commercial banks' (He, 2005) and are believed to have played a key role as policy banks.[5] If the government had allocated funds for investment in infrastructure, the 'big four' would not have extended loans to investment where commercial profitability was low. Therefore, in spite of the financial reforms, policy lending – which can be considered synonymous to directed credit – has remained a characteristic of the Chinese financial system. For this reason, NPLs in China are fundamentally different from those of privately owned banks in market economies. Lau (1999, p. 74) postulates

> The fact that the loans become 'non-performing' is not in general a surprise to either the lenders or the borrowers – most of the lenders do not expect the loans to be collectible even at the time they are first made and most of the borrowers know full well at the time that they will not be able to repay these loans. The truth of the matter is that most of these loans are actually government subsidies for loss-making SOEs disbursed in the form of bank loans. These are, in fact, policy loans.

There is little disagreement among scholars that policy lending is one of the reasons for huge NPLs in the SOCBs. However, the reason is not sufficient on its own to explain the dismal performance of the Chinese banking industry. The accepted view has overlooked an important dimension of the problem offered by modern banking theories. For instance, the financial restraint model argues in this particular regard that a satisfactory level of bank rent is necessary to create compatible incentives for banks. It will be argued in the context of this theory that the Chinese financial system has apparently failed to provide banks with sufficient rents to function profitably.

## 3. The financial-restraint model and rent creation

The seminal works of McKinnon (1973) and Shaw (1973) can be considered as the breakthrough in the analysis of the relationship between financial deepening and economic development. Their proposed theory states that an increase in monetary stock relative to the level of economic activity increases financial intermediation, followed by productivity increases and economic growth. Following this contribution, many economists – especially those believing in market power – advocate for financial liberalisation in developing countries. Markets in developing countries are unable to cope with fundamental problems of asymmetry of information and transaction cost that may lead to market failure. The possibility of market failure may require an alternative model to the market model. In other words, government intervention in the financial market as opposed to the free market doctrine may be required for enhancing financial stability and deepening.

The financial restraint model is one of such alternatives, advocating for state intervention in a specific pattern. It proposes that the government will control deposit and lending rates so that an excess spread compared to the market equilibrium is created as rent for banks. As stated in Chapter 1, the basic premise of this model is that the real interest rate remains positive, while inflation should be low and predictable so that the rent is transferred to financial intermediaries and borrowers (Hellmann et al., 1997). The Stiglitz and Weiss (1981) model is of particular importance in this perspective because it shows that credit is rationed due to asymmetric information and transaction cost. Since lenders cannot perfectly and costlessly monitor the behaviour of borrowers, the price mechanism does not clear the excess demand for loanable funds. Hellmann et al. (1997) expand this theory by arguing that if government-imposed ceiling on the deposit rate is below the market-clearing rate, rent opportunities could emerge, which will provide banks strong incentives to monitor their portfolios effectively.

Although financial-restraint policy now receives less attention, it worked well in helping the financial progress of some advance economies, particularly Japan. Japanese capitalism, which Dore (2000) refers to 'a system with its internal coherence', is composed of relationship and cooperation between lenders and borrowers. Social coherence of the system has paved the way for development of some distinct characteristics like an informal relationship between and among firms, banks, and regulatory authorities (Aoki, 1994; Aoki and Saxonhouse,

2000). Earlier, a system was designed by the regulatory authority in which a particular bank worked as main bank for a group of borrowers. The main bank was committed to supply necessary funds for corporations, even at the time of financial distress of those corporations. This committed relationship acted as a fuelling element to help financially distressed firms overcom bad times. Banks became involved and even sent board members to firms when such necessity emerged. Of course banks had an important instinct that motivated them to behave this way. Every main bank used to earn more than the market competitive rate from their client firms during the time of client's favourable business period. Because of this excess earning, main banks were ethically and professionally committed to rescue their client firms at the time of financial distress. All these arrangements took place under the direct auspices of the regulatory authority.

The model's success in some bank-based economies – especially during their rapid growth period – offers some appeals to test other cases under this framework. In this tradition, we can consider the Chinese case to test the theory. This will help us identify the linkage between banking sector rent and bank performance, with a particular focus on NPLs. Despite the high liquidity in the financial system of China, lending and deposit rates are still controlled by the central bank[6] – the People's Bank of China. The central bank has lowered the base rate for lending and deposit eight times since May 1996. The difference between the deposit and lending rates – bank rent opportunity – has been expanded as the base rate for deposits has been lowered without changing the lending rate. The difference reached 3.33 per cent per annum as of 2005. Moreover, the increase in bank rent opportunity is reflected in the government's assistance to Chinese banks in writing off huge NPLs (Tamaki and Yamazawa, 2005). However, majority of this rent was transferred to the SOEs, particularly during the period of 1978 through the mid-1990s (see Table 5.3).

*Table 5.3* A synopsis of interest rate spread and reform characteristics

|  | *1978–1982* | *1983–1994* | *1995–2001* |
| --- | --- | --- | --- |
| **Average interest spread (%)** | −2.02 | 0.44 | 2.87 |
| **Reform initiatives** | Gradual opening up | Bo Gai Dai policy (policy loans 1984) | Commercial banking law (1995) |
|  | Still favouring SOEs while hampering the profitability of SOCBs (transfer of rent) | Government budgetary allocations replaced by commercial lending | Began to resolve NPLs of SOCBs |

Source: Figure 5.2.

## 4.   Removing distortions in the Chinese banking system

While China made magnificent progress in opening up its economy to the outside world, the financial sector remained moribund for a long period of time. Channelling financial resources from the budget to financial intermediaries dominated the reform agenda during the first phase of the reform. Lending and deposit activities of state-owned financial institutions were highly concentrated on some special sectors. For example, a substantial portion of bank lending was given to SOEs at a subsidised rate. Easy availability of scarce funds to SOEs means that private entities did not have sufficient access to finance which, in turn, led the sector to suffer from financing constraint. Investment opportunities for firms other than those patronized by the state were neither available nor encouraged. Government strongly restricted the circulation of financial instruments especially by private organizations.

Because of the lax competition in the financial market as well as the certainty of tapping deposits, SOCBs were transformed into a symbol of inefficiency. They rarely focused on commercial viability of the projects they funded, perhaps because loan decisions were not motivated by profit motives but rather policy and directive lending from the top. Moreover, monopoly right was allowed for state-owned financial institutions. As a result, more than 90 per cent of Chinese household savings were deposited with the SOCBs (Lal, 2006). This fund was then transferred to state-owned enterprise, leaving zero or negative spread for banks. This implies that the Chinese financial system in the early reform period could be characterised by financial repression.

In terms of bank rent, the post-1978 period of China can be distinguished by three distinct phases (see Table 5.3 and Figure 5.2): (1) the period of negative interest rate spreads, 1978–1982; (2) the policy loan period of close-to-zero interest spreads, 1983–1994; and (3) the period of positive interest rate spreads since 1995.

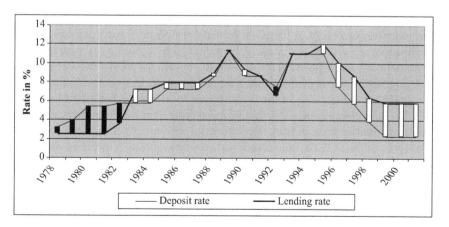

*Figure 5.2* Interest rate spread 1978–2001

Source: Construction based on People's Bank of China 2006 and Imai and Watanabe (2006).

## 4.1  *The negative and zero interest rate regimes*

Figure 5.2 clearly shows that the period of 1978 to 1982 can be characterized by a negative interest rate regime. During this time, commercial viability of the lending activities was not given much emphasis in the reform measures. The financial relationship between the SOCBs and SOEs remained unchanged, and they were governed by the state. The profitability of banks was not taken into serious consideration in financial intermediation. As a result, banks were not privileged to enjoy rents simply by extending loans to SOEs. While banks had to accept negative interest rates, averaging more than 2 per cent annually during the first phase of the reform, SOEs increased their muscle mainly from subsidized borrowing from the SOCBs. Banks could not perform the required monitoring activities because they were not provided with any incentive in the form of rent.

However, such a repressed financial regime was reformed in 1984 when the PBC was designated as the central bank of China. This reform removed the mandate of financial authority from the banks and established the PBC as the monetary authority. The interest rate on lending was, however, increased slightly. Banks therefore did not suffer negative rents, although the interest rate spread was not significantly different from zero.

The mild financial repression from 1978 to 1994 facilitated the flow of financial resources from savers to users. The policy, however, failed to provide banks with sufficient incentive to undertake commercially viable projects by utilizing large volume of savings available at low deposit rates.

The belief behind the government's mild financial repression policy – implemented through the state monopoly of the financial system – was that the monopoly would provide banks with the capability to capture deposits while curbing the growth of aggregate demand. This in turn will ensure financial deepening (Li, 2001). Moreover, the low interest rate on deposits while keeping the lending rate low was intended to resurrect the moribund SOEs. Toward this end, the policy was successful, as there was substantial increase in bank deposits during the financial repression. For instance, banks in China enjoyed an average increase of household bank deposits of more than 30 per cent for almost two decades.

Dying SOEs were kept alive at the cost of high inefficiency in the financial sector, which we argue is one of the main reasons for the skyrocketing NPLs of the SOCBs. Li's (2001) conclusion that financial repression has facilitated capturing this substantial increase in bank deposits is not without criticism. Because of the monopoly of the SOCBs, households had very little choice in investing their savings. Capital flight was not possible because of government restrictions on capital movement. Moreover, in a state of zero or negative profits, banks had little incentive to facilitate the flow of funds to productive sectors.

Chinese government targeted the commercial banks as a source of funds to offset the decline in fiscal revenues during the reform period. The reforms shifted the tax base away from the sources traditionally relied on by the tax system. Government revenue fell from more than 34 per cent of the gross national product (GNP) in 1978 to less than 13 per cent in 1994 (Hofman, 1998). This has compelled the government to look for alternative sources of revenues. Undoubtedly, SOCBs were easy prey. Extra-budgetary funds as well as the quasi-fiscal activities of the central banks were so significant that they protected the government from encountering any possible macroeconomic shock ensued from budget deficits (Hofman, 1998). If we assume zero opportunity cost of capital, the real resource transfer to banks due to negative real interest rate was, on average, 2.1 per cent of GDP for the period of 1986 to 1994 (Hofman, 1998).

### 4.2 The regime of positive interest rate spread

The period of near-zero interest rate ended in 1995 when the third set of reforms took place in China. Since 1995, banks have been enjoying positive interest rate margins. A true financial restraint policy was therefore implemented, which resulted in a critical transformation of the financial system. However, it can be argued that China was late in bringing the much needed changes in the banking system. This has lingered the process of cleaning up the messes from the banking system. Also, banks could not show instant performance improvement, even at the inception of positive interest rate. By the time the Chinese government put the financial-restraint model into effect, SOCBs already accumulated a huge volume of NPLs. It is usual for financial institutions that a certain portion of the profit has to be reserved as a provision against bad debt. Moreover, the additional burden for Chinese banks was to cover already accumulated NPLs. At this circumstance, an average spread of less than 3 per cent was not sufficient to allocate an adequate amount to cover up total bad debts. The Japanese experience can help prove a point here. After opening up the Japanese financial markets to the outside world, the rent-based banking system faltered because rent opportunity was abolished (Suzuki, 2005). This was followed by economic slowdown, even though the volume of NPLs of the Japanese banks was much lower than what the Chinese SOCBs are carrying now on their balance sheet. If we expect a positive relationship between financial sector development and economic growth, how can we explain the so-called China paradox? In other words, how has China been able to accelerate its GDP growth while keeping its formal financial sector mostly ailing?

## 5. Limited role of state-owned commercial banks

The problems with SOCBs in China are not new. As noted earlier, commercial banks' contribution to total financial intermediation was still substantial, given the underdevelopment of capital markets. Moreover, a lion's share of this financing by the banking sector was concentrated on the loss-making SOEs, whose economic health was worsening. Not only has the amount of losses incurred by SOEs increased over the years but the number of loss-making firms has also increased at the same time. The share of loss-making SOEs declined in the early years of reform to less than 10 per cent in 1985 (Lardy, 1998). Since then the percentage has skyrocketed, reaching an all-time high by the mid-1990s, with total losses amounting to RMB 80 billion. Taking these facts into account, one might wonder how it is possible for China to maintain such a lofty GDP growth rate. Investment in China averages more than 40 per cent of GDP. Who finances this investment?

Let us turn back to the status of private business entities. The performance of the private sector has risen sharply, and its contribution to GDP has intensified. The value added of the private sector to the total output increased from 50.4 per cent in 1998 to 59.2 per cent in 2003 (OECD, 2005). The average growth of value added to industry by private enterprises stood at more than 76 per cent for the period of 1999 to 2005, whereas the contribution by state-owned and state-holding enterprises staggered at about 24 per cent in the same period (Table 5.4).

It was mentioned earlier that the formal financial institutions do not serve the non-state sector to a mentionable extent, even though these private businesses are the growth drivers of the Chinese economy. Only a small volume of short-term financing from the formal financial institutions is channelled to the non-state sector. For example, short-term loans to township and village enterprises accounted for about 9 per cent of the total short-term financing in 2005, while the same statistics for private enterprises and individuals was 2.5 per cent. The reason is that the banks' monopoly power in the financial market has given them the discretionary power to extend loans even though the projects are not financially viable.

We argue that the absence of rent opportunities, which provide primary motivation for banks to accept profitable projects, is the fundamental reason that explains why a thriving private sector is deprived of formal financing. It is logical for banks to extend their credit at a suppressed interest rate to the state sector instead of private sector. In case a loan extended to SOEs becomes default, loan managers might be excused at the pretence of directive and policy lending. However, if the same happens to a loan extended to a non-state sector, the manger him/herself is to be responsible for the decision. In a no-rent state, loan managers might wish to avoid such a cumbersome situation. In contrast, if rents are created for banks and performance works as an indicator of successful lending,

*Table 5.4* Contributions to industrial growth (industry value added)[*]

|  | *State-owned and state-holding industrial enterprises (%)* | *Private industrial enterprises (%)* |
| --- | --- | --- |
| **1999** | 19.11 | 80.89 |
| **2000** | 23.52 | 76.48 |
| **2001** | 13.16 | 86.84 |
| **2002** | 19.51 | 80.49 |
| **2003** | 28.08 | 71.92 |
| **2004** | 34.93 | 65.07 |
| **2005** | 29.11 | 70.89 |

Source: National Bureau of Statistics (NBS) 2006.

[*] Each year's increase in industrial value added is scaled to 100.

it would be worthwhile for managers to consider projects initiated by private enterprises. Thus private enterprises suffered from lack of financing in China. A survey by 'All China Federation of Industry and Commerce', which is conducted mainly to identify financing behaviour in the private sector, reveals a sorry figure. In its 2002 survey, the federation showed that the number of firms relying on formal financing has been in decline. During the period of 1984 to 1989, 24.5 per cent of the private firms surveyed reported that they received finance from formal financial intermediaries. This ratio declined to 19.6 per cent during the period of 1990 to 2001. Tsai (2002, p. 2) argues: '[A]s of the end of 2000, less than 1 per cent of loans from the entire national banking system had gone to the private sector. Business owners take their exclusion from formal sources of credit for granted'.

He (2005) analyses the changes in four categories of funding sources of investment in China: 'budgetary funds', funds mainly from government; 'domestic credits', long-term borrowings by firms from domestic banks and non-bank financial institutions; 'foreign funds', long-term international loans, mainly in the form of official development aid, which have been used for investment projects, and foreign direct investment inflow; and 'all others', miscellaneous means of long-term financing. He (2005) reports data by the State Statistics Office, showing that in 1979, for what was called 'basic construction investment',[7] the share of budgetary funds was 75.8 per cent, while that of domestic credit was 1 per cent, foreign funds was 3.1 per cent and 'all others' was 20.1 per cent. In 1990, the share of budgetary funds was about 10 per cent, while that of domestic credit was about 20 per cent. Since then, the share of domestic credit has remained virtually unchanged. Throughout the period of 1979 to 2004, the share of budgetary funds was shrinking and the share of domestic credit was rising. The most notable change took place for the share of 'all others' which increased steadily and reached as high as more than 70 per cent of the total fixed asset investment. He (2005) places the following components in this category: (1) funds raised from equity markets, domestic and abroad, by issuing debentures or stocks; (2) funds raised internally, either from undistributed profits or retained funds, for some specific purposes; (3) funds raised from authorised surcharges such as 'coal for oil' fees and airport construction duty; (4) funds raised from borrowing in less-regulated markets, including borrowings from non-financial firms and individuals; (5) funds raised from issuing debt/share certificates to employees; and (6) in collectively owned or private enterprises, funds raised from personal savings. Formal financial intermediation does not play a significant role in the present-day Chinese economy.

In order to overcome the entrenched default culture and to ensure the SOCBs' increased participation in economic progress, the government has implemented some reform measures aimed at boosting market-oriented commercial banking. The importance of non-state commercial banking, although still at an embryonic stage, has increased recently. For example, joint-stock commercial banks (JSCBs) and city commercial banks (CCBs), which are diverse in terms of ownership structure and geographical location, have been prioritised in financing private industrial enterprises.

There are currently 12 JSCBs owned partially by local governments and SOEs with growing shares of private as well as foreign enterprises ownership. They held only 4.4 per cent of total outstanding loans in 1993, which rose to 15 per cent by the end of 2004. These banks meet largely the financing requirement of small and medium enterprises through an extensive branch network in the fast-growing coastal areas. As of 2004, deposits in these banks amounted to RMB 4,143.6 billion, which accounted for 16 per cent of the total deposits; whereas their loans disbursement amounted to RMB 2,926.1 billion, or 15 per cent of the total banking-sector loans.

The CCBs were created by restructuring and merging urban credit cooperatives. Although plenty in number, they play a very limited role since their operations are restricted to urban areas. In 2004 all CCBs combined accounted for only 5 per cent of total banking assets. Needless to say, increased rate of growth of the JSCBs and CCBs has led to a decline in the SOCBs' share of total banking assets from 73.9 per cent in 1993 to 54.6 per cent in 2004. Scholars are prompt to deny the probability that these non-state banks – no matter how efficiently they are driven by the market spirit – will supersede the long-lasting SOCBs in the near future.

## 6.   Concluding remarks

We have attempted to explore a potential cause for the persistent, appalling state of China's banking sector, especially the SOCBs, from a perspective overlooked by the existing literature. We argue that proper incentives can motivate incumbent banks to undertake activities that are compatible with the maximisation of social benefits. Financial repression that prevailed in China from the start of the reform period until the mid-1990s can explain, to a great extent, why Chinese banks are carrying an enormous volume of NPLs. Negative or zero interest rate margins along with the government expropriation by imposing implicit taxes on deposits through rate ceiling gave little incentive to banks for considering commercial viability of the projects they financed.

We have argued that banks are different from other industries. They need special attention from policymakers in the question of financial stability and soundness. It is more so in the case of China, because Chinese SOCBs account for a substantial part of total formal financial activities. However, they are not the active partners of the private business enterprises. Rather, informal financing sources are critically important for financing private enterprises that have been the life-blood of rapid GDP growth.

What constitutes the sources of informal finance and how the sector has accumulated such an enormous volume of funds are the issues we leave for our future research. A hint can be pointed out that the savings by households constitute more than 40 per cent of GDP. Of course, the Chinese economy can resort to that accumulation to keep the private sector growing vigorously. Still, there remains a crucial question: can China rely on this financing source for growth at its current level while its formal financial sector remains in trouble? The simple answer is no.

At this point in time, it seems that China's long-lasting rapid economic growth could undercut any cautionary remarks regarding an imminent financial crisis or economic slowdown. However, the need for a bold step to redress the current financial mess is quite essential. Otherwise, economic growth rate will be slowed down due to lack of sound backing from the financial system. Our presumption is that the Chinese economy has already reached the saturation level of informal finance. Thus redressing the current mess in the banking system is critical to sustain its rapid economic growth.

## Notes

1  This chapter is reproduced from Y. Suzuki, M.D. Miah, and Y. Jinyi (2008) 'China's Non-Performing Bank Loan Crisis: The Role of Economic Rents', *Journal of Asian Pacific Economic Literature*, 22(1), pp. 57–70.
2  We define 'formal financing' in the narrow sense as 'funding from formal external resources', which includes borrowing from formal financial institutions, typically commercial banks. Therefore 'informal finance' typically constitutes equity or shareholders' funds, loans from relatives and friends, and other informal sources, including internal reserves. Since our purpose is to estimate the contribution of commercial banks to total financing, this definition does not contradict the literature
3  From its inception, until 2005, stock-market capitalisation as share of the GDP hovered at about 40 per cent. With the prices of stocks in the major exchanges soaring, however, it experienced such an astounding rise that, in 2007, market capitalisation surpassed the GDP. At its peak, market capitalisation accounted for 1.2 times China's 2006 GDP. Some economists argue that the rampant speculative activities have contributed to a stock-market frenzy that is fuelling an unsustainable bubble, and they warn of the possible repercussions if the regulatory authority fails to prevent the bubble swelling. On the contrary, such overwhelming success could give the market more room to play its role in smoothing financial intermediation. Even if the sharp increase is temporary, firm conclusions cannot be drawn at this juncture. It would, however, be practical to conclude that the increase in market capitalisation will not cause China to shift its financial regime from bank-based to market-oriented in the near future.
4  Domestics credit increased from 13,487.6 billion yuan in 2001 to 28,873.78 billion yuan in 2006 (International Financial Statistics), whereas government total expenditure in 2005 stood at 3393.03 billion yuan (NBS, 2006)
5  He (2005) further points out that the big four banks were called 'specialised commercial banks' before 1994, when three large policy banks were established for the purposes of reducing 'policy burdens' on the 'big four'.
6  The foreign deposit rate for more than US$3 million has been deregulated since September 2000.
7  This is a statistical category smaller than 'fixed asset investment'.

# 6   Bank rent, bank performance, and financial stability in Sri Lanka

*Manjula K. Wanniarachchige*

## 1.   Introduction

Sri Lanka, as a country with an emerging economy, is endowed with immense opportunities for economic expansion and banking system development. Since the late 1970s, Sri Lanka has implemented open economic policies through liberalizing almost all the regulatory barriers in the economy. Along with these initiatives, the financial system also underwent a series of reforms, particularly during the 1990s, aimed at fostering competition and enhancing private sector participation. This reform package can be considered as the most comprehensive such package implemented in the South Asian region. Currently, Sri Lanka has already adopted most of the recommendations suggested by the Basel Committee on Banking Supervision (BCBS) for fostering the soundness of the financial system. However, Sri Lankan banking system has remained substantially stagnant, with a gradual decline in financial depth. For example, the size of the banking system relative to the country's GDP is continuously declining. By comparison, under very similar conditions, the Indian banking system has attained satisfactory growth. This chapter argues that the main cause behind such sluggish performance in Sri Lankan banking system is the lack of adequate incentives for the players.

The discussion in this chapter is organized into eight sections, including this introduction. Section 2 overviews the Sri Lankan macroeconomic context and banking system to illustrate its transition over previous decades. Section 3 highlights the nature and degree of banking system stagnation and questions the suitability of conventional bank rent literature in explaining the shallow financial depth in Sri Lanka. Sections 4 and 5 discuss the effects of interest rate, bank branch network, and ownership on bank performance and financial development, since these are the core elements of price and operating rent opportunities, as argued in Chapter 3 of this book. Further, sections 6 and 7 discuss the effects of inflation and political turbulence as core elements of macroeconomic rent opportunities on financial development. Finally section 8 concludes with a discussion on implications.

## 2.   Sri Lankan macroeconomic context and banking system

Historically, the economic evolution of Sri Lanka was marked by several European invasions and the British colonial era. The British, who started their own settlements in the early 1790s, acquired full control over Sri Lanka in 1815. Since then, the focus of the Sri Lankan economy shifted to export oriented agriculture. Even though the export oriented agricultural sector was heavily labor intensive, the Sri Lankan peasant cultivators hesitated to work in the plantation sector because of the low wages and social status associated with paid labor. The resulting labor shortage in the plantation sector was filled by recruiting labor from southern India. As a result, the migration of south Indian Tamils and their settlements in Sri Lanka increased, causing a drastic and rapid change in Sri Lankan demography. Concurrently, most of the lands used for export oriented agriculture had been previously used for cultivating traditional agricultural products or remained unutilized. Not only had the British not given enough attention to the traditional agricultural sector, but also most of the irrigation systems used for paddy cultivation was abandoned. Hence the productivity of these sectors plummeted. As a result, the domestic production was no longer sufficient to fulfill the consumption needs of the country. As a consequence, the country was transformed from a self-governed, self-sufficient economy to an import dependent colony of the British Empire. Sri Lanka subsequently gained independence in 1948. Even though the majority of the British immigrants left the country after independence, the majority of the Tamil immigrants continued to stay. Moreover, the export oriented agricultural sector continued to dominate the economy even after independence. Further, the basic structure of the governance established by the British continues to exist even today. Thus the century-long colonial period under the British marked a crucial point of transition in Sri Lanka's history and created a lasting effect on its economy as well as on other social dynamics.

During the British colonial period, most of the enterprises in Sri Lanka had been operated by the private sector. Even after independence, the United National Party (UNP) government continued to maintain a market economy. The UNP government even privatized a number of state-owned enterprises during that time (Balasooriya, Alam, and Coghill, 2008). However, the succeeding coalition government in 1956 initiated import substitution policies under a closed economic regime where most of the enterprises including banks and insurance firms were nationalized. As a result, until 1977, the Sri Lankan economy remained under excessive state ownership and control. During this period, the majority of the economic activities were carried out by the government or by state-owned enterprises. Due to excessive government regulation and political intervention, the pre-deregulation economy in Sri Lanka was highly inefficient. Huge supply shortages and public unrest were the inevitable consequences. Widespread public discontent toward the coalition government led the opposition UNP, in 1977, to a remarkable victory. Thereafter, the UNP government, capitalizing on its large majority, brought about considerable changes to the constitution and re-implemented open economic policies by liberalizing most of the regulations that restricted private sector activities. These initiatives were backed by the International Monetary Fund (IMF) recommendations package aimed at four different objectives – namely, market reforms, price liberalization, macroeconomic stability, and institutional reforms (Balasooriya et al., 2008).

Along with these deregulatory initiatives, the financial system also underwent a series of reforms from 1977 (Edirisuriya, 2007), which were further intensified during the early 1990s. In general, the financial system reforms focused on the promotion of private ownership and removing excessive regulatory restrictions. As a result, numerous private banks and foreign banks commenced operations in Sri Lanka. Even though state ownership in the banking system has declined substantially since the early 1980s, they collectively act as the major player, even in the current context, by holding nearly half of the assets in the banking system. Significantly, the shares of deposits and loans of the state-owned banks are disproportionately higher than their share of the total assets in the banking system, compared to other ownership groups. Even though the operations of the banking system have not yet fully shifted to the private sector, the performance of state-owned banks increased substantially due to restructuring initiatives implemented along with the financial reforms. For example, the Non-Performing Loans (NPL) ratios of these banks have been substantially dropped during the last decade. Despite the rapid increase in their operations (i.e., increased outreach of branch network, etc.), the number of employees has been drastically reduced due mainly to improved productivity. For example, the number of employees in the two largest state-owned commercial banks has dropped from 11,577 and 9,473 to 8,399 and 8,204, respectively, even though their branch network and fixed assets base increased substantially during the 2000–2010 period. These improvements can be directly attributed to the financial liberalization and improved competition created by the private-domestic and foreign banks.

As illustrated in Table 6.1, the Sri Lankan banking system, by the end of 2013, comprised thirty-three banks, of which twenty-four are commercial banks while the remaining nine are specialized banks. Commercial banks dominate the market, holding around 84 per cent of the total banking sector assets. Furthermore, in terms of ownership, eight banks belong to the government while the number of banks belonging to the private sector is twenty-five (of which twelve are foreign banks). Two state owned commercial banks, the People's Bank and the Bank of Ceylon, remain the largest banks in Sri Lanka. Apart from these banks, forty-eight finance companies authorized to accept public deposits were serving in the financial system by the end of 2013. The Sri Lankan financial system has emerged into a new era and acquired the majority of the institutional elements required for a modern banking system, due mainly to the successful implementation of reforms (Asian Development Bank, 2005). More importantly, the Sri Lankan financial system remained fairly resilient, even under the heavy pressures created by the US subprime crisis during 2007–2008. In view of the above facts, the Sri Lankan financial system can be identified as a bank-dominated financial system undergoing rapid transformation, with a huge potential for further development.

*Table 6.1* Banking system in Sri Lanka, 2013

| | Banks | | Branches | | Assets (%)[a] | |
|---|---|---|---|---|---|---|
| **By bank type** | | | | | | |
| Licensed commercial banks | **24** | | **2,803** | | **84** | |
| *State owned banks* | | *2* | | *1,356* | | *34.4* |
| *Private domestic banks* | | *10* | | *1,226* | | *37.1* |
| *Foreign banks* | | *12* | | *221* | | *12.0* |
| Licensed specialized banks | **9** | | **645** | | **17** | |
| *State owned banks* | | *6* | | *534* | | *14.0* |
| *Private domestic banks* | | *3* | | *111* | | *2.5* |
| Total | **33** | | **3,448** | | **100** | |
| **By bank ownership** | | | | | | |
| State owned banks | **8** | | **1,890** | | **48** | |
| *Licensed commercial banks* | | *2* | | *1,356* | | *34.4* |
| *Licensed specialized banks* | | *6* | | *534* | | *14* |
| Private domestic banks | **13** | | **1,337** | | **40** | |
| *Licensed commercial banks* | | *10* | | *1,226* | | *37.1* |
| *Licensed specialized banks* | | *3* | | *111* | | *2.5* |
| Foreign banks | **12** | | **221** | | **12** | |
| *Licensed commercial banks* | | *12* | | *221* | | *12* |
| Total | **33** | | **3,448** | | **100** | |

Source: FSSR (2013).

[a] As of 2010.

## 3.   Banking system stagnation in Sri Lanka

The Sri Lankan banking system has maintained a sizable interest spread of around 5.6 per cent on average during the period 2000–2010, as illustrated in Table 6.2. However, total assets in the banking system relative to GDP were only 69 per cent, whereas the market capitalization in the equity market relative to GDP was as low as 18.8 per cent on average during 2000–2010. Even though the equity market gained significantly after 2009 with the ending of the three-decade long civil conflict,[1] the banking system did not expand sufficiently. More specifically, the relative significance of financial intermediation through banks is decreasing. For example, the size of the banking system relative to GDP, measured in terms of total assets in the banking system, declined to 63.2 per cent in 2010 from 75.1 per cent in 2000. This was a contraction of nearly 16 per cent in banking system assets when taken together with the phase of economic growth. These facts collectively indicate the relatively shallow financial depth and sluggish development in the Sri Lankan financial system in general and in the banking system in particular.

*Table 6.2* Interest rates, inflation, banking system and equity market in Sri Lanka

| Year | AWDR | AWPR | Spread | Inflation (CCPI) | Market capitalization | | Banking system assets | |
|---|---|---|---|---|---|---|---|---|
| | | | | | Value[a] | %[b] | Value[a] | %[b] |
| 2000 | 9.9 | 21.5 | 11.6 | 6.2 | 88.8 | 7.1 | 944.5 | 75.1 |
| 2001 | 10.8 | 14.3 | 3.5 | 14.2 | 124.0 | 8.8 | 1,018.9 | 72.4 |
| 2002 | 7.5 | 12.2 | 4.7 | 9.6 | 162.6 | 10.3 | 1,099.2 | 69.5 |
| 2003 | 5.3 | 9.0 | 3.7 | 6.3 | 262.8 | 14.4 | 1,265.3 | 69.4 |
| 2004 | 5.3 | 10.2 | 4.9 | 9.0 | 382.1 | 18.3 | 1,464.0 | 70.0 |
| 2005 | 6.2 | 12.1 | 5.9 | 11.0 | 584.0 | 23.8 | 1,781.0 | 72.6 |
| 2006 | 7.6 | 14.7 | 7.1 | 10.0 | 834.8 | 28.4 | 2,142.2 | 72.9 |
| 2007 | 10.3 | 17.0 | 6.7 | 15.8 | 820.7 | 22.9 | 2,504.2 | 70.0 |
| 2008 | 11.6 | 19.2 | 7.5 | 22.6 | 488.8 | 11.1 | 2,697.5 | 61.2 |
| 2009 | 8.0 | 11.1 | 3.1 | 3.4 | 1,092.1 | 22.6 | 3,013.3 | 62.4 |
| 2010 | 6.2 | 9.3 | 3.0 | 5.9 | 2,210.5 | 39.5 | 3,539.1 | 63.2 |
| **Average** | **8.1** | **13.7** | **5.6** | **10.4** | **641.0** | **18.8** | **1,951.7** | **69.0** |

Source: CBSL (2010).

Note: AWDR, average weighted deposit rate; AWPR, average weighted prime rate; CCPI, Colombo consumer price index.

[a] LKR billions.
[b] As a percentage of GDP.

Due to this stagnation in the banking system, a sizeable unmet credit demand exists in Sri Lanka. As illustrated by a survey conducted by the German Technical Cooperation (initiated with the support of the Ministry of Finance and Planning in Sri Lanka), 50 per cent of Sri Lankan households have claimed that they are in need of credit to be used in SMEs and microenterprises in addition to other consumption requirements (Daily News, 2008). Moreover, despite the rapid increase in the market capitalization in the equity market after the ending of the three-decade long civil war, the number of companies listed in the capital market has increased only marginally. This is an indication of the lack of qualified and willing firms to access capital market financing through achieving sufficient scale and reputation. Consequently, a majority of the firms depend on bank financing. Therefore an expansion in bank lending to the corporate sector can stimulate economic activities because it enables the firms to undertake investment opportunities which would have otherwise been foregone due to the financial constraints.

Significantly, India and Sri Lanka have adopted very similar financial reforms and strategies during very similar time periods. Moreover, the financial system infrastructures of both countries remarkably improved in recent years, due mainly to economic and financial reforms, restructuring of the state-owned banks, and increased competition in the banking system. However, as illustrated in Figure 6.1, the extent of growth in the banking systems in India and Sri Lanka are remarkably

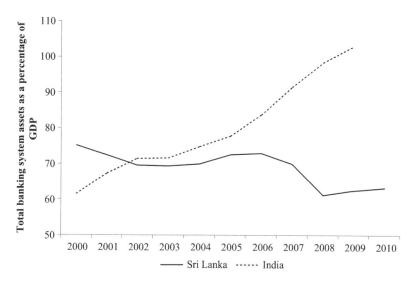

*Figure 6.1* Size of banking systems relative to GDP in India and Sri Lanka

different, despite the very similar levels of interest spreads available to the banks in both countries. For example, the relative size of the banking system in India compared to its GDP has increased from 61.6 per cent in 2001 to 102.9 per cent in 2010, while that of Sri Lanka has decreased from 75.1 per cent to 63.2 per cent. Nevertheless the average interest spread has been very similar in the two countries: the average interest spread in Sri Lanka during 2000–2010 was 5.6 per cent, while that of India during 2001–2009 was 4.8 per cent.

The bank rent opportunity available to the banks in terms of interest spreads, the key endogenous variable in the financial restraint model, has remained remarkably similar in both countries. As noted previously, the average interest spread during 2000–2010 in Sri Lanka was 5.6 per cent, while the average interest spread in India during the same period was around 4.8 per cent. Therefore India and Sri Lanka should have enjoyed similar levels of financial deepening in an abstract sense, if the arguments pertaining to the financial restraint model are applicable. This explains how current bank rent models fail to appropriately explain such difference in the extent of financial development when the conditions pertaining to the endogenously treated variables remain substantially similar.

Nevertheless, some of the conditions prevailing particularly in Sri Lanka have violated the key assumptions of the financial restraint model – namely, macroeconomic stability and low levels of inflation. Thus it can be argued that the differences in the financial development in the two countries are due to the variations of factors other than the bank rent opportunities represented by the interest spreads. Yet the financial restraint model has failed to accommodate these factors endogenously. As a consequence, the explanatory power of the financial restraint model is poor with regard to numerous developing countries with turbulent socio-economic environments.

Therefore this chapter makes an attempt to explain the conditions prevailing in Sri Lanka and possible reasons for its shallow financial depth using the integrated bank rent model introduced in Chapter 3. To this end, section 4 discusses the availability of price rent opportunities, in terms of interest spread, and its consequences on the bank branch network and credit expansion. Section 5 discusses the operating rent opportunities available to Sri Lankan banks, given the ownership of banks. Sections 6 and 7 discuss the nature and effects of macroeconomic rent opportunities prevailing in terms of economic and political stability.

## 4.   Interest rates and branch network expansion

Nominal deposit rates in Sri Lanka were comparatively higher during the period 1990–2009 (on average, around 8 per cent). However, due to high inflation rates, the real deposit rates have remained at very low levels with huge fluctuations. Significantly, inflation has surpassed the nominal deposit rate from 2001 until the end of 2008, causing negative real deposit rates as illustrated in Table 6.2. In contrast, substantially higher lending rates can be observed during the period 1990–2009. For example, the average lending rate amounted to around 14 per cent. As a result, the interest spread remained as high as 6 per cent on average, as illustrated in Table 6.2. As argued in this chapter, such interest spread may not necessarily indicate the availability of excess profit opportunities for the Sri Lankan banks. It can rather be an indication of the existence of operating and macroeconomic losses which forced all the banks to maintain higher spreads to cover excessive operating costs and credit risk, regardless of other factors like competition. Nevertheless, lower deposit rates and higher lending rates might have had negative effects on both deposit mobilization and lending.

As illustrated in Figure 6.2 and Figure 6.3, nominal interest rates have remained relatively stable during 1990–2009. Nevertheless, due to heavy fluctuations in the inflation, the real interest rates have experienced remarkable fluctuations. A noticeable correlation does not exist between nominal interest rates and deposit collection or lending. As expected, bank credit negatively responds to the real interest rate. Interestingly, however, Figure 6.3 indicates the existence of a negative relationship between real deposit rate and quarterly change in bank deposits. For example, during periods with higher real deposit rates, lower increases in bank deposits can be observed and vice versa. Further, even during the periods with negative real interest rates, marginal increases in the bank deposits could be observed. This observation is quite contradictory to the conventional theory. Nevertheless, this could be an indication of the lower responsiveness of deposits to deposit interest rates, as also argued in the financial restraint model. This suggests that factors other than the interest rate have a substantial effect on bank deposits.

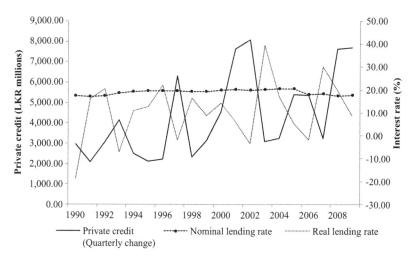

*Figure 6.2* Interest rates and credit in Sri Lanka during 1990–2010

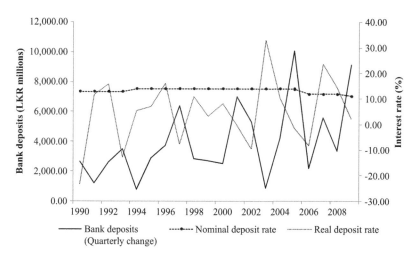

*Figure 6.3* Interest rates, and time and savings deposits in Sri Lanka during 1990–2010

To statistically investigate the effect of interest rate on bank deposits and lending, the regression models expressed in equation 6.1 and 6.2 were used. Bank branch network, bank rate, and domestic savings rate were also used as control variables. Quarterly banking statistics in Sri Lanka over twenty years during the period 1990–2009 (4 × 20 = 80 observations) were used as data. Monthly bulletins and annual reports published by the CBSL were used as the main sources of secondary data concerning the financial system and other macroeconomic parameters.

$$LDEPO_t = \alpha + \beta_0 DR_t + \beta_1 BRANCH_t + \beta_2 BR_t + \beta_3 DSR_t + \varepsilon_t \qquad (6.1)$$

$$LCREDIT_t = \alpha + \beta_4 LR_t + \beta_5 BRANCH_t + \beta_6 LDEPO_t$$
$$+ \beta_7 SPREAD_t + \beta_8 INF_t + \varepsilon_t. \qquad (6.2)$$

Equation 6.1 investigates the impact of deposit interest rates on the amount of deposits accumulated in the banks. Here, $DR$ denotes the weighted average deposit rate per annum in real terms after adjusting for inflation. The real deposit rate is used instead of nominal deposit rate based on McKinnon's (1973, p. 39) concept of "real return on holding money". Similar to the specification by Beck et al. (2007), $BRANCH$ stands for the extent of the branch network in terms of the number of people (in thousands) per bank branch.[2] Hence higher values of $BRANCH$ indicate lower levels of outreach in the branch network and vice versa. For example, as illustrated in Table 6.3, the number of people per bank branch was 3,640 in 2009, compared to 18,480 in 1990. Given the low level of population growth prevailing in Sri Lanka, this is an indication of a healthy expansion of the bank branch network. When the branch network is extensive, the bank can offer a diversified set of services while forming closer relationships with their clients. Moreover, the physical distance between the clients and the bank also tends to decrease when the branch network is extensive. Due to these reasons, an expansion of the branch network is often considered as a quality adjusted measure of bank performance (Wu, 2005). More precisely, these conditions enhance the convenience benefits and other non-financial gains of clients, which sometimes can substitute for the gains expected in terms of higher deposit rates.

Among the other variables, $BR$ accounts for the changes in the bank rate. Banks may face higher borrowing costs when the bank rate is higher. Concurrently, an increase in the bank rate may contribute to increasing other interest rates in the market. Therefore, due to the increased cost of alternative sources of funds, banks may make additional efforts to mobilize more deposits through various strategies that may or may not involve adjustments to the deposit rates. $DSR$, on the other hand, represents the domestic savings ratio, which is used to control the impact associated with the changes in domestic savings propensities. Finally, the dependent variable, $LDEPO$, denotes the quarterly change in bank deposits held by the public in real terms. The deposits in this case include both time and savings deposits. To correct the distribution, this variable was log transformed. The symbols $\alpha$, $\beta$, and $\varepsilon$ respectively denote intercepts, regression coefficients, and error terms. The time frame, which is indexed by $t$, ranges between 1990Q1 and 2009Q4.

Further, Equation 6.2 assesses the effects of the lending rate on the level of bank credit. The dependent variable, $LCREDIT$ measures the quarterly change in credit extended to the private sector. To obtain the characteristics of a normal

*Table 6.3* Descriptive statistics

| Variable | Description | Minimum | Maximum | Mean | Std. Deviation |
|---|---|---|---|---|---|
| LDEPO[a] | Logarithm of the real value of quarterly change in time and savings deposits | 2.84 | 4.86 | 3.77 | 0.41 |
| | *Real value of quarterly change in time and savings deposits (LKR millions)* | −44,995 | 71,826 | 8,203 | 13,411 |
| LCREDIT[b] | Logarithm of quarterly change in credit to private sector | 2.00 | 5.10 | 4.06 | 0.52 |
| | *Quarterly change in credit to private sector (LKR millions)* | −44,734 | 127,063 | 18,475 | 27,140 |
| DR | Real deposit rate | −40.60 | 42.90 | 0.40 | 15.42 |
| BRANCH | No. of persons per bank branch ('000) | 3.64 | 18.48 | 11.51 | 4.65 |
| BR | Bank rate | 14.00 | 25.00 | 16.63 | 2.13 |
| DSR | Domestic savings ratio | 15.20 | 24.00 | 20.73 | 2.24 |
| LR | Nominal lending rate | 8.95 | 22.30 | 15.91 | 3.46 |
| SPREAD | Spread between nominal lending rate and nominal deposit rate | 2.76 | 11.57 | 5.91 | 1.62 |
| INF | Inflation | −31.27 | 51.07 | 9.60 | 15.13 |

Note: N =80.
[a] Contains two missing values.
[b] Contains six missing values.
LKR = Sri Lankan rupees.

distribution, this variable was log transformed as well. In general, banks in developing countries face loanable fund constraints rather than constraints on the demand for credit. Therefore *LDEPO*, as used in the previous equation, is also used in this model to investigate the effect of an expanded deposit base on credit expansion. The nominal lending rate denoted by *LR* is used to capture the effect of interest rates on the level of lending. Some studies like Amor-Tapia et al. (2010) argue that inflation positively contributes to credit expansion and bank profitability. Moreover, unlike depositors, borrowers may not be discouraged when the general price levels are increasing. More precisely, increasing price levels may positively affect the credit demand. Therefore inflation (*INF*) is used as a separate variable together with the nominal lending rate, instead of integrating them together to get the real lending rate.

Further, an expanded branch network can enhance the level of credit extended by the banks through mitigating the information asymmetry and through promoting relationship-based lending. *BRANCH* accounts for this effect, and its specification is the same as used in equation 6.1. *SPREAD* captures the effect of interest spread. As already discussed in Chapter 3, interest spread constitutes the price rent opportunities. Moreover, the key arguments pertaining to the financial restraint model emphasize the importance of interest spreads for banking system development. Using price rent opportunities, banks can invest more resources in enhancing their screening and monitoring systems, thereby leading to an expansion of credit.

The Kolmogorov-Smirnov test was used to test for the normality of the distribution. Some of the variables (i.e., *LDEPO* and *LCREDIT*) were log transformed to correct the distribution as mentioned before to ensure the robustness of the regression models. The issues associated with serial correlation were diagnosed using the Durbin-Watson (DW) test. Significantly, instead of using the consumer price index, this investigation uses the Wholesale Price Index (WPI) in accordance with McKinnon's (1973) arguments. More precisely, inflation, here, was calculated by annualizing the quarterly changes in the WPI (base year 1990). Therefore both the interest rates and the inflation rates are expressed on an annual basis. However, there is a possibility that annualized quarterly inflation rates may appear substantially higher than actual annual averages. Nevertheless, the study relies on the quarterly inflation rates because the depositors and the borrowers are more responsive to short-term price fluctuations rather than annual averages. Moreover, future expectations about the inflation tend to be based on monthly or quarterly price changes rather than the annual inflation rate of the previous year. While the descriptive statistics relating to these regressions are illustrated in Table 6.3, the results are discussed separately in sections 4.1 and 4.2.

### 4.1 Deposit collection

The regression model illustrated in equation 6.1 indicates that the explanatory variables are capable of explaining around 43.1 per cent of the fluctuations in the quarterly changes in the deposit base [$F(4, 73) = 13.81$, $p < .01$, $DW = 1.99$]. The Breusch-Pagan/Cook-Weisberg test ($\chi^2 = .61$, $p = .434$) provides adequate assurance of the absence of issues concerning heteroskedasticity. Table 6.4 summarizes the regression results. Quite surprisingly, the effect of the deposit rate (*DR*) on quarterly change in deposits (*LDEPO*) is negative and negligible ($\beta = -.007$; $p = .006$). Moreover, nominal interest rate (when substituted for real deposit rate) did not show any statistically significant effect on deposits. Hence the banks seem to stimulate more deposits when the interest rates decrease, by offering other benefits since the capacity of banks to offer variety of non-financial benefits (such as gifts) increases when the deposit rates are lower because they can use the savings on interest costs to offer other benefits. Therefore the overall effect of interest rate on bank deposits is negligible in Sri Lanka, as also claimed in the financial restraint model.

*Table 6.4* Regression results

| Variable | Description | Coefficients | | | |
|---|---|---|---|---|---|
| | | *ß* | *Std. error* | *T* | *Sig.* |
| **Dependent variable: LDEPO** | | | | | |
| α | Constant | 3.180 | 0.608 | 5.232 | 0.000 |
| DR | Real deposit rate | −0.007*** | 0.002 | −2.858 | 0.006 |
| BRANCH | No. of persons per bank branch ('000) | −0.043*** | 0.011 | −4.022 | 0.000 |
| BR | Bank rate | 0.030* | 0.017 | 1.745 | 0.085 |
| DSR | Domestic savings ratio | 0.028 | 0.022 | 1.305 | 0.196 |
| **Dependent variable: LCREDIT** | | | | | |
| α | Constant | 3.546 | 0.564 | 6.282 | 0.000 |
| LR | Nominal lending rate | −0.071*** | 0.021 | −3.433 | 0.001 |
| BRANCH | No. of persons per bank branch ('000) | −0.026* | 0.013 | −1.980 | 0.052 |
| LDEPO | Logarithm of the real value of quarterly change in time and savings deposits | 0.268** | 0.122 | 2.189 | 0.032 |
| SPREAD | Spread between nominal lending rate and nominal deposit rate | 0.152*** | 0.041 | 3.681 | 0.000 |
| INF | Inflation | 0.005* | 0.003 | 1.900 | 0.062 |

Note: LDEPO denotes logarithm of the real value of quarterly change in time and savings deposits, and LCREDIT denotes the logarithm of quarterly change in credit to the private sector. The symbols (***), (**), and (*) indicate statistical significance at 1 per cent, 5 per cent, and 10 per cent levels, respectively.

*BRANCH* has a statistically significant ($p < 0.001$) negative effect on the level of deposits. In other words, banks are able to mobilize 4.3 per cent more deposits on a quarterly basis when the number of people per bank branch decreases by one thousand. This should not be confused with a reduction in the number of bank clients. It is rather an indication of a decrease in the share of the population to be served by each branch due to an increase in the number of bank branches. When the branch network is extensive, banks are better able to provide more diversified sets of services at a relatively lower cost due to economies of scope and scale (Cohen and Kaufman, 1965). Hence their ability to attract more deposits and clients increases when the number of branches increases. These increased deposit bases and clienteles tend to create more rent opportunities. Therefore the banks are able to recover higher costs associated with establishing new branches relatively quickly. More precisely, expanded branch networks tend to create strong operating rent opportunities as argued in Chapter 3.

The bank rate denoted by *BR* positively affects the amount of bank deposits ($p$ = .085). For example, one unit increase in the bank rate can cause an increase of around 3 per cent in bank deposits on a quarterly basis. This suggests that the banks try to collect more deposits when the money market rates increase, regardless of an increase in the deposit rate. The moderate levels of competition prevailing in Sri Lanka do not push the deposit rates upward when other money market rates increase. Hence when the bank rate increases, the spread between the bank rate and the deposit rate tends to increase. Therefore banks, without entering into price competition, tend to provide other benefits in attracting deposits, particularly during special social and cultural events such as the New Year and Christmas. On the other hand, when the bank rate moves upward, the costs of borrowing from the central bank increase. Hence, banks are incentivized to increase their deposit bases in an attempt to minimize potential liquidity problems. The effects of changes in the domestic savings ratio as indicated by *DSR*, however, were not statistically significant ($p$ = .196). The implication is that, irrespective of the level of savings in a society, the desire to keep savings in bank deposits is influenced more by banking system specific variables rather than by the extent of savings in Sri Lankan economy.

These findings support the idea that an expansion of the branch network contributes to enhancing the capacity of the banks to mobilize more deposits. This is explained in terms of two main factors. First, when the number of branches increases, inevitably the number of branches located in the rural and semi-urban areas tends to increase. Therefore banking services spread into the rural areas. When the banking services are not available, people may hoard money or accumulate savings in non-financial assets instead of bank deposits. Therefore an expanded branch network facilitates the flow of savings from the informal sector and from other non-financial assets toward the banking system.

Second, the extent of the branch network affects the ability of the banks to offer a diversified set of services to a wide range of clients. For example, the geographical spread and the size of the banks affect their ability and cost effectiveness in implementing services like ATMs, electronic fund transfer services, credit card facilities, and other online services. When these services become popular among the public, the demand for currency tends to diminish because the public tends to shift from currency toward forms of near money like bank deposits. The debit and credit card facilities allow them to transact using the money in their bank accounts instead of carrying cash all the time. Hence the average deposit holdings of individuals tend to increase.

The presence of banks in the rural areas was limited in Sri Lanka in previous decades. As a result, the CBSL imposed a regulation on the establishment of new branches, which required the banks to establish at least two branches in rural areas for each branch they established in the Colombo metropolitan area. This policy may have contributed to expanding the branch network, particularly in the rural areas. Moreover, it can be seen that, along with the rapid improvements in the banking system, an increasing number of firms have started paying their employees' salaries and remunerations through the banks.

This may also have contributed to increasing the average deposit holdings of the banks. Hence, in general, when banking services are efficient and developed, the demand for money in terms of the transactions and precautionary motives tends to decline as the amount of bank deposits increases.

## 4.2 Credit expansion

The regression model illustrated in equation 6.2 provides more concrete evidence on the effect of the interest rates and other variables in determining the amount of credit extended to the private sector by the banks. The model indicates that nearly 60 per cent of the variation in *LCREDIT* is explained by the explanatory variables [$F(5, 68) = 20.79$, $p < .01$, $DW = 1.80$]. The Breusch-Pagan/Cook-Weisberg test ($\chi^2 = .01$, $p = .916$) confirms the absence of issues associated with heteroskedasticity. Table 6.4 provides details of the regression coefficients and their statistical significance.

As expected, the nominal lending rate (*LR*) has a negative impact on the extent of bank lending ($p = .001$). The coefficient indicates that a one unit increase in *LR* can cause nearly a 7 per cent decrease in bank credit on a quarterly basis. When the interest rate increases, the costs of borrowing for the investors tend to increase, and thereby the returns on their investments tend to decrease. Therefore firms decrease their borrowings and investments when interest rates are increasing. This finding is consistent with the existing literature as well.

Quite similar to its influence on deposits, the branch network has a positive effect (a negative coefficient for *BRANCH*) on the level of credit as well. However, as indicated by the magnitude of the coefficient and its statistical significance ($p = .052$), the effect of the branch network on credit is relatively weaker than its effect on deposits. When the number of branches increases, each branch tends to serve only a limited number of clients. This does not indicate a decline in the client base for the entire bank because *BRANCH* decreases merely because the client base is distributed among more branches. Moreover, when the branch network is extensive, the physical distance between the bank and its clients tends to decrease. These factors strengthen the relationships between bank staff and more active clients. This results in an increase in relationship-based lending and a reduction in screening and monitoring costs.

The relatively weak relationship between the branch network and credit can be explained based on the unique characteristics pertaining to the Sri Lanka banking system. Even though the banks now mobilize more deposits from rural areas by capitalizing on their extensive branch networks, their lending activities are mainly concentrated on the metropolitan cities mainly because the majority of the firms located in rural areas are SMEs. These SMEs are informationally opaque, and hence monitoring and screening become costly for the banks compared to their dealings with the informationally transparent larger firms located in the metropolitan cities. Hemachandra (2003) also argues that the Sri Lankan banks tend to extend more credit to the formal sector compared to the informal sector, due to different risk levels associated with those sectors. Due to these reasons, the effect of branch network on credit expansion is slightly lower than its effect on the mobilization of deposits. However, an indirect effect of the expanded branch network on credit expansion is also noteworthy. As discussed previously, banks in most of the developing countries face loanable fund constraints which limit their ability to extend more credit. Hence when the deposit base expands as a result of the branch network expansion, the lending capacities of the banks tend to increase. For example, *LDEPO* positively affects bank credit ($p = .032$). More precisely, when the deposit base increases by 1 per cent, the amount of credit tends to increase by 0.27 per cent. Therefore the overall effect of the expanded branch network on the bank credit is certainly higher than the magnitude of *BRANCH*.

Further, *INF* positively affects the level of credit ($p = .062$). Seemingly, rising price levels positively affect the profitability of firms. As a consequence, firms tend to borrow more during the periods of inflation because, given the relatively stable nominal lending rates, the borrowing costs in real terms tend to decrease when inflation increases. Significantly, as suggested in the financial restraint model, the *SPREAD* positively affects the level of credit ($p < .001$). Higher spreads seem to provide the Sri Lankan banks with additional profit opportunities (in terms of the price rent as argued before), which they can use in improving their screening and monitoring systems, and technology. This in turn increases their ability to lend because the lack of resources to be utilized in the screening and monitoring process remains a major bottleneck in extending credit. In other words, when adequate profit margins are absent, banks prefer to extend credit to a well-known group of large firms rather than to the SMEs located in rural areas, particularly when obtaining information is costly.

In addition to information problems associated with SMEs, extending many small loans to the SMEs is costly for the banks, compared to extending fewer large loans to the large enterprises. When extending fewer bulky loans, banks need to monitor and screen only a few firms. Therefore they can minimize their monitoring and screening costs when extending credit to large firms usually located in the cities. However the rates of return on the SME projects may be higher than those of large firms. Hence when the information problems are greater, the credit may not necessarily flow to the sectors with the highest returns. On the other hand, the outcomes associated with growing SME sectors are multifaceted and facilitate the achievement of a wide range of economic and social objectives such as reducing unemployment, mitigating income disparity, and poverty alleviation. Therefore, in terms of achieving socially optimal outcomes, the expansion of opportunities available for the SMEs in accessing credit is vital.

## 5.   Bank ownership

The arguments pertaining to the principal-agent framework, the property rights approach, and public choice theory provide the theoretical foundation necessary for hypothesizing the effects of ownership on the performance of firms (Altunbas, Evans, and Molyneux, 2001; Figueira, Nellis, and Parker, 2009; Starr, 1988). However, the existing debate on the relation between ownership and performance is not straightforward, and the empirical evidence remains largely mixed (Wanniarachchige and Suzuki, 2011). Despite the drastic banking and financial system reforms that have substantially reshaped the banking system in Sri Lanka during recent decades, rigorous attempts have not been made to explore the effects of bank ownership on performance. Nevertheless, as argued in Chapter 3, bank ownership is one of the factors in the operating environment that affects the operating rent opportunities.

There is no straightforward method for assessing the performance of banks. The techniques based on the X-efficiency literature have attracted substantial popularity in measuring bank performance in recent decades. Such measures usually rely on advanced statistical and mathematical programming techniques and are concerned with identifying an efficient frontier against which the performances of individual banks can be assessed. Data envelopment analysis (DEA), the distribution-free approach, the stochastic frontier approach, the thick frontier approach, and the free disposal hull approach are some of the well-known techniques in the X-efficiency literature (Berger and Mester, 1997). Each method has its own pros and cons.

Among these techniques, DEA has attracted widespread attention and was extended and applied in various fields by various researchers (Coelli, 1996). Further, it has become a popular benchmarking technique in differentiating the performance of different firms. DEA is a non-parametric approach based on liner programming techniques which constructs an efficient frontier and adopts piece-wise linear technology. Under DEA, the performances of different firms are estimated relative to the efficient frontier on which the most efficient firms with efficiency scores of one lie. Thus the efficiency scores generated by DEA always range between 0 and 1. DEA has the capability to deal with multiple inputs and outputs simultaneously without having to aggregate them using some arbitrary weights. This is one of the reasons for its superiority over simple ratio based measures. Concurrently, DEA is unit-invariant. Hence it is not required to measure all the inputs and outputs in one homogeneous unit of measure. Each input or output can be measured using the most appropriate unit of measure. As far as the banks are concerned, these features entail numerous advantages, because the banks inevitably use different types of inputs and produce numerous outputs which are difficult to be measured using a homogeneous unit of measure in such a way that an aggregation into a single figure is feasible. Moreover, DEA does not require researchers to specify the functional form of the model in advance, unlike most of the parametric approaches where such specification is mandatory. Further, as DEA is a non-parametric technique, it may be used even with small samples without raising serious concerns about the robustness of results. Thus DEA has several merits compared with various other parametric techniques (Avkiran, 1999). As a consequence, the technique gives substantial flexibility to the researcher in application and has emerged as a leading tool for measuring the performance of financial institutions (Colwell and Davis, 1992).

Nevertheless, DEA has several limitations as well. First, DEA fails to filter out the effect of statistical noise from efficiency measures. In fact, DEA measures gross performance rather than net performance. Thus DEA may under- or over-estimate the true performance. Second, efficiency scores of DEA can be seriously affected by outliers and measurement errors. Third, DEA efficiency scores are calculated by comparing different decision-making units (DMUs) within the selected sample. Hence such scores are less meaningful when compared with DMUs outside the sample. More precisely, DEA efficiency scores are comparable only within the sample considered for estimating the efficiency scores. These can be viewed as serious defects associated with DEA (Figueira et al., 2009). However, compared to other available techniques, the merits of DEA outweigh the demerits in numerous ways.

Further, revenue-based efficiency estimated using DEA tends to align better with the bank rent concept, which is also associated with additional revenue opportunities. Banks with higher revenues relative to their costs are able to generate more profit than their less efficient counterparts. As a consequence, even when the banks are operating in a competitive market, more efficient banks are able to enjoy greater rent opportunities due to their efficiency. Additional revenues available to efficient banks tend to enhance their franchise values and thereby create additional incentives for pursuing prudent strategies. This type of approach was first suggested by Berger and Mester (1997), and was followed up by other researchers like Drake, Hall, and Simper (2009) and Hadad et al. (2008). In fact, revenue efficiency is also a partial measure of bank performance. However, DEA-based efficiency measures take a broader perspective than simple financial ratios like ROA or ROE. Thus, despite the fact that it does not directly capture the aspects of stability, revenue efficiency gives a reasonable approximation of the performance of a bank compared to other traditional techniques (Berger and Mester, 2003; Drake et al., 2009; Hadad et al., 2008). Therefore revenue-based efficiency is used here to measure profitability of banks in Sri Lanka and India, which in turn is used as a signal of the availability of bank rent opportunities. This study applied the slack based model (SBM) in estimating revenue efficiency. SBM was pioneered by Tone (2001) and can be considered superior compared to other DEA models since it explicitly treats both input and output slacks and assigns an efficiency score of 1 only if a particular DMU is neither associated with output shortages nor input excesses. Banks typically produce multiple outputs using multiple inputs, despite the fact that there is no universal consensus on defining what constitutes outputs and inputs (Avkiran, 2006; Colwell and Davis, 1992). Therefore researchers usually identify different combinations of inputs and outputs based on the purpose for which the performance is measured. The production approach and intermediation approach are two theoretical approaches that assist in modeling bank operations and in identifying their inputs and outputs (Avkiran, 2006; Wu, 2005). Given the nature and objectives of banks, the intermediation approach is widely applied and is consistent with the majority of the DEA literature (Sathye, 2003; Worthington, 2000). Therefore this study follows the intermediation approach.

The input-output specification of this study, although not identical, closely follows that in two other recent studies. For example, Hadad et al. (2008) specify net interest income, net trading income, and net off-balance sheet income as outputs, whereas personnel expenses, non-personnel expenses, and provisions for losses on earning assets are identified as inputs. Further, Drake et al. (2009) in their study recognize net interest income, other operating incomes and net commissions, and fees and trading incomes as outputs, while non-interest expenses, other operating expenses, and provisions are treated as inputs. Taking net interest income is inappropriate because the banks transfer deposits and other resources into loans and other types of investments. Therefore interest income and interest expenses have to be treated separately as an output and an input respectively. Further, instead of considering provisions as a separate input, here the provisions are pooled with other operating expenses due mainly to lack of separate data on different kinds of provisions. On the output side, all incomes other than interest income are categorized as non-interest income, given their relative insignificance as separate items, particularly in developing countries. In summary, interest expenses (IE), overhead expenses (OE), and personal costs (PC) were recognized as inputs, while interest income (IIN) and non-interest income (NIN) were recognized as outputs in this study.

Special care was taken to draw a balanced sample by selecting the same banks in different periods. Here, banks which were involved in mergers and/or acquisitions and banks which entered or exited from the market during the selected time frame were dropped from the sample, in addition to the banks for which data was not available over all the periods. Hence four out of the thirty-five banks were dropped due to lack of data. Moreover, the data on six regional banks were consolidated on an annual basis, and they were treated as one bank, because these banks share common characteristics and operate mainly on a regional basis. Moreover, the government has already taken steps to consolidate these six regional banks into a single bank. Thus the data set contains data on twenty-six banks over a period of eight years, from January 2000 through December 2007. These twenty-six banks are composed of five state-owned banks, ten private banks, ten foreign banks, and the Regional Development Bank.[3] Data since 2008 were dropped because the performance of the banks may have been affected by the global financial crisis. The variations in performance may be distorted during a crisis, because the crisis may affect the different ownership groups differently.

In the first stage, the revenue efficiencies of individual banks were estimated using the SBM model of DEA. Hence the efficiencies of the banks were measured on an annual basis relative to the efficiency frontier for that particular year rather than relative to the global efficiency frontier for the entire eight year period. However, this may result in the limitation that the efficiency scores are not directly comparable across different periods. To overcome potential issues associated with such limitations, another supplementary performance measure (i.e., ROA) was used so that a comparison between the DEA revenue efficiency scores and ROA was possible. In the second stage, one-way ANOVA was used to identify statistically significant performance variations among different ownership groups. Dunnet's C post hoc estimation technique was used regarding the data that did not meet the homogeneity of variance assumption. The null hypothesis used for

*Table 6.5* ANOVA results on revenue efficiency and ROA

| Results | Bank group | Mean | S.D. | Mean differences |
|---|---|---|---|---|
| **Revenue** | Foreign (F) | .868 | .179 | S*, P* |
| **efficiency** | Domestic private (P) | .462 | .214 | F* |
| | State-owned (S) | .585 | .345 | F* |
| **Return** | Foreign (F) | 2.515 | 1.872 | P*, S** |
| **on assets** | Domestic private (P) | .451 | 4.609 | S**, F* |
| | State-owned (S) | 1.769 | 1.286 | P**, F** |

Note: * and ** indicate groups with significant mean differences at .01 and .05 levels, respectively.

this investigation states that the mean efficiency scores among different groups are equal. As the objective of this investigation was limited to the identification of the effect of ownership, other explanatory variables were not considered.

As indicated by the ANOVA results shown in Table 6.5, ownership explained around 18.7 per cent of the performance variation in Sri Lankan banks [$F(2, 207) = 59.6$, $p < .01$, $\eta^2 = .36$]. According to Cohen's $f^2$, the effect size of ownership is large (.6).[4] The foreign banks have higher mean revenue efficiency scores than all others. Further, these mean differences are statistically significant. Statistically significant performance differences between other groups of banks could not be observed, although the mean revenue efficiency scores for domestic-private banks were slightly lower than those for state-owned banks.

As a supplementary analysis, the same tests were performed, replacing the DEA revenue efficiency scores with ROAs. As shown in Table 6.5, the ownership accounted for around 1.6 per cent of the performance variation in Sri Lankan banks [$F(2, 207) = 8.75$, $p < .01$, $\eta^2 = .079$]. According to Cohen's $f^2$, the effect size of ownership is medium (.09). Further, the foreign banks outperform their domestic counterparts in terms of ROA as well. The performance of the domestic-private banks was significantly lower than that of state-owned and foreign banks. The results based on both DEA revenue efficiency scores and ROA suggest that the foreign banks outperform the domestic banks in Sri Lanka. These findings are consistent with those of Bhattacharyya, Lovell, and Sahay (1997) and Clarke et al. (2002). However, it is worth noting that the foreign banks operate only in the metropolitan areas of Sri Lanka. Further, the branch network of foreign banks is trivial (Mittal and Dhade, 2007), and most of the foreign banks have less than five branches (Wanniarachchige and Suzuki, 2011; Wanniarachchige, Suzuki, and Kjærland, 2011). For example, each foreign bank has established only one branch in each district (more precisely, in the main city of each district), except in urbanized districts like Colombo, Gampaha, Kalutara, and Kandy. Moreover, the foreign banks basically deal only with large corporate clients. On the other hand, compared to conventional technologies in the domestic banks, the cutting-edge technologies available to the foreign banks allow them to further lower their operating costs. Due to these reasons, the foreign banks have been able to maintain relatively low NPL ratios and lower operating costs. These can be recognized as the main reasons for higher profitability associated with the foreign banks.

In contrast, the state-owned banks contribute heavily to extending the banking services to the rural areas by establishing branches there. Domestic banks (both state-owned and private) deal with small scale borrowers and savers as well. In particular, the state-owned banks are involved in financing backward industries and less creditworthy SMEs, with the aim of improving their financing conditions in line with national objectives (Kumbhakar and Sarkar, 2003; Sathye, 2003). Moreover, domestic banks are still in the process of adopting modern technologies while restructuring their operating systems. Hence their operating costs are relatively higher. The higher efficiencies associated with the foreign banks are not surprising. But, surprisingly, according to both DEA revenue efficiency and ROA, the performances of domestic private banks are lower than those of the state-owned banks. This goes against the well-established theoretical predictions of the property rights approach and public choice theory. Nevertheless, this conflicting situation can be further explained based on several factors that have characterized the banking system in Sri Lanka during the past decades.

First, banking systems based on arm's length transactions in a deregulated setting require the banks to be sufficiently large if they are to be efficient (Hellmann and Murdock, 1998). State-owned banks have been the major players in the banking system for decades. Hence by now, these banks have been able to expand their branch networks, acquire large market shares, and have already achieved substantially large scales. In contrast, domestic private banks are still in their expansionary stage. At this stage, they have to make heavy investments and incur higher costs in extending the branch network, adopting the latest technologies, and expanding their scales. Hence even now, state-owned banks have been able to hold onto the lion's share in the market by capitalizing on their extended branch networks and established reputations. But relatively small private banks with narrow branch networks have failed to acquire market share rapidly under current conditions, even though their shares have increased substantially in recent years.

Second, people seem to favor the state-owned banks due to their perception of the safety of deposits. Seemingly, this perception is more common among the elderly population than the younger population. In general, a promise made by a government is more credible than a promise made by an individual or even a private corporation (Hellmann and Murdock, 1998). This reputation has enabled the state-owned banks to pool large amounts of deposits at a lower cost.

Finally, state-owned enterprises still perform a key role in Sri Lanka and carry on their banking activities through state-owned banks. As a result, state-owned banks have an additional advantage in mobilizing deposits and in lending compared to the domestic private banks. A large proportion of credit extended to state-owned enterprises contributes partly to keep the NPL ratios of state-owned banks low, even when they incur heavy NPLs on the credit extended to the private sector.

## 6.   High and volatile inflation

Like most of the developing countries, Sri Lanka has experienced substantially higher and turbulent inflation rates throughout its history since the initiation of open economic policies in 1977. For example, the average inflation during 1955 and 1969 was as low as 1.7 per cent. Moreover, the average inflation during 1970–1977 was around 5.8 per cent. The period particularly during 1970–1977 was characterized by severe government intervention and price controls. This was the main reason for substantially lower inflation rates during this period. With the economic deregulation in 1977, most of the government interventions and price controls were abolished. Thereafter, the general price level started to rise rapidly due to the substantial supply shortage prevailed during the 1970–1977 period characterized with import substitution policies. The period between 1978 and 1993 can be recognized as a period of high inflation, during which almost all years recorded double digit inflation rates (except during 1985–1987). Later the regulators tamed inflation to some extent. As a consequence, inflation slowed down substantially during 1985–1987 before it increased again in 1988.

From 1987 until around 1991, the political climate was relatively more unstable in Sri Lanka, mainly due to the conflicts that arose between the *Janatha Vimukti Peramuna* (JVP)[5] and the government. This created an upward pressure on inflation, mainly through curtailing economic activity. Political situation started to recover again since 1991, and Sri Lanka entered into a relatively stable political period, particularly after 1994 under the newly elected government.[6] As a consequence, inflation rate decreased gradually. For example, inflation rate remained below 10 per cent during 1994–2004 (except for 15.9 per cent in 1996 and 14.2 per cent in 2001).

Inflation skyrocketed again during 2005–2008 and reached 22.6 per cent by the end of 2008. A rapid increase in government expenditure and a substantial decline in unemployment can be held accountable for the increased inflation during this period. For example, government expenditure increased by around 20 per cent on average annually during 2004–2009. Increased defense expenditure, government sector employment, and wages and salaries can be held mainly responsible for the rapid increase in government expenditure during this period. Further, the unemployment rate fell to an average of 6 per cent during 2005–2010, from an average of 8.2 per cent during 2000–2004.

However, the inflation rate sharply decreased to 3.5 per cent in 2009 from 22.6 in 2008. Declining prices of imports resulting from the global financial crisis also contributed to lower inflation in Sri Lanka, particularly in 2009 and 2010. Further, the ending of the three-decade-long civil conflict in the first half of 2009 has contributed to expanding the supply of goods and services, due mainly to the increased economic activities, particularly in former war-torn areas (i.e., the Northern and Eastern Provinces). This can be considered as another reason for the sudden decline in inflation.

Despite the slight decline in the inflation rate in recent years, the overall level of inflation in Sri Lanka has been very high. In this context, regulators of financial

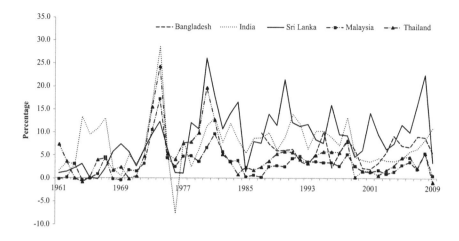

*Figure 6.4* Inflation in Sri Lanka and selected nearby countries (1961–2009)

markets cannot implement the recommendations of the financial restraint model because it was intrinsically difficult to set deposit rate ceilings in such a way that the real interest rates remain positive and adequate. Moreover in addition to being high, as illustrated in Figure 6.4, the inflation rate in Sri Lanka was highly volatile compared to some of the nearby countries. For example, the average annual inflation in Sri Lanka during 1990–1999 was 11.3 per cent. In contrast, the inflation rates in India, Bangladesh, and Thailand were 9.5, 5.7, and 5.0 per cent, respectively. Moreover, the annual inflation in Sri Lanka during 2000–2009 remained at 10.7 per cent on average when the average annual inflation rates during the same period for India, Bangladesh, and Thailand were 5.5, 6.0, and 2.5 per cent, respectively. This type of highly volatile inflation aggravates the fundamental uncertainty associated with the economic environment.

In view of these facts, the macroeconomic instability associated with inflation is relatively high in Sri Lanka. This makes decision making more difficult for the banks. For example, forecasting the profitability of a project becomes more difficult due to increased uncertainty caused by volatile inflation. Hence the determination of appropriate lending rates and deposit rates becomes cumbersome for the banks. As a consequence, banks may seek to maintain extra margins in interest rates (i.e., the required risk premiums increase). This results in higher lending rates as well as lower deposit rates than could have been available under stable and low levels of inflation. Hence these volatile macroeconomic conditions may hinder deposit mobilization as well as credit expansion by the banks.

Nevertheless, these higher spreads by no means represent the availability of actual rent opportunities for the banks. They merely signal that excessive uncertainty prevailed in the economy. Figure 6.5 illustrates the correlation between

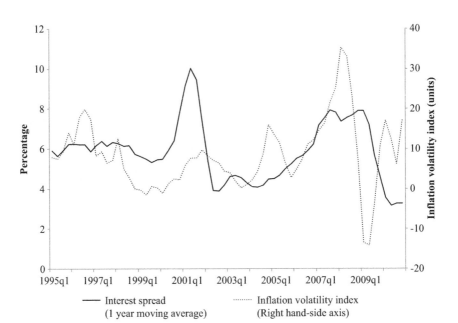

*Figure 6.5* Volatility of inflation and bank interest spreads

the interest spread and the volatility of inflation, estimated using the volatility index of inflation. This index was designed so that it accounts for both the magnitude and the degree of volatility of inflation. A one-year moving average of the quarterly inflation rates (calculated based on WPI) is used as the magnitude of inflation, while a five-year moving window standard deviation of the quarterly inflation rates is taken as the degree of volatility. Finally, volatility is multiplied by the magnitude to calculate the inflation volatility index. Figure 6.5 suggests that the interest spread is substantially responsive to the inflation volatility index.[7] In other words, banks tend to widen their interest spreads when the uncertainty is increased due to unpredictable movements in the general price levels, though these higher spreads may not necessarily materialize as profits for the banks. Significantly, in a high inflation environment, banks may try to increase the lending rates instead of lowering the deposit rates in response to increased uncertainty, because decreased deposit rates may result in negative real interest rates and hence discourage deposit mobilization. Hence high and volatile inflation may reduce a substantial portion of economy's investments.

Therefore the interest spread alone cannot appropriately predict the extent of rent opportunities available for the banks because higher interest spreads may alternatively reflect the higher levels of uncertainty and transaction costs. More precisely, high and volatile inflation creates macroeconomic losses, which eventually erode the price rent opportunities available in terms of interest spreads.

## 7. Socio-political instability associated with civil war

The macroeconomic instability associated with civil war in Sri Lanka has been high. The civil war has aggravated the fundamental uncertainty in Sri Lanka, in addition to creating substantial property damage and threats to human life. Despite the existence of a few periods of relatively peaceful politics, Sri Lanka has witnessed political turbulences since the early days of independence. The root causes for the recently ended civil war can be traced back to Sri Lanka's colonial period. For example, as discussed in section 2, the export oriented agricultural sector instigated by the British paved the way for a huge migration of Tamil workers from the southern parts of India, contributing to the increase in the Tamil population in Sri Lanka. Some of the political reforms initiated after independence, including the first constitution of Sri Lanka, contributed to polarizing these ethnic groups (Bouffard and Carment, 2006). In particular, the declaration of *Sinhala* (the native language of the ethnic majority of Sri Lanka) as the official language in 1956 aggravated the tensions among the minority Tamils. These ill-planned and inappropriate policy initiatives have been widely held responsible for laying the initial foundation for the conflicts between Sinhalese and Tamils.

The Liberation Tigers of Tamil Elam (LTTE) was one of the organized militant groups that attempted to mobilize the Tamil population in Sri Lanka to claim a separate state in the Northern and Eastern Provinces. The state proclaimed by the LTTE comprised of 28.7 per cent of the landmass and around 60 per cent of the coastal areas in Sri Lanka (Ministry of Defense, 2011). The LTTE was initially proscribed by the Sri Lankan government in 1978 and later banned by thirty-two other countries, including India, the United Kingdom, and the United States on different occasions (Ministry of Defense, 2011). Initial conflicts between the LTTE and the Sri Lankan government can be traced back even to the 1970s, though a majority of the sources claim that the war officially started in 1983. Though the conflicts were mainly confined to the Northern and Eastern Provinces, the terrorist activities of the LTTE frequently caused severe damage to people and property in the capital city of Colombo and other major cities as well. The LTTE assassinated a large number of political leaders and leading government officials, regardless of their ethnicity, creating enormous pressure on the political climate in Sri Lanka.

In addition, the JVP was a radical Sinhalese political group with a Marxist ideology responsible for the political turbulence that prevailed in the southern parts of Sri Lanka during the early 1970s and late 1980s. Their struggle was mainly focused on establishing a communist regime in Sri Lanka. During these periods, they entered into armed struggle against the government to achieve their objectives, which eventually failed due to strong resistance from the government. This turbulence did, however, aggravate the political situation and cause instability in Sri Lanka during these periods. Though most of the militant groups, including the JVP, subsequently entered the democratic political process, the LTTE consistently refused to do so. Together, these two conflicts contributed to make the political climate in Sri Lanka very unstable in the past few decades and caused severe damage to resources and human life. This adverse political climate aggravated macroeconomic instability in Sri Lanka, while intensifying the fundamental uncertainty in the economy. Due mainly to these reasons, Sri Lanka became recognized as one of the most politically unstable countries in the region (Younis et al., 2008).

Similar to high and volatile inflation, the socio-political instability had a substantial impact on the performance of the banking system and credit markets through affecting the level of fundamental uncertainty in the economy. The uncertainties resulting from uprisings and civil wars can affect the financial system and the economy in a number of ways (Baddeley, 2008; Blattman and Miguel, 2010; Nagarajan, 1997; Rodrik, 1999). Nevertheless, the identification of civil wars and measurement of their intensity and impacts are quite controversial because, in the first place, there is no universally accepted definition for civil war in the literature. Sambanis (2004) highlights a number of difficulties in arriving at such a definition. Therefore "the distinction between civil wars and other forms of political instability has largely been assumed rather than demonstrated" (Blattman and Miguel, 2010, p. 6). As the focus of this study is not to distinguish civil wars from other type of conflicts, a relatively loose definition was used based on the discussions in Sambanis (2004). Hence a civil war in this context refers to an armed conflict between a politically organized militant group with a clearly stated political objective and the government within a sovereign state over a sustained time period, causing substantially large number of deaths for both military forces and civilians.

Based on this definition, the conflicts that prevailed between the government and the LTTE since the early 1980s until early 2009 can be identified as the main civil war in Sri Lanka after independence.[8] In addition, the conflicts that existed in the early 1970s and again in the late 1980s between the JVP and the Sri Lankan government also loosely fit the definition of this study. However, due to the unavailability of a comprehensive data set beyond the year 2000, the analysis in this section is confined to the period between 2000 and 2010. Hence the impact of the turbulence caused by the JVP and the impact of the violence created by the LTTE prior to 2000 remain unexplored in this study.

Some studies have attempted to measure the intensity of civil war based on the geographical spread of the conflict or its duration. However, the exact geographical spread of the civil war in Sri Lanka cannot be clearly identified. In fact, the effects of civil war were widespread across the country. If the war intensity is measured based on the duration of the war, only the long-term effects can be observed. Therefore this investigation primarily draws on the number of deaths caused by the civil war (measured on a quarterly basis) as an indication of the intensity of the civil war.

The risk perceptions of foreign and domestic investors were substantially higher during the war period due to frequent and unexpected terrorist attacks in many parts of the country. Sri Lanka's missed growth potential during this period can be directly attributed to the prolonged civil war (World Bank, 2000a). The continued civil war suppressed GDP growth in Sri Lanka by around 2–3 per cent on an annual basis (CBSL, 1998). These negative consequences mainly resulted from the inefficient allocation of resources, damages to infrastructure, under-utilization of scarce resources, and other productivity losses attributable to deteriorating investor confidence and human suffering (CBSL, 2002; Suzuki, Dulal, and Wanniarachchige, 2010). The following discussion explores the impact of socio-political stability or instability on banking system development, drawing upon the Sri Lankan experience, mainly during two important periods of political stability.

The first period of political stability commenced in 2001 when the initial steps for a seemingly viable ceasefire agreement (CFA) between the Sri Lankan government and LTTE were implemented with the mediation of the Norwegian government.[9] As a consequence of a series of negotiations, the Sri Lankan government and the LTTE signed a memorandum of understanding in 2001 as an initiative to facilitate further political negotiations. Subsequently, the parties officially entered into the CFA in February 2002.[10] This led to a 'no war–no peace' period, which can be considered as the longest such period after the commencement of war in the early 1980s (Crisis Group Asia, 2006; Fair, 2006; NORAD, 2011; Podder, 2006; Suzuki et al., 2010). The CFA along with the ongoing discussions on peace with wide support from both international and domestic parties fostered optimism among investors about the possible end of the war in the near future.[11]

The number of deaths caused by the war decreased dramatically during 2002–2005 as a result of the CFA. As shown in Figure 6.6, according to the statistics published by the Institute for Conflict Management (2011), the number of deaths fell to fifteen in 2002 from 1,822 in 2001, having been as high as 3,791 in 2000. However, deaths started to rise gradually again since 2003, due mainly

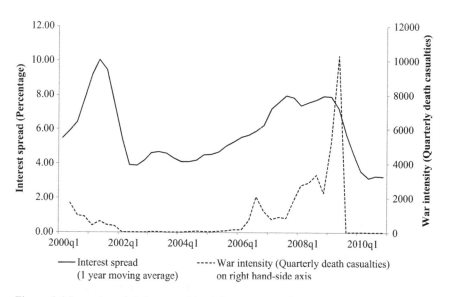

*Figure 6.6* Intensity of civil war and bank interest spread

to the CFA violations by the LTTE. Nevertheless, the number of deaths attributable to the war remained comparatively lower until the end of 2005. However, due to frequent violations of the CFA conditions by the LTTE,[12] initial signs of a possible CFA failure started appearing from early 2003, particularly since the withdrawal of the LTTE from the peace negotiations in April 2003 (Bouffard and Carment, 2006). But the violence did not escalate suddenly, because the Norwegian facilitators and the government of Sri Lanka were making rigorous attempts to restart the peace negotiations. Moreover, the catastrophic consequences caused by the 2004 tsunami also forced the parties to suppress the hostilities temporarily while opening up a window of opportunity for peace negotiations (NORAD, 2011, p. 3). Nevertheless, the period of effective peace directly attributable to the CFA seemed to last only until 2005. Thereafter, the mutual trust between the parties started to collapse and tensions began to rise. Moreover, the role of the Norwegian government as the peace broker was questioned frequently by various parties including some of the Tamil groups (not affiliated to LTTE) in Sri Lanka, given the perceived bias of the Norwegian team toward the LTTE (NORAD, 2011, p. 7).

In response to the CFA violations by the LTTE, the Sri Lankan government commenced its "Humanitarian Operation" in 2006.[13] The Humanitarian Operation aimed at liberating and freeing affected Sri Lankan civilians in the North and East from LTTE terrorism (Ministry of Defense, 2011). After that, the number of deaths increased again, even beyond the pre-CFA figures. Subsequently, the CFA officially ended in early 2008 when the government explicitly stated its withdrawal from the agreement due mainly to the frequent violations of agreed conditions by the LTTE and its withdrawal from the peace negotiations in 2003. Hence Sri Lanka entered a relatively unstable socio-political climate again after 2003, which was further intensified after 2007 and lasted until the first half of 2009. During this period, the number of deaths increased rapidly due to intensified attacks from the Sri Lankan government forces toward the end of the war. This can be observed in Figure 6.6 as a sharp spike around 2009.

The second period of political stability commenced in 2009. More specifically, after completely withdrawing from the CFA in early 2008, the Sri Lankan government initiated a series of aggressive attacks against the LTTE. As a result, the government was able to liberate the Eastern Province and then gradually took full control over the Northern Province by completely defeating the LTTE in mid-2009. This marked the end of the prolonged civil war, yet without a permanent and mutually agreeable political solution for the underlying issues. However, after 2009, the number of deaths attributable to the war fell to zero. Since then, a remarkably peaceful environment emerged all over the country, while massive development projects started in the war-torn areas.

Significantly, as illustrated in Figure 6.6, the interest spreads (marked on the left axis) show an observable response to the intensity of the civil war (marked on the right axis).[14] For example, the interest spreads declined and remained relatively low during the period between 2002 and 2005. With the collapse of the optimism about the CFA after 2003 and then with the re-escalation of

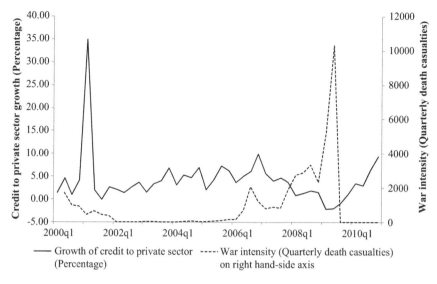

*Figure 6.7* Intensity of civil war and credit growth

violence particularly after early 2007, the interest spread started to rise again and reached its peak during 2007–2008, where the intensity of the war was highest. Subsequently, due to the hope of possible ending of the war around 2008 (combined with the monetary easing of the CBSL in response to the worsening global financial situation), the interest spread started decreasing sharply.[15] Finally, after the end of the war in mid-2009, the interest spread recorded historic low levels during the second half of 2009 and in 2010.

Further, as illustrated in Figure 6.7, the growth rate of credit increased sharply with the initiation of peace talks in 2002 due to the optimism generated by the CFA. For example, credit to the private sector increased by around 35 per cent from LKR 364 billion in 2000Q4 to LKR 491 billion in 2001Q1. However, the credit growth slowed down again due to a substantial increase in the lending rates in 2001. Nevertheless, annual credit growth rate remained around 5.5 per cent on average during 2000–2006. In other words, point-to-point credit growth between 2000Q4 and 2006Q4 was 245 per cent. With the re-intensification of the war after early 2007, the credit growth rates started to decline rapidly and recorded negative growth rates during the first three quarters of 2009. Nevertheless, part of the decline in the credit growth during 2008 and first half of 2009 was attributable to the US subprime issue.[16]

The growth rate of credit regained its strength since the last quarter of 2009, when the war came to a complete halt. Simultaneously, the aggregate investments by the banking system increased by 32.5 per cent and 25.8 per cent, respectively, in 2002 and 2003 compared to a 13.7 per cent increase in 2001. As a consequence, the risk weighted assets of the banking sector increased by 30 per cent in 2003, compared to minor increases like 3 per cent and 0.1 per cent in the two preceding years. Furthermore, it remained above 20 per cent on average during the five subsequent years.

Nevertheless, the government might have increased the borrowings from the banking system to finance its budget deficits, widening due to increasing defense expenditures. If so, banks would have been unable to provide sufficient amounts of credit to the private sector. But this has not been the case in Sri Lanka. For example, despite the fluctuations, net borrowings of the government from the banks for financing the budget deficit and the defense expenditure as a percentage of total government expenditure remained relatively constant. Therefore the intensity of the war did not significantly affect the net bank borrowings of the government for war finance. Significantly, government borrowing also shows a similar pattern to the growth of credit to the private sector. Hence credit to both sectors has expanded equally during politically stable periods.

Credit expansion that occurred alongside the progress of the CFA has created a positive effect on the ROAs of the banking system. For example, the ROA of the banking system increased to 1.9 per cent in 2006 compared to 1.0 per cent in 2001, and further increased to 2.7 per cent by the end of 2010 despite the declining interest spreads (from an average of 6.5 per cent during 2000–2002 to 6 per cent during 2003–2009Q2 and finally to 3 per cent during 2009Q3–2010Q4). Consistently increasing ROAs despite the declining interest spreads provide evidence contrary to the conventional argument in the bank rent literature, which postulates a close positive association between interest spreads and rent opportunities available for the banks. Actually, this signaled the positive macroeconomic rent opportunities (or declining macroeconomic losses) emerging within the country due to the increased conduciveness of the socio-political climate, which actually augmented the declining price-rent opportunities in a way that preserved and enhanced the profitability of the banks.

Due to the improved domestic political climate, foreign currency transactions were also improved since 2001 concurrently with the initiation of the aforementioned memorandum of understanding. For example, bank deposits denominated in foreign currencies nearly doubled during 2001 and 2002. The return of the war risk deposits maintained abroad by the government also contributed to increasing the foreign currency deposits (Suzuki et al., 2010). Other positive economic outcomes resulting from the positive socio-political climate during this period included the following: net-positive inflows of foreign investments in 2002, which had remained negative since 1998; removal of the war risk insurance premiums by insurance companies on port services and on external trade; a decrease in the national security levy by the government (by 1 per cent); and decreased pressures on the national budget from defense expenditures. Similar to other performance indicators, the banks' branch network expansion also shows a significant correlation with the intensity of the war. In contrast to the adjustments in the interest rates and amount of credit, decisions to expand the branch network are long term in nature. Therefore a substantial time lag may be expected because banks need to plan and establish new branches, which necessitates substantial

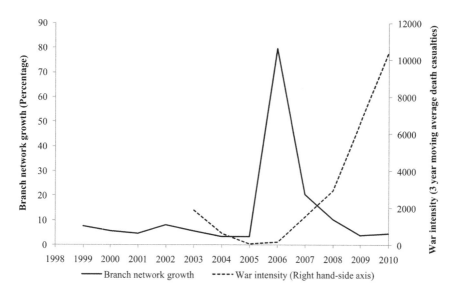

*Figure 6.8* War intensity and branch network expansion

new investments in both fixed assets and in human resources. After several trials, it was found that the branch network expansion in a particular year was highly correlated with the average number of death casualties in the war during the three preceding years. Hence the three year moving average of the number of deaths was taken as a proxy for socio-political stability from a long-term perspective. Figure 6.8 plots the growth rate of the number of bank branches (percentage) and the war intensity (i.e., the three year moving average of the number of deaths). The growth rate of the branch network remained below 10 per cent before 2005. However, when the war intensity fell substantially after 2002 with the CFA, a potentially long-term peaceful environment emerged in Sri Lanka. This created confidence among bankers and reduced the overall risk perceptions in the country. Hence banks took steps to rapidly expand their branch network in 2005, with a short time lag since 2002. The branch network grew by nearly 80 per cent in 2006, compared to less than 10 per cent annual growth before. Some of the districts had recorded relatively higher bank branch growth rates even earlier, in 2002 and 2003 in some cases. The growth rate remained at around 20 per cent and 10 per cent in 2007 and 2008, respectively.

Increases in the number of bank branches outside Colombo metropolitan city during 2006–2008 remained considerable. More precisely, most of the districts located very near to war-torn areas have recorded over 100 per cent expansion in the number of branches, while most of the war-torn districts also have recorded substantially higher growth rates in the number of branches than the districts located in the Western Province.[17] Substantial increases in the number of bank branches in the districts directly exposed to the war like Ampara, Batticaloa,

Jaffna, Kilinochchi, Mullaitivu, and Vavuniya are particularly noteworthy. In comparison, no new branches were established in Mullaitivu and Kilinochchi districts from 1998 until 2005.

Subsequent decline can be mainly attributable to the escalation of the war again since around 2005. Even though substantial increases in the branch network could not be observed in other districts after 2009, almost all war-torn districts recorded substantially higher branch network growth rates again along with the ending of the war toward 2009. For example, the expansion of branch network re-intensified in Batticoloa (16.7 per cent in 2008), Trincomalee (9.6 per cent in 2009), Mannar (22.2 per cent in 2009), Vavuniya (28.6 per cent in 2009), and Kilinochchi (35.7 per cent in 2010); and such substantially higher growth rates prevailed till 2014 in most of those districts. Interestingly, this gradual spread of bank branches in each area follow a close link with the gradual ending of the war in each area, showing a clear link between political instability and branch network expansion.

Concurrently, the equity market also responded actively to the socio-political stability during the time periods discussed previously. Figure 6.9 shows the movement of the All Share Price Index (ASPI) and the market capitalization of the equity market from January 1993 to June 2009. There was a remarkable growth in the equity market after 2002 with the initiation of the CFA. This slowed down again after 2005 due to the increased instability and then started to decline after 2007 particularly due to the global economic slowdown and the intensified civil war. Interestingly, the growth quickly recovered after May 2009, responding to the ending of the civil war. The market responded even before the actual ending of the war due to the confidence emerging since the beginning of 2009, given the remarkable progress the Sri Lankan government forces were making in the battle. However, despite previous stagnation, the number of

*Figure 6.9* Performance of equity market in Sri Lanka (January 1993–June 2009)

companies listed in the equity market increased gradually from 191 in January 1993 to 234 in June 2009.

The discussion in this section shows that the stable socio-political climate that prevailed during the CFA and after the ending of the civil war substantially stimulated the banking system development in Sri Lanka. Socio-political instability increased the risk perceptions of local and foreign investors while increasing the uncertainty in the domestic markets. As a consequence, like the effect of high and volatile inflation, the required risk premiums increased and the demand for, and supply of, financial services tended to decline. Generally, an unstable socio-political environment creates macroeconomic losses for the banks. Thereby, overall rent opportunities tend to decrease. As a consequence, either the required level of incentives cannot be maintained or disincentives may emerge.

In contrast, a stable socio-political climate facilitates economic activity in several ways and hence creates positive macroeconomic rent opportunities for the banks and other enterprises as well. First, expected risk premiums decline due to the lowered risk perceptions of both bankers and investors. Second, costs in the corporate sector reduce due to the removal of additional taxes imposed by the government solely for the purpose of financing the war expenditures; additional insurance premiums imposed by the insurance companies; other direct losses resulting from property damage; and the reduction in business opportunities due to the conflict. In this sense, a stable socio-political climate helps reduce the transaction costs in the economy and hence lowers the friction in the economic system. Third, new opportunities for investments emerge in the areas left abandoned due to the war. These factors collectively have affected the financial and banking system development in Sri Lanka, though it is hard to analyze the magnitude of their individual effects and test their significance statistically.

Similar evidence on the effects of socio-political stability on the financial system with regard to Georgia can be found in Suzuki et al. (2010). They see socio-political instability caused by ethnic violence, civil unrest, and soaring inflation as the main factor that hindered financial development in Georgia. They further illustrate how the relatively stable climate that emerged after the Rose revolution[18] contributed to the expansion of credit and economic activity in Georgia. Moreover, they state that macroeconomic stability results in increased lender confidence. As a consequence, banks become less hesitant to channel funds to long-term investment projects with large learning effects. In other words, banks in a volatile environment prefer short-term over long-term lending. Therefore, in conclusion, positive macroeconomic rent opportunities resulting from the favorable macroeconomic environment enhance the overall rent opportunities available for the banks. Nevertheless, the discussion in this section does not aim to attribute the entire positive outcome directly to one single factor (i.e., the CFA in 2002 and the ending of the civil war in 2009). However, the optimism created after the initiation of the CFA in 2002 and after the end of the three-decade long civil war in 2009 has played a crucial role in improving the banking system performance and financial system activities.

## 8.   Conclusions and implications

The interest spreads in the Sri Lankan banking system have decreased during the last decade (2000–2009). If interest spread was a good proxy for the level of bank rent opportunities, the profitability of Sri Lankan banks should have been decreased along with the interest spread. However, the profitability of the banking system has been consistently increasing. This emphasizes the inappropriateness of the interest spread as a proxy for the overall bank rent opportunities. Hence the rent opportunities created in terms of the interest spreads only reflect the availability of price rent opportunities. These price rent opportunities may or may not be captured by the banks, due to the extent of operating and macroeconomic rent opportunities.

Concurrently, despite the gradual decrease, Sri Lankan banks have enjoyed healthy interest spreads which have been even higher than those enjoyed by the Indian banks. However, the size of the Sri Lankan banking system relative to GDP is gradually decreasing when the size of Indian banking system relative to GDP is consistently increasing. Given the similar rent opportunities prevailed in terms of the interest spreads, these two countries should have experienced similar patterns of banking system development according to the conventional bank rent literature. The contrasting experiences adequately demonstrate the failure of conventional bank rent models to explain the relative banking system underdevelopment in Sri Lanka. In contrast, however, along with the implementation of financial reforms and gradual developments in the banking infrastructure, operating rent opportunities available for the banks have changed favorably. Increasing operating rent opportunities, in turn, have offset the erosion of price rent opportunities so that the banks could maintain and enhance their profitability, even when the interest spreads were decreasing. Nevertheless, the operating environment in Sri Lanka is not yet satisfactory. For example, current operating environment creates more operating rent opportunities for state-owned banks and foreign banks. Some of the larger domestic private banks also seem to enjoy higher rent opportunities compared to other small and newer domestic private banks. More specifically, ownership creates operating rent opportunities for both state-owned and foreign banks. These operating rent opportunities should be distinguished from the price rent opportunities available in terms of the interest spread.

Further, due to the heavy concentration of the banking system in a few state-owned banks and few large domestic private banks, the actual level of competition remains relatively lower. This situation has allowed the state-owned banks to remain inefficient instead of making attempts to be more efficient. Therefore, despite the higher rent opportunities available, state-owned banks have failed to capture them in terms of profits. Hence such rent opportunities remain unproductive and are wasted. Nevertheless, the magnitude of operating rent opportunities attributable to ownership tends to decrease with development in the banking system because better operating environments create a level playing field for all ownership groups so that they can operate under the same operating conditions and technology. If a level playing field can be created for the entire banking system to compete on similar ground, these unproductive rents can be transformed into productive rent opportunities. Moreover, Sri Lanka has consistently experienced macroeconomic losses due to economic as well as socio-political instabilities. These macroeconomic losses can be directly attributed to government failures to contain inflation and achieve political stability. These macroeconomic losses may have eroded price and operating rent opportunities.

This chapter makes four main implications for the financial regulators in less developed economies: First, the incentives available for Sri Lankan banks were certainly inadequate for fostering a healthy banking system development due mainly to inadequate operating rent opportunities and macroeconomic losses. Second, the effectiveness of increased deposit rates as a tool for attracting more deposits is intrinsically weak. Bank deposits become increasingly less responsive to the interest rates in light of the expanding convenience benefits associated with banking. Third, encouraging the banks through different policy initiatives is vital for fostering an extended bank branch network with advanced technologies to enhance the quality and diversity of the services offered by the banks. Price rent opportunities created in terms of the interest spreads can partly contribute to these objectives. Finally, maintaining an appropriate level of competition is also crucial for encouraging the banks to upgrade their operating systems and information systems, which ultimately improve the quality of the services offered to bank clients (Wanniarachchige and Suzuki, 2010). Meanwhile, the policies aimed at minimizing direct price competition within the banking system are also essential, because it is price competition that erodes most of the rent opportunities available for the banks.

## Notes

1   The share market activity almost doubled after the end of civil conflict in 2009. With the momentum of growth of the Colombo Stock Exchange during 2010, the market capitalization as a percentage of GDP reached the level of some of the other stock exchanges in the region (e.g., the Colombo Stock Exchange 40 per cent, the Indonesia Stock Exchange 46 per cent, the Philippine Stock Exchange 67 per cent, etc.). Nevertheless, this momentum reversed gradually.
2   Bank branches, in this case, include banking outlets that offer limited set of banking services as well.
3   The new Regional Development Bank established by consolidating these six banks started its operations in July 2010.
4   Cohen's $f^2 = \eta^2/(1-\eta^2)$. As cited in Murphy and Myors (2004, p. 52), an $f^2$ of .35 a large effect size, .15 a medium effect size, and .02 represents a small effect size.
5   The conflicts between the JVP and the government started around 1987 and almost ended by the end of 1989.
6   However, the political turbulences associated with the civil war were higher until 2009.
7   The substantial increase in the interest spread during the period 2000Q4–2001Q3 can be attributed to the upward adjustment of policy interest rates by the CBSL. According to the CBSL (2001), these policy interest rates were increased as an attempt to curb the inflationary pressures created by the increased food and fuel

prices in the international market and the shortage of food supply in the domestic market due to prolonged drought. Heightened terrorist risk also contributed to the abrupt increase in interest spreads. However, when the conditions became favorable, the CBSL reduced the policy rates back to normal levels gradually on several occasions in the second half of the year. For example, the bank rate was increased to 25percent in 2000Q4 from 16 per cent in 2000Q3. It was reduced to 23 per cent in 2001Q3 and then to 18 per cent in 2001Q4.

8  Ministry of Defense (2011) and NORAD (2011) discuss the dimensions of the war between the Sri Lankan government and LTTE in more detail.

9  Actual involvement of the Norwegian government in the peace process began in 1997 (NORAD, 2011, p. 3). After the initial studies and discussions, a significant outcome of the Norwegian involvement emerged only around 2001.

10  The CFA in 2002 was only one of the many attempts between the two parties to resolve the conflict. For example, the earlier attempts in 1957, 1965, 1984, 1985, 1987, 1989, and 1995 failed without sustainable solutions (Bouffard and Carment, 2006).

11  Nevertheless, the LTTE refused to participate in peace negotiations and subsequently withdrew in 2003 (Crisis Group Asia, 2006; Fair, 2006; NORAD, 2011, p. 3; Podder, 2006).

12  It is often claimed that the LTTE used the CFA (the one in 2002 and previous attempts) "to regroup, rearm and strengthen its military capabilities" (Ministry of Defense, 2011, p. 2). Further, according to the Ministry of Defense (2011), the Sri Lanka Monitoring Mission (SLMM) documented that the LTTE had violated the CFA 3,830 times compared to 351 CFA violations attributable to the Sri Lankan government.

13  For detailed official information about the Humanitarian Operation and the civil war in Sri Lanka, refer to the Ministry of Defense (2011).

14  As mentioned in footnote 7, the higher interest spreads that prevailed around 2001 can be attributed to the upward adjustments in policy interest rates by the CBSL.

15  It should be noted, however, that the interest spread is expected to rise due to increased risk perceptions about the financial markets resulting from the global financial crisis, though the lending rates are expected to decrease due to the reduction in the policy interest rates by the government in response to the global financial crisis. Hence the decrease in the interest spread is directly attributable to the lowered risk perceptions resulting from the ending of the civil war.

16  This credit contraction, however, was much smaller than that occurred in most of the developed countries.

17  The Western Province is the economically most prosperous province in Sri Lanka, and it contributes nearly half of the total GDP of the country (45 per cent in 2009).

18  "The Georgian people's Rose Revolution of November 2003 strove to achieve a democratic society, improve human rights and living conditions, reduce corruption, and enhance the national economy" (Papava, 2006, p. 657).

# 7 Islamic bank rent

## Comparison among Bangladesh, Indonesia, Malaysia, and Pakistan

*Yasushi Suzuki, S. M. Sohrab Uddin, Sigit Pramono, and Shoaib Khan*

## 1. Introduction

The absence of market mechanism to clear imbalances in the financial market not only makes it intrinsically different from the commodity market but also urges for a special attention for its smooth functioning (Stiglitz, 1994). Maintaining adequate rent (surplus) opportunity is regarded as an ideal way of patronizing smooth functioning of the financial market, in particular, the banking market (Hellmann et al., 1997). Many East Asian countries including Japan have experienced the positive impact of financial sector rents (bank rents) during their rapid industrialization process (Khan, 2000; Suzuki, 2011). However, the bursting of bubble in these countries elucidates the necessity of monitoring bank rents for protecting the 'franchise value' of banks as prudent lenders. Consequently, the analysis of monitoring rents has provided a new outlook for investigating the role of banks in accelerating the financial development and thereby the economic prosperity of an economy.

The rise of Islamic banking has been noticed both in Islamic and non-Islamic countries during the last few decades. This rise attracted the attention of non-Muslims to a great extent to the Islamic mode of financing, which is evident by the fact that around 40 per cent of the cliental base of Islamic banks is now consisted by non-Muslims (Ariff, 2014). In around seventy countries, there are more than three hundred Islamic financial institutions, which include five Islamic banks in the United Kingdom and nineteen institutions in the United States. Iran, Saudi Arabia, and Malaysia altogether hold the majority of the *Shari'ah* compliant capital (Amirzadeh and Reza Shoorvarzy, 2013, p. 66; Johnes, Izzeldin, and Pappas, 2014). However, this rise cannot be attributed to the pure *Shari'ah*-based *mudaraba* (trust based contract) and *musharaka* (partnership/ equity based contract). As a matter of fact, the profit-and-loss sharing investments of Islamic banks accounted for less than 20 per cent (Abdul-Rahman et al., 2014, p. 140). Islamic banks all around the world put their credit preference to the *murabaha* asset-based financing, which has been criticized by the Islamic scholars and regarded as the so-called *murabaha* syndrome.

Rather than identifying the real scenario for such dominance of asset-based financing, most of the existing literature attempts to shed analytical light on the divergence of *Shari'ah*-compliant *murabaha* (mark-up contract), *bai-muajjal* (variant of *murabaha*), *bai-salam* (forward sale contract), and *ijara* (leasing) from the *Shari'ah* prescription. As a variant approach upon theoretical speculations, El-Gamal (2007) considers the dependency of Islamic banks on asset-based financing as an opportunity for *rent-seeking*. In Chapter 4, Suzuki and Uddin put forward a new conceptualization of 'Islamic bank rent' by linking the financing pattern of Islamic banks in Bangladesh with the global trend of *murabaha* dominance (see also Suzuki and Uddin, 2014). We argue that beyond the rent opportunity held by conventional banks, Islamic banks as sensible *Shari'ah*-compliant lenders need to seek for an extra profit opportunity for absorbing unexpected loss and unique commercial risk exposed to them. They insist that the credit portfolio preference to repeated *murabaha* financing in Islamic banks is due partly to their credit strategy for seeking an appropriate balance between risk and return and for responding to the periodic volatility in transaction costs of monitoring and profit-and-loss sharing. However, we have to accumulate the empirical studies to see the rent opportunity to be captured by Islamic banks. In this regard, this chapter aims at drawing the evidence from the banking sector of Bangladesh, Indonesia, Malaysia, and Pakistan, where Islamic banking is in a state of rising, and both Islamic and conventional banking operate simultaneously. This chapter thus contributes to the promulgation of an appropriate road map for patronizing the acceleration of profit-and-loss sharing modes of financing of Islamic banks.

The remaining part of this chapter is organized as follows: section 2 reviews the Islamic bank rent approach and attempts to identify whether Islamic banks need more bank rent opportunities than their conventional counterparts. Section 3 provides an overview of the Islamic banking sector in Bangladesh, Indonesia, Malaysia, and Pakistan. Section 4 highlights the quantitative and qualitative evidence from the Islamic banking sector of these countries. Section 5 concludes this chapter by raising several policy options for regulators to design an appropriate regulatory framework for making Islamic banks as prudent financial intermediaries for the society.

## 2. A review of the concept of Islamic bank rent

From the perspective of Islamic banking, Suzuki and Uddin (2014, p. 174) define Islamic bank rent as "the extra profits enough to compensate for the unexpected loss and the displaced commercial risk which Islamic banks are facing; in other words, as the excess profits required for maintaining their franchise value and reputation as prudent *Shari'ah*-compliant lenders" (see section 4.2 for details). Here, the unexpected loss is concerned with the difficulties in profit-and-loss sharing, whereas the displaced commercial risk is associated with the possibility of withdrawal of funds by the depositors due to higher loss of Islamic banks compared to their conventional counterparts. The term 'Islamic bank rent' (in a *narrower* sense) is denoted by α in the following equation:

*Spread earned by Islamic banks = (Risk-adjusted) risk premium + α,* where

*Spread = Rate of profit received – Rate of profit paid.*

The risk-adjusted risk premium in the equation is sought in the same way for both conventional and Islamic banks. As long as banks develop adequate skills for screening and monitoring of borrowers, there is no need of bank rent opportunity in the competitive market. However, it is almost impossible to acquire such skills under conditions of uncertainty. In order to cover unmeasurable risk or uncertainty, banks need to earn extra profit by adding a subjective risk premium. In contrast, Islamic banks need to earn an extra profit to maintain their franchise value as prudent *Shari'ah*-compliant lenders, due to the existence of unique risks like the profit-and-loss sharing risk and the displaced commercial risk. As discussed in Chapter 1, we presume that the rent opportunity is reflected in the expected return, including a risk premium to cover unspecified adverse events. In this context, the role of bank rent as a buffer or cushion in responding to unexpected losses should be argued. In this context, we can also call the overall bank rent opportunity as *surplus* (see section 1.2) to be captured by Islamic banks so as to cover the general uncertainty 'plus' α as 'Islamic bank rent' in a *broader* sense. However, do Islamic banks really need more bank rent opportunities?

The products of Islamic banks can be categorized as *Shari'ah*-compliant fixed-return or markup modes and pure *Shari'ah*-based modes (Çizakça, 2011). The incentive and sanction mechanisms embedded in *Shari'ah*-compliant products are likely to be similar to conventional banking, as these products are borrowed from the West and financial engineering has been done for making them compliant to Islamic *Shari'ah*. But the situation of Islamic banks is still far different from that of conventional banks. This is because Islamic banks engage in risk sharing under existence of morality, transparency, ethics, and fairness and under prohibition of not only *riba* (interest) but also *maysir* (gambling), *rishwah* (corruption), *gharar* (ambiguity), and *jahl* (ignorance); whereas convention banks deal with risk-shifting only (Ariff, 2014, p. 735). With regard to the *Shari'ah*-based *mudaraba* mode of financing, Islamic banks are subject to severe information asymmetry and transaction costs unless borrowers are ethical and fair. The management of such mode is fully based on trust. On the other hand, at least theoretically, the *Shari'ah*-based *musharaka* mode of financing exposes to relatively less information asymmetry and lower transaction costs, since Islamic banks have the opportunity to participate in supervision and monitoring of the borrowers' business (Abdul-Rahman et al., 2014). However, the real scenario is entirely different. This is because of a number of reasons.

First, even though the willingness of having *halal* (*Shari'ah*-based) financial products has been growing during the recent years, the desire to share losses does not match with such demand of depositors of Islamic banks (Abdul-Rahman et al., 2014). As a result, Islamic banks remain concerned about the post-lending effect of losses from their modes of financing and prefer to engage in less risky projects for avoiding risk sharing, even though it is prescribed by the Islamic *Shari'ah*. Second, Islamic banks need to absorb both credit risk and *Shari'ah* compliance risk. Consequently, the difference between the rates of profit received and profit paid cannot guarantee necessary rent for Islamic banks. In order to protect their franchise values, they have to manage an extra cushion for capturing unwanted losses against *Shari'ah* compliance, which has been denoted α in our new concept of Islamic bank rent. Third, the well-functioning of the profit-and-loss sharing mode depends on the well-structured system of property rights and the system of tax allowance (Abdul-Rahman et al., 2014). Debt is considered as tax deductible, whereas equity is not. Thus, from the demand-side perspective, borrowers show their disinclination toward an equity-based mode of financing. Fourth, Islamic banks refrain from taking collateral for reducing credit risk under profit-and-loss sharing mode, which is a common phenomenon under asset-based lending (Zaher and Hassan, 2001). Fifth, continuous monitoring and supervision required under equity-based financing, along with the periodic determination of the profit-and-loss sharing ratio, can accelerate the transaction costs of Islamic banks (Sundararajan and Errico, 2002). On the other hand, we should note that even though Islamic banks cannot adopt the risk management techniques, including financial derivatives and sale of debt applied by the conventional banks for managing their profit-and-loss sharing mode, they are still exposed to market competition under the liberalized financial atmosphere (El-Hawary et al., 2007).

## 3.   Islamic banking in Bangladesh, Indonesia, Malaysia, and Pakistan: an overview

Before comparing the Islamic bank rent opportunity situation in the banking sector of Bangladesh, Indonesia, Malaysia, and Pakistan, let us have a look at the current penetration level of Islamic banking in these countries. The size of the banking sector assets relative to gross domestic product (GDP) compared to that of the stock market represented by the market capitalization relative to GDP in Bangladesh, Indonesia, Malaysia, and Pakistan reflects similar situation in these countries. For instance, by the end of 2010, the size of the banking sector was 69.96 per cent of the total financial sector's assets, whereas the share of stock market accounted for 32.79 per cent in Bangladesh (Uddin and Suzuki, 2015). In case of Indonesia, the size of the banking sector and the stock market was 72.07 per cent and 44.30 per cent, respectively, in 2013 (FSA, 2014). In Malaysia, the size of the banking sector relative to GDP was 303.83 per cent in 2010, compared to 165.85 per cent of the stock market (BNM, 2014). Similarly, the size of the banking sector and the stock market was about 37 per cent and 27.48 per cent, respectively, at the end of 2014 in Pakistan. As discussed in Chapter 2, the financial sector, particularly the banking sector, is expected to play an important role for the economic prosperity in developing countries.

Immediately after the independence in 1971, the banking sector of Bangladesh went through a massive transformation process, mainly through the nationalization order issued by Bangladesh Bank, the central bank of the country, for six state-owned banks. During the initial stage, the state-directed credit policy was patronized by the government with the help of these banks. Later, private banks were allowed to start their operations in 1982, followed by the denationalization of two state-owned banks consecutively in 1983 and 1984 as part of the financial liberalization policy. The operation of the first Islamic bank was allowed in 1983, followed by four other banks, which initiated their operations as full-fledged Islamic banks in the country. In addition, two other banks shifted to Islamic banking practice respectively in 2004 and 2008, even though they started their operations as conventional banks. Thus, by the end of 2012, the number of full-fledged Islamic banks increased to seven (see Table 7.1). In addition, sixteen conventional banks also offer simultaneous Islamic banking operations by maintaining separate windows/branches. Thus, out of forty-seven banks, 48.93 per cent are fully or partially engaged in Islamic banking. In aggregate, these banks controlled 18.86 per cent and 21.07 per cent of the banking sector deposits and credits, respectively.

After continuing the financial repression policy for the banking sector, initiated immediately after the national independence in 1945, the government of Indonesia began banking deregulation program in the early 1980s. The Indonesian government launched a significant banking deregulation package known as Package 27 October 1988 Policy (Pakto 88) in 1988. The Pakto 88 covered broad essential deregulation issues, including abolition of the entry barriers, reduction of the reserve requirements to encourage liquidity, and introduction of the legal lending limit in banking credit. Undoubtedly, a massive banking deregulation program has contributed immensely toward the improvement of the financial sector, which was reflected in the access to financial services and financial deepening. In addition, the financial performance of the banks increased sharply, especially during the 1990s. Unfortunately, due to the weaknesses of asset quality and the accumulation of non-performing loans, and also due to the external shock in the economy, Indonesia's banking sector was exposed to a vulnerable position (Sastrosuwito, 2010). Consequently, we witnessed the occurrence of a currency crisis after the collapse of Thai Bath that finally evolved into a full-blown financial crisis and brought severe financial devastation in many Asian countries, which also hit Indonesia in 1997. In response to the financial crisis, the Indonesian government under the International Monetary Fund (IMF) took some intervention policies in the banking sector, including the closure and takeover of the unhealthy banks, introduction of the banking recapitalization scheme, and establishment of the Indonesian Banking Restructuring Agency (IBRA; Binhadi, 1995; Suzuki and Sastrosuwito, 2011, 2012). Meanwhile, considered as a relative latecomer in introducing Islamic banking in comparison with other Muslim countries, the operation of Islamic bank was started in 1992 in Indonesia. By the end of 2012, the number of full-fledged banks was eleven and the number of conventional banks with Islamic banking windows/branches was twenty-four, leading to a total of thirty-five banks with Islamic banking operations (see Table 7.1). In aggregate, they represented 29.17 per cent of the banking sector. The total market share of these

*Table 7.1* Comparative position of the Islamic banking sector in Bangladesh, Indonesia, and Malaysia by the end of December 2012, and in Pakistan by the end of December 2014

|  | Islamic banks | Banks with dual banking | Islamic banking sector | Banking sector |
|---|---|---|---|---|
| **Bangladesh** | | | | |
| No. of banks | 7 (14.89) | 16 (34.04) | 23 (48.93) | 47 |
| Deposits | 961.2 (17.81) | 56.7 (1.05) | 1,017.9 (18.86) | 5,396.0 |
| Credits/ financing | 858.9 (19.89) | 51.2 (1.19) | 910.1 (21.07) | 4,318.6 |
| **Indonesia** | | | | |
| No. of banks | 11 (9.17) | 24 (20.00) | 35 (29.17) | 120 |
| Deposits | 117,817 (3.65) | 29,695 (0.92) | 147,512 (4.57) | 3,225,198 |
| Credits/ financing | 112,396 (4.12) | 35,109 (1.29) | 147,505 (5.41) | 2,725,674 |
| **Malaysia** | | | | |
| No. of banks | 5 (8.93) | 11 (19.64) | 16 (28.57) | 56 |
| Deposits | 66,658 (4.41) | 319,538 (21.19) | 386,196 (25.60) | 1,508,578 |
| Credits/ financing | 39,605 (3.24) | 275,386 (22.56) | 314,991 (25.80) | 1,220,825 |
| **Pakistan** | | | | |
| No. of banks | 5 (13.51) | 17 (45.94) | 22 (59.45) | 37 |
| Deposits | 988.1 (11.75) | 81.9 (0.97) | 1,070 (12.73) | 8,403.4 |
| Credits/ financing | 713.1 (13.73) | 51.9 (0.99) | 765 (14.72) | 5,191 |

Source: Constructed by the authors based on the annual report 2012–2013 of Bangladesh Bank; Bank Indonesia's Indonesian Banking Statistics and Islamic Banking Statistics in 2012; BNM's The Financial Stability and Payment Systems Report, 2014; and Islamic Banking Bulletin and Statistics on Scheduled Bank in Pakistan, 2014, published by State Bank of Pakistan.

Notes: Amounts are in billion BDT (local currency of Bangladesh), in billion Rupiah (Indonesian currency), in billion Ringgit (Malaysian currency), and in billion Rupees (Pakistani currency), except number of banks. Figures in parentheses represent the percentage of the respective sectors in terms of banking sector as a whole.

banks was 4.57 per cent of the banking sector's deposits and 5.41 per cent of the banking sector's credits.

Bank Negara Malaysia (BNM) as the central bank was established in 1958 under the Central Bank of Malaya Ordinance. According to the Central Bank of Malaya Ordinance, BNM has the authority to supervise the commercial banks' activities in Malaysia. Moreover, through the amendments of the Insurance Act 1963 and the Banking Act 1973, BNM has had full mandate as a financial regulator and authority for all the financial institutions in Malaysia covering finance companies, merchant banks, money market operations, and insurance companies (Muda, 1996). Following the financial and monetary crisis in 1997 that also adversely affected the Malaysian economy, BNM undertook restructuring, consolidation, and rationalization policies for the financial sector including the banking sector. These policies have brought significant results for the Malaysian financial system, and accordingly it has become less fragmented through consolidation and rationalization programs (BNM, 2011). For instance, the total number of domestic financial institutions was seventy-seven during 1980s, which reduced to thirty-four by the end of 2011. Concerning Islamic banking, the first bank initiated its operations in 1983 in Malaysia. By the end of 2012, there were sixteen banks, of which five banks were involved with full-fledged Islamic banking and eleven banks continued separate windows (see Table 7.1). The current regulation regarding the issuance of Islamic bank license in Malaysia is quite unique. This is because BNM requires every single bank that offers Islamic banking products or services to hold a full-fledged Islamic bank license, irrespective of the fact that it works as a full-fledged Islamic bank or as a conventional bank with Islamic windows. By the end of December 2012, Islamic banking sector accounted for 28.57 per cent of the banking sector's assets, which constituted 25.60 per cent and 25.80 per cent of total deposits and credits, respectively. In fact, Malaysia is acknowledged as one of the pioneering countries where the development of Islamic finance and banking in terms of regulatory framework ratification and product innovation are immensely noticeable. Clearly, the Malaysian government has been successfully contributing toward the realization of the goal of becoming one of the leading global hubs for Islamic finance and banking.

In the case of Pakistan, State Bank of Pakistan (SBP) started its operation as a central bank on July 1, 1948. Commercial banking has grown favorably after independence till the time of nationalization in 1974. Pakistan Banking Council was set up for the monitoring of six national banks that were consolidated from thirteen banks under the nationalization policy. Under financial liberalization, the nationalization act was amended in early 1990s with the privatization of state owned banks and the issuance of licenses for the establishment of new banks. Most of the reforms made during the latter half of 1990s empowered the regulatory power of SBP. In contrast to conventional banking, Islamic banks initiated their operations in 1980. According to Table 7.1, twenty-two banks out of a total of thirty-seven engaged in Islamic banking either fully or partly by the end of 2014. Among twenty-two banks, five were full-fledged Islamic banks and seventeen were conventional banks with Islamic banking windows and branches. Thus the Islamic banking sector as a whole constituted 59.45 per cent of the banking sector. In total, these banks held 12.73 per cent and 14.72 per cent of the sector's deposits and credits, respectively.

## 4. Evidence from the banking sector of Bangladesh, Indonesia, Malaysia, and Pakistan

Now let us compare the situation of Islamic bank rent opportunity in the banking sector of Bangladesh, Indonesia, Malaysia, and Pakistan. In order to compare the performance of the Islamic banks and the banking sector as a whole, two performance measures – namely, return on assets (ROA) and non-performing loans (NPL) / non-performing financing (NPF) – of Bangladesh, Indonesia, Malaysia, and Pakistan during the period 2007 to 2012 are used in this section. Table 7.2 shows the performance comparison on the basis of ROA, which suggests that Islamic banks in Bangladesh have been performing better than the overall banking sector during the whole period under study. For instance, unlike the conventional banking sector, the ROA of Islamic banking sector is greater than or equal to 1.27 per cent for the entire period. In contrast, the ROA of the Islamic banking sector in both Indonesia and Pakistan has been consistently lower than that of the banking sector during the full period.

*Table 7.2* The averages of ROA and NPL of Islamic banks in Bangladesh, Indonesia, Malaysia, and Pakistan

|  | 2007 | 2008 | 2009 | 2010 | 2011 | 2012 |
|---|---|---|---|---|---|---|
| **Bangladesh*** | | | | | | |
| ROA (in %) | 1.27 | 1.44 | 1.67 | 2.26 | 1.40 | 1.62 |
|  | (0.90) | (1.20) | (1.40) | (1.80) | (1.50) | (0.60) |
| NPL (in %) | 3.38 | 2.68 | 2.17 | 2.33 | 2.15 | 2.98 |
|  | (13.20) | (10.80) | (9.20) | (7.30) | (6.10) | (10.00) |
| **Indonesia** | | | | | | |
| ROA (in %) | 2.07 | 1.42 | 1.48 | 1.67 | 1.79 | 2.14 |
|  | (2.78) | (2.33) | (2.60) | (2.86) | (3.03) | (3.11) |
| NPL (in %) | 4.05 | 3.95 | 4.01 | 3.02 | 2.52 | 2.22 |
|  | (4.07) | (3.20) | (3.31) | (2.56) | (2.17) | (1.87) |
| **Malaysia** | | | | | | |
| ROA (in %) | 1.30 | 1.00 | 1.30 | 1.30 | 1.00 | 1.40 |
|  | (1.50) | (1.50) | (1.20) | (1.50) | (1.60) | (1.60) |
| NPL (in %) | 3.30 | 2.30 | 2.20 | 2.10 | 1.60 | 1.20 |
|  | (3.20) | (2.20) | (1.80) | (2.30) | (1.80) | (1.40) |
| **Pakistan**** | | | | | | |
| ROA (in %) | 0.08 | −0.11 | −0.72 | −1.14 | 0.65 | 0.46 |
|  | (1.50) | (0.80) | (0.90) | (1.00) | (1.50) | (1.30) |
| NPL (in %) | NA | NA | 6.30 | 7.30 | 7.60 | 7.60 |
|  | (7.51) | (8.63) | (13.75) | (14.84) | (14.93) | (13.98) |

Source: Constructed by the authors based on the annual report 2012–2013 of Bangladesh Bank and respective banks' annual reports.

Note: Figures in parentheses represent the averages of the banking sector. NA stands for not available.

* In the case of Bangladesh, six full-fledged Islamic banks are considered for the computation. Indonesian data are collected from Indonesian Banking Statistics and Islamic Banking Statistics, published by Bank Indonesia, in 2012. Data of Malaysian banks are collected from BNM's The Financial Stability and Payment Systems Report, 2014. Data of Pakistani banks are collected from the Balance Sheet Analysis of Financial Sector and the Financial Stability Review published by State Bank of Pakistan.

** In case of Pakistan, five full-fledged Islamic banks are considered for the computation.

However, we note that the ROA of the Islamic banking sector in Malaysia is slightly lower in comparison with the banking sector as a whole. Thus, based on ROA, it can be argued that Islamic banks in Bangladesh are performing better than their conventional counterparts, whereas the scenario is reverse in the case of Indonesia, Malaysia, and Pakistan.

Similar performance of Islamic banks can also be observed in Bangladesh in terms of NPL, since it remains much lower for the Islamic banks compared to the banking sector as a whole during 2007–2012. The situation in Indonesia also remains the same as a result of a consistently higher NPL than that of the overall banking sector. However, the NPL of Islamic banks in Pakistan is much lower than the NPL of the banking sector whereas the NPL of Islamic banks in Malaysia have been fluctuating and showing a lower tendency than that of the banking sector.

Thus, in aggregate, it can be noted that Islamic banks in Bangladesh dominate their conventional counterparts in terms of performance demonstrated by higher ROA and lower NPL. On the other hand, consistently lower ROA followed by a higher trend of NPL indicates the fact that Islamic banks in Indonesia have failed to catch up with the banking sector in terms of performance. In the case of Malaysia, it is noted that the aggregate performance of Islamic banks in terms of ROA and NPL is slightly lower than the overall banking sector. Finally, performance indicators in Pakistan dictate a dual scenario because of a lower ROA followed by a lower NPL, which is almost half of the ratio of the banking sector. It is also evident that the NPL of the Islamic banking sector in Malaysia has been consistency lower than other countries, whereas that of Bangladesh is lower than Indonesia and Pakistan. On the other hand, the Islamic banks in Pakistan have been holding the highest NPL among these countries.

The differences shown by the performance indicators in these countries postulate a strong likelihood of a further disparity in their lending patterns. In order to explore the issue in these countries, the income from different Islamic financing modes such as profit-and-loss sharing *mudaraba* and *musharaka*, and asset-based financing modes including *murabaha* during 2008 to 2012, are given in Table 7.3. The income of Islamic banks in Bangladesh predominantly comes from asset-based financing. Only one of the reported banks has been engaged in profit-and-loss sharing modes, with a very insignificant percentage of less than 5 per cent during the period of study, which reflects a pure dominance of the *murabaha* mode. On the other hand, Islamic banks in Indonesia and Pakistan engage with the profit-and-loss sharing modes to a higher extent compared to the situation in Bangladesh. However, the dominance of the *murabaha* mode is still prevalent in both countries, as it is reflected by the percentages of its income in most of the reported banks under each case. Thus the lending patterns of the Islamic banks in each of the countries can be linked with their respective performance indicators. In line with Bangladesh, Malaysian Islamic banks are significantly engaged in sales based transactions, especially *murabaha* and *baibithamanajil* (deferred sales) contracts, even though Malaysia is recognized as one of the pioneering countries

*Table 7.3* Income from *murabaha* (as a percentage) of different Islamic Banks in Bangladesh, Indonesia, Malaysia, and Pakistan

| Name of the bank | Year | | | | |
|---|---|---|---|---|---|
| | 2008 | 2009 | 2010 | 2011 | 2012 |
| **Bangladesh** | | | | | |
| Islami Bank Bangladesh Ltd. | 60.00 | 54.82 | 54.25 | 58.20 | 58.68 |
| | (1.70) | (2.58) | (3.63) | (4.13) | (3.78) |
| First Security Islami Bank Ltd. | 77.78 | 81.36 | 79.83 | 75.22 | 75.22 |
| | (0.00) | (0.00) | (0.00) | (0.00) | (0.00) |
| Export Import Bank of | 22.82 | 21.48 | 38.98 | 42.51 | 40.09 |
| Bangladesh Ltd. | (0.00) | (0.00) | (0.00) | (0.00) | (0.00) |
| Shahjalal Islami Bank Ltd. | NA | 20.32 | 15.39 | 15.63 | 17.10 |
| | | (0.00) | (0.00) | (0.00) | (0.00) |
| Social Islami Bank Ltd. | NA | 20.74 | 18.41 | 6.03 | 4.63 |
| | | (0.74) | (0.66) | (0.42) | (0.41) |
| Al-ArafahIslami Bank Ltd. | 34.74 | 29.98 | 35.15 | 25.66 | 15.93 |
| | (0.01) | (0.01) | (0.01) | (0.00) | (0.00) |
| **Indonesia** | | | | | |
| PT. Bank Syariah Mandiri | 47.00 | 45.00 | 49.00 | 58.00 | 66.00 |
| | (41.00) | (39.00) | (36.00) | (32.00) | (26.00) |
| PT. Bank Muamalat | 45.00 | 43.00 | 43.00 | 47.00 | 48.00 |
| Indonesia | (50.00) | (47.00) | (49.00) | (43.00) | (42.00) |
| PT. Bank Mega Syariah | 81.00 | 86.00 | 88.00 | 88.00 | 85.00 |
| Indonesia | (6.00) | (4.00) | (3.00) | (2.00) | (0.00) |
| PT. Bank Rakyat Indonesia | 87.00 | 66.00 | 66.00 | 59.00 | 66.00 |
| Syariah | (11.00) | (18.00) | (26.00) | (16.00) | (18.00) |
| PT. Bank Negara Indonesia | NE | NE | 51.00 | 51.00 | 56.00 |
| Syariah | | | (11.00) | (13.00) | (13.00) |
| PT. Bank Central Asia Syariah | NE | NE | 5.00 | 31.00 | 36.00 |
| | | | (9.00) | (14.00) | (27.00) |
| **Malaysia** | | | | | |
| Bank Islam Malaysia Berhad | 55.26 | 69.08 | 59.66 | 59.66 | 59.10 |
| | (0.08) | (0.08) | (0.04) | (0.04) | (0.04) |
| Bank Muamalat Malaysia | 41.57 | 36.47 | 40.46 | 41.67 | 49.43 |
| Berhad | (0.07) | (0.21) | (0.41) | (0.31) | (0.00) |
| Al Rajhi Banking and | 99.88 | 99.90 | 99.91 | 99.90 | 99.93 |
| Investment Corporation | (0.00) | (0.00) | (0.00) | (0.00) | (0.00) |
| (Malaysia) Berhad | | | | | |

| Name of the bank | Year | | | | |
|---|---|---|---|---|---|
| | *2008* | *2009* | *2010* | *2011* | *2012* |
| **Pakistan** | | | | | |
| Al Baraka Bank Pakistan | 72.06 | 78.92 | 55.89 | 56.90 | 48.05 |
| | (11.31) | (8.55) | (17.70) | (16.43) | (19.54) |
| Bank Islami Pakistan | 35.34 | 30.89 | 40.41 | 31.00 | 27.03 |
| | (31.99) | (34.37) | (35.93) | (38.33) | (26.10) |
| Burj Bank Ltd. Pakistan | 42.86 | 30.42 | 51.91 | 53.68 | 29.88 |
| | (38.57) | (45.12) | (34.01) | (34.64) | (26.98) |
| Dubai Islamic Bank Pakistan Ltd. | 13.96 | 11.59 | 13.01 | 11.81 | 13.72 |
| | (6.45) | (6.82) | (1.58) | (1.38) | (1.62) |
| Meezan Bank Pakistan | 35.70 | 35.63 | 33.28 | 27.00 | 21.36 |
| | (19.70) | (17.23) | (12.15) | (10.93) | (0.07) |

Source: Calculated by the authors based on the annual reports of respective banks.

Notes: Figures in parentheses represent the income from profit-and-loss sharing *mudaraba* and *musharaka* in Bangladesh, Indonesia, and Malaysia; and diminishing *musharaka* only in the case of Pakistan. NA and NE stand for not available and not established respectively.

where the development in Islamic finance and banking has been prevalent since 1983, and accordingly it placed itself as an Islamic financial hub in the international financial market.

In order to analyze the Islamic bank rent opportunity captured by the Islamic banking (*riba*-free banking) operation in Bangladesh, Indonesia, Malaysia, and Pakistan, we compare the cost to income ratio from the conventional banking (*riba*-based banking) with that under the Islamic banking. For this analysis, banks operating conventional branches simultaneously with the Islamic banking windows/branches have been considered. Accordingly, we use the data of nine banks in Bangladesh, six banks in Indonesia, three banks in Malaysia, and ten banks in Pakistan. The purpose of this approach is to compare the ratio of profit paid and received by Islamic banking operation, with the ratio of interest paid to depositors and interest received from borrowers in conventional banking operation on a non-risk adjusted basis (see Table 7.4). Thus this approach represents the underlying idea of the gross value of any bank-rent opportunity. Interestingly, the cost to income ratio of *riba*-free banking operations of conventional banks is consistently lower than the *riba*-based banking operations for all the countries. It can be argued that the complete dominance of the *murabaha* mode in Bangladesh and Malaysia, and a partial dominance of the *murabaha* mode in Indonesia and Pakistan provides some form of bank rent opportunity for the Islamic banks in these countries.

*Table 7.4* Cost to income ratio in *riba*-based banking[a] and Islamic banking[b] of conventional banks

| Name of the bank | Year | | | | | |
|---|---|---|---|---|---|---|
| | 2007 | 2008 | 2009 | 2010 | 2011 | 2012 |
| **Bangladesh** | | | | | | |
| Prime Bank Ltd. | 75.07 | 80.29 | 80.42 | 64.74 | 75.76 | 76.69 |
| | (62.79) | (65.22) | (59.84) | (53.88) | (64.72) | (65.98) |
| Bank Asia Ltd. | 73.86 | 75.18 | 72.13 | 65.11 | 75.59 | 73.47 |
| | NE | NE | (50.15) | (45.15) | (67.22) | (69.38) |
| The City Bank Ltd. | 78.16 | 68.02 | 63.43 | 49.27 | 52.75 | 61.29 |
| | (54.11) | (57.65) | (81.44) | (81.75) | (104.39) | (73.20) |
| Dhaka Bank Ltd. | NA | 71.05 | 73.58 | 67.14 | 76.06 | 77.90 |
| | NE | (86.78) | (83.45) | (60.07) | (75.20) | (110.93) |
| Jamuna Bank Ltd. | NA | 82.30 | 78.07 | 72.67 | 75.25 | 81.27 |
| | NE | (58.78) | (58.79) | (58.69) | (60.89) | (68.61) |
| Premier Bank Ltd. | 79.68 | 75.50 | 77.30 | 69.48 | 77.52 | 81.09 |
| | (77.93) | (78.97) | (84.95) | (72.43) | (70.31) | (69.18) |
| Southeast Bank Ltd. | 76.51 | 84.04 | 86.55 | 75.09 | 86.81 | 90.11 |
| | (68.88) | (70.30) | (66.97) | (64.32) | (67.85) | (71.95) |
| AB Bank Ltd. | 72.69 | 72.49 | 67.49 | 61.99 | 76.21 | 77.11 |
| | (72.75) | (71.63) | (67.11) | (59.10) | (70.67) | (73.57) |
| HSBC Bank Ltd. | 45.41 | 45.37 | 48.71 | 40.92 | 35.51 | 41.12 |
| | NE | (0.00) | (0.00) | (1.47) | (7.36) | (10.36) |
| **Indonesia** | | | | | | |
| PT. Bank BTN | 53.01 | 56.24 | 60.02 | 48.18 | 50.79 | 48.67 |
| | (46.96) | (35.26) | (38.05) | (44.39) | (48.59) | (42.79) |
| PT. Bank DKI | 43.06 | 51.92 | 52.29 | 41.70 | 40.53 | 41.81 |
| | (23.11) | (15.05) | (19.02) | (19.82) | (20.34) | (12.29) |
| PT. Bank Danamon | 37.00 | 36.41 | 33.25 | 24.73 | 26.32 | 23.34 |
| | (31.49) | (36.77) | (26.66) | (16.33) | (18.01) | (21.42) |
| PT. Bank BII | 45.41 | 44.40 | 36.77 | 32.01 | 35.50 | 35.08 |
| | (30.24) | (30.47) | (33.85) | (35.39) | (32.69) | (19.36) |
| PT. Bank Permata | 34.26 | 42.11 | 46.80 | 39.86 | 44.55 | 47.02 |
| | (36.95) | (40.28) | (31.04) | (18.31) | (20.27) | (14.39) |
| PT. Bank BTPN | 31.31 | 40.98 | 41.13 | 36.02 | 37.05 | 34.30 |
| | NE | (16.68) | (35.69) | (27.34) | (16.33) | (10.44) |
| **Malaysia** | | | | | | |
| Hong Leong Bank Berhad | 59.18 | 55.31 | 53.83 | 45.91 | 49.95 | 52.19 |
| | (57.08) | (54.39) | (53.66) | (46.51) | (58.02) | (55.22) |
| Affin Bank Berhad | 57.71 | 54.33 | 45.12 | 50.33 | 56.85 | 60.27 |
| | (54.18) | (58.89) | (45.51) | (50.41) | (55.96) | (59.12) |
| CIMB Bank Berhad | NA | 49.38 | 39.23 | 38.67 | 44.92 | 45.84 |
| | NA | NA | (49.77) | (53.94) | (55.01) | (52.48) |

| Name of the bank | Year | | | | | |
|---|---|---|---|---|---|---|
| | *2007* | *2008* | *2009* | *2010* | *2011* | *2012* |
| **Pakistan** | | | | | | |
| Askari Bank Ltd. | 57.68 | 58.00 | 60.27 | 64.47 | 69.52 | 71.52 |
| | (36.29) | (55.93) | (57.78) | (55.93) | (63.34) | (58.39) |
| Bank Alfalah Ltd. | 64.71 | 66.15 | 70.91 | 65.68 | 58.90 | 60.93 |
| | (61.14) | (58.03) | (54.23) | (49.44) | (53.90) | (54.74) |
| Bank Al Habib Ltd. | 57.94 | 54.84 | 58.97 | 60.69 | 61.42 | 63.22 |
| | (53.93) | (52.55) | (60.99) | (61.54) | (55.36) | (52.61) |
| The Bank of | 77.52 | 69.07 | 79.17 | 78.52 | 72.98 | 71.40 |
| Khyber Ltd. | NE | (39.36) | (35.77) | (34.44) | (31.52) | (33.89) |
| Habib | 69.18 | 68.80 | 68.04 | 69.57 | 71.85 | 68.98 |
| Metropolitan | (62.15) | (66.70) | (76.39) | (79.09) | (69.33) | (73.07) |
| Bank Ltd. | | | | | | |
| MCB Ltd. | NE | 28.09 | 29.99 | 32.21 | 33.93 | 39.50 |
| | NE | (65.45) | (67.01) | (66.81) | (68.86) | (79.59) |
| National Bank of | 33.51 | 39.20 | 50.66 | 50.97 | 50.69 | 55.96 |
| Pakistan | NE | (33.56) | (50.09) | (33.65) | (52.94) | (47.98) |
| Soneri Bank Ltd. | 69.11 | 61.89 | 70.44 | 69.85 | 69.16 | 64.58 |
| | NE | (85.18) | (81.57) | (83.44) | (89.26) | (90.71) |
| Standard Chartered | 28.40 | 29.71 | 39.02 | 38.61 | 36.49 | 38.24 |
| Bank Ltd. | (20.13) | (25.60) | (36.18) | (30.79) | (26.65) | (29.86) |
| United Bank Ltd. | 40.74 | 45.91 | 46.24 | 42.24 | 43.72 | 47.18 |
| | (122.18) | (22.86) | (22.91) | (49.42) | (69.46) | (68.33) |

Source: Calculated by the authors based on the annual reports of respective banks.

Notes: Figures in parentheses represent the ratio from Islamic banking operations. NA and NE stand for not available and not established, respectively.

[a] (Interest paid/Interest received) × 100.

[b] (Profit paid/Profit received) × 100.

In passing, it is worth noting our interviews with the directors and managers of Islamic banks in Indonesia to seek for the answer to the question as to why Islamic banks in Indonesia have been successful in sanctioning higher percentage of equity-based financing compared to that of Bangladesh and Malaysia.

First, we consider Indonesian Islamic banks' innovation of a two-step *mudaraba* and *musharaka* financing. Acknowledging the huge demand from the consumer products in the Muslim community of Indonesia, Islamic banks have made a strategic alliance with non-bank Islamic financial institution. Under this strategic financing, Islamic banks arrange *mudaraba* and *musharaka* contract with the non-bank financial institution, and then the consumer financing company will channel this fund to the end users by using a *murabaha* financing contract. This type of financing is reported by Islamic banks under the *mudaraba/musharaka* mode.

Second, we consider Indonesian Islamic banks' flexibility in Islamic opinion (*fatwa*) in developing Islamic banks' products. The National *Shari'ah* Council (Dewan Syariah Nasional/DSN) in Indonesia as the highest authority in the functioning of the *Shari'ah* Supervisory Body (SSB) for Islamic financial institutions turns out to have a policy that is quite accommodating and flexible to encourage the development of *mudaraba/musharaka* financing products in Islamic banks. We underline two progressive practices of Islamic banks in Indonesia which have obtained approval from the National *Shari'ah* Council, the first of which is the application of the penalty to the *mudaraba/musharaka* financing in the case of business due to negligence or moral hazard. The imposition of this penalty will be reported in Islamic banks' accounting treatment as "non-*halal* (impermissible) income" and will be donated to the *Zakat* organization (DSN, *Fatwa* no. 17). Besides, Indonesian Islamic banks perform an innovative *mudaraba/musharaka* financing in construction or manufacturing projects by using working capital financing, which can be categorized as 'project during construction' after a certain period of time. This type of transaction is also reported under *mudaraba/musharaka* financing. When the project is completed, the financing will be reconverted into *murabaha* financing by a refinancing contract between the Islamic bank and the entrepreneur (DSN, *Fatwa* no. 89).

Interestingly, the nature of the *musharaka* financing adopted by Islamic banks in Indonesia is not of the type of purely 'participatory' financing. Rather, it is a unique variant approach of *musharaka* financing mode. Thus we observe the *murabaha* syndrome in the Islamic banking sector of Bangladesh and Malaysia and the partial or *quasi-murabaha* syndrome in Indonesia and also in Pakistan.

Going back to examine the sustainability of Islamic banks' rent opportunity, we further compare the ratio of operating expenses to income in both conventional and Islamic banking. All banks reported in Table 7.4 with a time period from 2007 to 2012 are considered for this section. The observations are presented in Table 7.5. It shows quite interesting and fluctuating trends in these countries. In the case of Bangladesh, the ratio is relatively higher in *riba*-based banking compared to the *riba*-free banking. On the other hand, in the case of Indonesia and Pakistan, the ratio in *riba*-free banking is higher, with ups and downs during the observed period. It is highly likely that an Islamic bank with a higher ratio of operating expenses to income is associated with a lower performance as compared to an Islamic bank with a lower ratio. This has happened to the Islamic banks in Indonesia and Pakistan, as they demonstrated a lower performance compared to those in Bangladesh. Similar to Bangladesh, the ratio of *riba*-free banking is significantly lower compared to the *riba*-based banking in the case of Malaysia. It indicates that the Malaysian Islamic banks have been successful in utilizing the conventional banks' infrastructure and network for leveraging their business operations, which results in a relatively efficient management of operating expenses.

*Table 7.5* Ratio of operating expenses to income in *riba*-based banking[a] and Islamic banking[b] of conventional banks

| Name of the bank | Year | | | | | |
|---|---|---|---|---|---|---|
| | 2007 | 2008 | 2009 | 2010 | 2011 | 2012 |
| **Bangladesh** | | | | | | |
| Prime Bank Ltd. | 25.29 | 24.77 | 31.49 | 33.91 | 28.12 | 24.25 |
| | (6.35) | (6.32) | (5.39) | (6.78) | (5.37) | (5.85) |
| Bank Asia Ltd. | 18.55 | 19.86 | 24.36 | 29.79 | 22.00 | 21.43 |
| | NE | NE | (50.45) | (18.42) | (12.18) | (9.54) |
| The City Bank Ltd. | 32.58 | 38.66 | 37.85 | 45.61 | 39.33 | 34.75 |
| | (12.49) | (13.58) | (8.57) | (28.29) | (30.48) | (6.40) |
| Dhaka Bank Ltd. | NA | 21.08 | 20.82 | 24.44 | 21.21 | 17.01 |
| | NE | (4.48) | (4.45) | (7.03) | (5.27) | (7.60) |
| Jamuna Bank Ltd. | NA | 26.90 | 29.56 | 27.86 | 25.81 | 23.25 |
| | NE | (11.99) | (9.81) | (9.06) | (9.07) | (6.56) |
| Premier Bank Ltd. | 22.54 | 25.04 | 27.50 | 42.82 | 54.43 | 41.19 |
| | (8.91) | (9.40) | (8.25) | (6.03) | (3.30) | (3.29) |
| Southeast Bank Ltd. | 15.71 | 15.40 | 15.68 | 19.00 | 16.87 | 15.22 |
| | (9.32) | (8.56) | (7.80) | (8.31) | (6.85) | (5.32) |
| AB Bank Ltd. | 26.74 | 26.91 | 29.40 | 36.57 | 28.54 | 27.71 |
| | (4.32) | (3.64) | (3.56) | (6.50) | (4.02) | (3.33) |
| HSBC Bank Ltd. | 21.76 | 23.40 | 28.04 | 31.72 | 32.84 | 27.68 |
| | NE | (9.32) | (6.56) | (2247.27) | (39.23) | (15.38) |
| **Indonesia** | | | | | | |
| PT. Bank BTN | 34.44 | 32.37 | 31.46 | 38.36 | 36.01 | 38.21 |
| | (38.55) | (36.52) | (47.49) | (52.89) | (5.61) | (31.50) |
| PT. Bank DKI | 46.97 | 38.35 | 43.00 | 52.96 | 43.75 | 45.31 |
| | (64.56) | (86.60) | (54.08) | (73.00) | (43.20) | (83.34) |
| PT. Bank Danamon | 36.62 | 47.89 | 52.33 | 50.64 | 50.72 | 54.65 |
| | (50.96) | (39.18) | (45.71) | (51.44) | (55.25) | (102.12) |
| PT. Bank BII | 51.25 | 50.42 | 64.64 | 60.91 | 57.73 | 53.57 |
| | (49.10) | (40.17) | (49.27) | (111.70) | (24.71) | (31.14) |
| PT. Bank Permata | 51.29 | 42.43 | 37.05 | 47.99 | 45.02 | 47.93 |
| | (60.00) | (24.45) | (29.62) | (41.68) | (54.10) | (68.28) |
| PT. Bank BTPN | 42.58 | 36.60 | 42.68 | 44.11 | 39.78 | 41.16 |
| | NE | (112.61) | (56.00) | (140.70) | (123.21) | (81.57) |
| **Malaysia** | | | | | | |
| Hong Leong Bank Berhad | 26.12 | 27.86 | 29.91 | 31.63 | 32.21 | 30.18 |
| | (17.75) | (17.16) | (17.60) | (21.14) | (19.28) | (17.92) |
| Affin Bank Berhad | 31.88 | 33.75 | 37.77 | 35.12 | 29.72 | 28.78 |
| | (20.65) | (25.42) | (33.77) | (32.77) | (24.22) | (19.51) |
| CIMB Bank Berhad | NA | 36.74 | 50.70 | 57.58 | 50.37 | 52.80 |
| | NA | NA | (27.98) | (16.68) | (18.86) | (22.28) |

(*Continued*)

*Table 7.5* (Continued)

| Name of the bank | Year | | | | | |
|---|---|---|---|---|---|---|
| | 2007 | 2008 | 2009 | 2010 | 2011 | 2012 |
| **Pakistan** | | | | | | |
| Askari Bank Ltd. | 32.20 | 33.67 | 32.73 | 29.12 | 27.74 | 29.56 |
| | (61.36) | (37.61) | (32.39) | (53.18) | (39.61) | (36.30) |
| Bank Alfalah Ltd. | 34.50 | 37.28 | 34.18 | 39.08 | 39.23 | 42.23 |
| | (32.95) | (33.16) | (30.85) | (29.30) | (23.52) | (22.89) |
| Bank Al Habib Ltd. | 32.78 | 30.52 | 23.98 | 23.50 | 21.93 | 22.36 |
| | (23.97) | (17.88) | (16.49) | (15.24) | (12.50) | (22.62) |
| The Bank of Khyber Ltd. | 22.84 | 38.75 | 33.91 | 28.41 | 27.99 | 31.51 |
| | NE | (31.62) | (26.93) | (27.81) | (33.96) | (41.41) |
| Habib Metropolitan Bank Ltd. | 19.54 | 21.39 | 18.04 | 19.79 | 21.96 | 24.30 |
| | (11.49) | (9.60) | (6.67) | (5.58) | (4.75) | (4.73) |
| MCB Ltd. | NE | 21.39 | 21.60 | 24.60 | 26.23 | 26.04 |
| | NE | (10.84) | (11.04) | (19.38) | (24.21) | (38.12) |
| National Bank of Pakistan | 28.47 | 32.07 | 30.23 | 30.54 | 33.05 | 37.05 |
| | (36.05) | (63.18) | (67.84) | (49.53) | (19.63) | (25.71) |
| Soneri Bank Ltd. | 20.62 | 25.46 | 22.83 | 27.03 | 28.02 | 32.94 |
| | NE | (12.74) | (32.07) | (40.93) | (41.91) | (39.26) |
| Standard Chartered Bank Ltd. | 55.80 | 56.28 | 48.74 | 46.97 | 46.74 | 50.10 |
| | (7.55) | (10.46) | (27.89) | (24.58) | (33.87) | (59.34) |
| United Bank Ltd. | 34.65 | 33.69 | 31.00 | 33.16 | 29.65 | 34.19 |
| | (219.51) | (106.21) | (62.80) | (46.91) | (36.37) | (42.29) |

Source: Calculated by the authors based on the annual reports of respective banks.

Notes: Figures in parentheses represent the ratio from Islamic banking operations. NA and NE stand for not available and not established, respectively.

[a] (Operating expenses / Interest received) × 100.

[b] (Operating expenses / Profit received) × 100.

## 5.  Conclusion

In order to identify the existence and the consequence of any variation in the financing patterns of banks engaged in Islamic banking in Bangladesh, Indonesia, Malaysia, and Pakistan, this chapter has attempted to shed analytical light on the comparative performance of Islamic banking and conventional banking. The findings report that the distinct lending patterns of Islamic banks are highly associated with their performance, which has contributed enormously toward the discrepancy with pure conventional counterparts. Even though profit-and-loss sharing *mudaraba* and *musharaka* financing modes have been highly encouraged by the Islamic *Shari'ah*, the actuality in the Islamic banking sector is highly divergent. Islamic banks are heavily engaged either in the *murabaha* syndrome or in the partial-*murabaha* syndrome due to the practical difficulties embedded in the profit-and-loss sharing modes.

The case of the Islamic banks in Bangladesh can be regarded as the *murabaha* syndrome. Such an approach helps them uphold the leading position in the banking sector in terms of performance, manifested by ROA and NPL. The higher bank rent opportunity generated by the syndrome, represented by a lower cost to income ratio (see Table 7.4), contributes immensely toward a constantly higher ROA than that of the banking sector as a whole. This has created sufficient incentive for the Islamic banks to monitor their borrowers, which is reflected by the consistently lower NPL. Like Bangladesh, Malaysian Islamic banks have a similar financing pattern, which is dominated by sales-based transactions. It can also be viewed as experiencing the *murabaha* syndrome. Even though the performance of Islamic banks represented by ROA and NPL has been slightly lower than the overall banking sector, still it can be argued that Islamic banks in Malaysia have been successfully utilizing their conventional banking infrastructure and network for leveraging their business operations.

On the other hand, a relatively higher adoption of the profit-and-loss sharing financing modes – in other words, the partial-*murabaha* syndrome – in Indonesia and Pakistan still creates some form of bank rent opportunity for the Islamic banks. However, such an opportunity has been eroded due to the higher operating expenses to income ratio (see Table 7.5). It is highly likely that higher transaction costs connected to the profit-and-loss sharing *mudaraba* and *musharaka* financing modes offset the bank rent opportunity created by the partial-*murabaha* syndrome for protecting the franchise value of Islamic banks. Accordingly, these banks in Indonesia and Pakistan have failed to catch up with their respective banking sectors' ROA. In particular, a very low level of market penetration by Islamic banking in Indonesia seems to have much to do with the insufficient bank rent opportunity to be captured by Indonesian Islamic banks. Presumably, these banks possess fewer incentives for monitoring the borrowers, which can be linked with their higher level of NPL as compared to the overall banking sector. Thus, as long as sufficient bank rent opportunities cannot be protected, it is hard to ask Islamic banks to patronize the *Shari'ah* driven profit-and-loss sharing *mudaraba* and *musharaka* financing modes in reality.

# 8 Financial sector rents in GCC countries

## Are Islamic banks different?

*Yasushi Suzuki and Mohammad Dulal Miah*

## 1. Introduction

Bank rent as an analytical tool has been applied to see if the rent opportunity is reasonably used as an incentive to improve banks' credit risk management and/or to maintain banks' franchise value/reputation. This model is undoubtedly applicable irrespective of the nature of financial institutions. However, Islamic banks deserve special attention in this regard for various reasons. First, information problems stemming from borrowers' uncertainty is possibly higher for Islamic banks than the conventional banks, owing to the fact that the investment pattern of the former, as per Islamic conventions, is based on profit-and-loss sharing agreements, whereas the latter lends upon a pre-agreed rate of return. Obviously, a profit-and-loss sharing agreement entails higher uncertainty and thus higher credit risk than the conventional pre-agreed rate lending. Second, Islamic banks should comply strictly with Islamic principles instilling proper *Shari'ah* board and other required institutions. Any deviation from this standard compliance might induce depositors to promptly withdraw their deposits from Islamic financial institutions. This situation is termed in the literature as 'displaced commercial risks' (El-Gamal, 2006).

A combined effect of these risks means that Islamic banks need to seek a higher spread as compensation than their conventional counterparts. As such, the net interest margin for Islamic banks should be higher than the conventional banks. In other words, Islamic banks should earn an 'extra' margin or 'rent' over conventional banks. In this pursuit, this chapter aims to investigate if Islamic banks really earn any rent. Since the concept of 'Islamic bank rent', as discussed in Chapter 4, is quite new, substantial literature on the issue does not exist. Suzuki and Uddin (2014) examine the existence of extra spread for Islamic banks in the context of Bangladesh and find that the asset-based financing provides Islamic banks with relatively higher rent (see Chapter 4).

Scholars point out the divergence between theory and practice; for instance, the excessive use of *murabaha* (*murabaha* syndrome), which gives a fixed rate of return to the banks (Ayub, 2007, p. 446), and the financial disintermediation toward small-scale enterprises (Visser, 2009, p. 139). Unless the portfolio preference of a vast majority of depositors particularly in developing countries is not so risk averse, it makes sense that Islamic banks that specialize in small-scale credit tend to restrict themselves to *murabaha* and *bai'salam* finance (Visser, 2009, p. 139). In Chapter 7, we observe that the share of *murabaha* operation, secured trading, or asset-backed financing with relatively low credit risk has been dominant in the credit portfolio of Islamic banks in Bangladesh, Indonesia, and Pakistan.[1] Islamic banks in these countries are heavily engaged either in the *murabaha* syndrome or in the partial-*murabaha* syndrome, due to the practical difficulties embedded in the profit-and-loss sharing modes. On the other hand, this syndrome can be considered as a rent-seeking of acceptable risk-adjusted returns as the Islamic bank rent in a broader sense.

With this tradition, the current chapter aims to contribute to further argument on the Islamic bank rent opportunity by examining the case of five GCC (Gulf Cooperation Council) countries, consisting of Bahrain, Kingdom of Saudi Arabia (KSA), Kuwait, Qatar, and the United Arab Emirates. Note that Oman is excluded because Islamic banks in the country are not providing sufficient data due to their short history. It is only in 2013 when two Islamic banks started formal operations in the country. Like other developing and emerging economies, the financial sector in the GCC is dominated by the banking sector, which is relatively concentrated on a few domestic players dominating the market. Moreover, Islamic banks have grown in recent years to become the prominent financial intermediaries, and have already been able to capture a substantial market share in the region. In this sense, an analysis of the absence or presence of Islamic bank rent and the behaviour of Islamic banks thereof, focusing on the region, is expected to contribute to the existing literature by providing new evidence and information. In so doing, this chapter basically shares the theoretical underpinnings on the concept of Islamic bank rent which were discussed in section 4.2 and section 7.2. The subsequent sections are organized as follows: Section 2 discusses in brief the financial systems of GCC countries. Section 3 takes the main issue of the chapter into account (i.e., examining the bank rent opportunity to be captured by Islamic banks), which is followed by an interim conclusion.

## 2. The financial profile of GCC

### 2.1 *The macroeconomic outlook*

GCC as an economic block retains a high profile in the global economic landscape for good reason. The combined GDP of the region grew from US$377 billion in 2000 to an all-time high of US$1,619 billion in 2013 before it finally tumbled down to US$1,399 billion in 2015 (Table 8.1). This decline can substantially be attributed to the recent nosedive of oil price. Blessed by the natural gift of oil, the economies in the GCC have been relying heavily on hydrocarbon products. For instance, contribution of hydrocarbon products still accounts for almost half of the total GDP of all countries in the GCC except Bahrain (Table 8.1).

*Table 8.1* Selected macroeconomic indicators, 2015

|  | Bahrain | KSA | Kuwait | Oman | Qatar | UAE |
|---|---|---|---|---|---|---|
| GDP (current US$ in billions) | 32.22 | 646.00 | 112.81 | 70.25 | 166.91 | 370.29 |
| GDP per capita (current US$) | 23,396 | 20,482 | 28,985 | 15,645 | 74,667 | 40,438 |
| CPI (base year 2010) | 110.56 | 118.23 | 118.17 | 109.6 | 112.45 | 109.35 |
| Contribution of hydrocarbon to GDP (in %) | 26.13 (2013) | 44.45 (2013) | 55.09 (2014) | 47.18 (2014) | 54.4 (2013) | 40.4 (2012) |

Source: WDI, except CPI, which is from IMF.

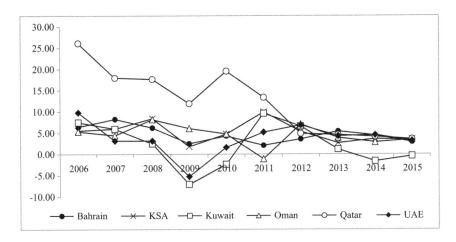

*Figure 8.1* GDP growth rate (annual percentage)
Source: Constructed based on WDI data.

In terms of total GDP, KSA is the largest economy in the GCC followed by UAE; Bahrain is the smallest one. However, Qatar has been able to reach the top of the list of richest nation in the world in terms of GDP per capita (PPP). Average inflation of the region is also stable hovering around 2 per cent to 3 per cent annually.

All the GCC countries have been experiencing declining GDP growth rate (year-on-year basis) since 2006, mainly due to the worldwide financial crisis (Figure 8.1) and most recently due to the declining oil price. Like other regions of the world, financial crisis has halted the growth momentum of GCC countries. Although Kuwait, Qatar, and UAE have experienced the biggest blow of decline in GDP growth rate, UAE and Kuwait saw a negative growth rate in 2009. Since then, the growth rate was in a recovery phase before the declining oil price forced the GDP growth rate of all the countries (except Kuwait) to decline again and converged around 3 per cent in 2015.

## 2.2 *The banking system*

Most countries in the GCC have been trying various policy revisions aiming at reducing their heavy reliance on hydrocarbon products. Despite the fact that oil has been creating the economic fortune of most GCC countries, the recent decline of oil prices has presented several issues to be seriously considered by the concerned policymakers. First, oil resources are finite and neither the price nor the demand for oil is stable. Second, the oil revenues quickly crowd out any other economic activities having strategic future potentials. Perhaps this has been the reason for the suboptimal economic performance of many resource-rich economies, proving the widely known adage 'the resource curse' (Auty, 1993). Realizing the consequence of the resource curse, policymakers of the GCC countries have placed the issue of economic diversification on the political agenda. As part of this strategy, developing the financial markets is on the priority list. It is believed that a thriving financial sector would be an attractive high-productivity sector by itself and would help develop business activity in other sectors through easier financing and better asset management (Kern, 2012).

As mentioned previously, the financial system of GCC is dominated by banking system. Banking sector assets as a percentage of GDP accounted for 260 per cent for Bahrain (as of September 2015), the highest in the GCC countries, followed by UAE (193 per cent) and Kuwait (166 per cent). In Qatar, the ratio is 149 per cent, just ahead of Oman (121 per cent) and the KSA (93 per cent), which is the lowest in the region (Khandelwal, Miyajima, and Santos, 2016). Owing to numerous reforms and supportive initiatives from the national government, the sector experienced almost double-digit growth throughout the last decade. Figure 8.2 shows an upward trend of domestic credit to the private sector by all

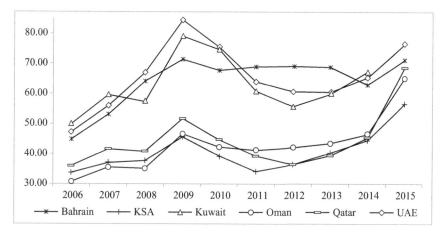

*Figure 8.2* Domestic credit to private sectors (percentage of GDP)
Source: Constructed from WDI data.

types of financial institutions, until the financial crisis adversely affected the region in 2009. Since then the ratio was declining until 2012, before finally a recovery trend has been observed. Taking into consideration only the banking institutions, credit to private sector grew from 38.69 per cent of GDP in 2005 to 51.56 per cent in 2013, an aggregate growth of more than 33 per cent. Bahrain recorded the highest growth (about 58 per cent), whereas Saudi Arabia experienced the lowest growth (about 14 per cent).

It is noteworthy that the behaviour of banking sectors in the GCC is intensely homogenous, which implies that the banking systems of the region are highly integrated. Two clusters of bank groups are visible in Figure 8.2, in which Kuwait, Bahrain, and UAE share almost similar ratio of domestic credit to GDP and are ahead of the second cluster to which Oman, KSA, and Qatar belong. Looking at the picture of the region as a whole, net credit grew around 14.33 per cent annually from 2001 to 2007 and then declined to about half of that level (7 per cent) for the period of 2008 to 2012. Afterward, an upshot was observed, averaging the growth rate about 25 per cent annually until 2015. Moreover, banking sectors are highly concentrated. In all six countries, the largest five banks are domestic and account for 50–80 per cent of total banking sector assets (Al-Hassan, Khamis, and Oulidi, 2010). They further report that the banking sector in Oman is highly concentrated. The largest bank of the country, Bank Muscat, accounts for more than 40 per cent of the total banking system's assets, whereas the share of top five banks is 81.1 per cent. This is followed by Kuwait (81 per cent) and Qatar (80 per cent). The lowest concentration is noted in UAE, where the top five banks account for 48 per cent of the total banking system's assets.

Like the banking concentration, credit concentration to some particular economic sectors is also clear from the lending activities of GCC banking. In Bahrain, the retail banking portfolio is highly exposed to construction, real estate, and the household sectors. Similarly, loan exposure to real estate and construction sectors is evident in Kuwait, Qatar, and the UAE. In Kuwait, real estate and construction sectors constitute about 50 per cent of the total loans disbursed (Al-Hassan et al., 2010). In contrast, the Omani banking sector is highly exposed to the household sector, followed by the real estate and construction sectors. A similar trend is noted for Qatar, where the majority of the loan portfolio is concentrated on the household sector, which is followed by construction and real estate sectors. On the other hand, the loan portfolio of banks in Saudi Arabia appears to be well diversified, even though lending is relatively skewed toward the government sector. The banking sector of UAE is highly exposed to the construction and real estate sectors.

Even if the banking system of GCC is highly concentrated and has disrupted significantly by the subprime mortgage crisis, no major bank in the region has failed because of the negative effect of the crisis. Of course, the crisis in real estate weighed heavily on many institutions, particularly in the UAE. Despite this setback, banks have been able to gradually recover from stresses. This can be attributed to banks' relative strength in financial capital. The capital adequacy ratio (CAR) of banks in the GCC is well above the minimum requirement.

Capital adequacy ratio averaged 17.38 per cent in 2013 (IMF, 2014). UAE had the highest level of CAR (18.8 per cent) followed by Bahrain (18.6) and KSA (17.7), whereas Qatar had the lowest (15.8) in the region. Also, a higher capital to asset ratio provides banks with sufficient buffer to absorb unanticipated economic and financial shocks.

## 2.3 The capital market

Development of the capital market in the GCC countries is not on par with the development of the banking system. Stock market capitalization accounted for about 63 per cent of GDP in 2015 (Figure 8.3). Qatar has the most developed stock market in the region, accounting for market capitalization of more than 85 per cent of GDP, whereas the ratio of market capitalization to GDP amounts to 53 per cent in UAE, the lowest in the region. However, the exchanges are dominated by a few sectors such as financial institutions and telecoms in terms of market capitalization, and free float tends to be limited, given that the largest firms are government related enterprises. The total value of initial public offerings in the GCC region has remained relatively small at about $35 billion in the 2004–2013 period, compared to $2.44 trillion globally (Gokkent, 2014). GCC markets generally lack institutional investors whose long-term horizons would provide a natural base for domestic debt market development. In addition, nonbank financial institutions have limited presence in the GCC, although they have witnessed rapid growth in recent years. Most mutual investment funds are bank-owned.

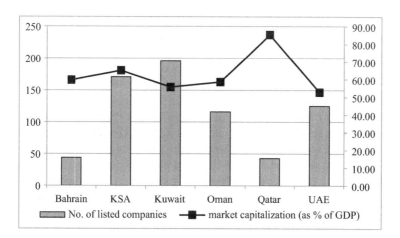

*Figure 8.3* Number of listed companies (left axis) and market capitalization (right axis), 2015

Source: All data are collected from WDI except for Kuwait, which is collected from the Central Bank of Kuwait. For Kuwait, data for market capitalization and number of listed companies are as of 2014 and 2013, respectively.

Bond markets in the region remain shallow, and investment in the secondary bond markets has not developed to a mentionable level, particularly as governments have drawn down outstanding debt in recent years. As of June 2016, the total outstanding bonds issued by GCC entities stood at approximately $263 billion (Deepak, 2016). Interestingly, the overall market composition is equally distributed between sovereign, banking, and other corporate issuers. Issuers in the UAE represent about 45 per cent of the total outstanding GCC bond market and are at the forefront of bond issuances in the region, followed by the issuers in Qatar (26 per cent), Saudi Arabia (15 per cent), Bahrain (8 per cent), Oman (4 per cent), and Kuwait (2 per cent) (Deepak, 2016). However, in the UAE, the bond market composition is largely composed of banking and financial services issuers, which constitute almost half of the UAE's outstanding bond issuance. This is an expected market characteristic, given the prominence that the UAE has achieved as a financial hub for the GCC.

## 3. Analysis of Islamic bank rents

Besides the economic importance of the GCC, this regional economic block provides an important test case for the Islamic bank rent issue. With the advent of Islamic financing, however, GCC banks have boosted their presence and investment in the private sector, particularly in previously untapped markets. With its greater importance in financial intermediation, the Islamic banking industry controls an average 35 per cent of the region's banking system assets, 40 per cent of lending, and 39 per cent of deposit (Table 8.2). It can also be observed based on the reported data (Table 8.2) that Saudi Arabia dominates the region in terms of Islamic banking assets, representing more than one-third in the total Islamic banking assets, 41 per cent in the loan market, and 37 per cent in the deposit market, followed by Kuwait and Qatar, respectively. Among the reported countries, Bahrain is lagging behind all other countries in terms of Islamic finance, representing about 6 per cent of lending, as well as deposit markets of the region. UAE ranks four among the five reported countries.

Table 8.3 reports the provision for loans and leases (PLL), return on average assets (ROAA), and net interest margin (NIM) of conventional and Islamic banks of five GCC countries. On average, the PLL is higher by ninety percentage points for conventional banks than Islamic banks in those five countries. This leads to the conclusion that Islamic banks are very cautious in expanding their investment portfolio. Low portfolio risk on the one hand and higher NIM on the other have helped Islamic banks enjoy higher return on average assets. For instance, the NIM is higher by 0.30 percentage points for Islamic banks than conventional banks. This is a rough indicator of the presence of Islamic bank rents in five GCC countries. However, a clear picture about the presence of Islamic bank rents can be derived by breaking down aggregate data across the countries.

Table 8.2 Descriptive statistics (average 2005–2014; in million US$)

| | Assets | | Loan | | Deposit | | Equity | | Net income | |
| --- | --- | --- | --- | --- | --- | --- | --- | --- | --- | --- |
| | *Conv.* | *Islamic* | *Conv.* | *Islamic* | *Conv.* | *Islamic* | *Conv.* | *Islamic* | *Conv.* | *Islamic* |
| **KSA** | 34788.52 | 20459.61 | 20055.77 | 16370.77 | 25654.36 | 16041.14 | 4498.00 | 3683.34 | 741.07 | 625.11 |
| **UAE** | 14613.64 | 10125.41 | 9467.95 | 6369.93 | 9384.53 | 7304.75 | 1833.56 | 1145.16 | 287.73 | 125.59 |
| **Kuwait** | 30264.66 | 15193.83 | 13324.71 | 8868.40 | 12472.23 | 10816.31 | 2763.56 | 2003.59 | 309.45 | 183.16 |
| **Qatar** | 19925.31 | 10153.74 | 12747.64 | 6168.26 | 13353.36 | 6472.50 | 2699.43 | 1924.06 | 448.58 | 272.32 |
| **Bahrain** | 10739.94 | 3614.89 | 5054.61 | 1927.01 | 5960.78 | 2366.59 | 1178.36 | 543.33 | 75.27 | 35.62 |

Source: Authors' calculation based on data from Bankscope.

Table 8.3 Year-wise aggregate data of PLL, ROAA, and NIM

| | 2005 | 2006 | 2007 | 2008 | 2009 | 2010 | 2011 | 2012 | 2013 | 2014 | Average |
|---|---|---|---|---|---|---|---|---|---|---|---|
| **PLL** | | | | | | | | | | | |
| Conventional | 4.79 | 4.12 | 3.52 | 2.88 | 3.89 | 4.52 | 4.33 | 4.25 | 4.46 | 4.63 | 4.14 |
| N | 42 | 43 | 47 | 47 | 48 | 48 | 48 | 48 | 48 | 29 | |
| Islamic | 4.06 | 2.89 | 2.42 | 2.27 | 2.95 | 3.33 | 3.71 | 3.74 | 3.67 | 3.42 | 3.24 |
| N | 12 | 14 | 14 | 17 | 20 | 22 | 22 | 27 | 27 | 14 | |
| **ROAA** | | | | | | | | | | | |
| Conventional | 3.68 | 2.91 | 2.75 | 1.62 | 1.54 | 1.66 | 1.70 | 1.86 | 1.90 | 1.89 | 2.15 |
| N | 41 | 44 | 47 | 49 | 49 | 49 | 49 | 49 | 49 | 31 | |
| Islamic | 3.87 | 4.82 | 4.61 | 2.85 | 0.44 | −0.40 | 0.92 | 4.39 | 1.11 | 1.43 | 2.40 |
| N | 17 | 18 | 19 | 23 | 25 | 25 | 26 | 27 | 27 | 14 | |
| **NIM** | | | | | | | | | | | |
| Conventional | 3.17 | 3.09 | 3.03 | 2.85 | 2.79 | 2.93 | 3.04 | 2.97 | 2.94 | 2.92 | 2.97 |
| N | 36 | 39 | 41 | 42 | 42 | 43 | 44 | 44 | 44 | 39 | |
| Islamic | 3.30 | 3.48 | 3.69 | 3.82 | 3.38 | 3.21 | 3.16 | 2.79 | 2.88 | 3.01 | 3.27 |
| N | 20 | 21 | 22 | 24 | 27 | 27 | 30 | 32 | 32 | 26 | |

Source: Authors' calculation based on data from Bankscope.

In four (KSA, Kuwait, Qatar, and Bahrain) of the five countries, Islamic banks are enjoying higher NIM than the conventional banks. The excess NIM on an average accounts for 1.16 per cent in KSA and 1.19 per cent in Qatar. Though the magnitude is not so substantial in Bahrain (0.30 per cent) and Kuwait (0.10 per cent), the difference of NIM between conventional and Islamic banks is still observed. Higher spread margin has helped Islamic banks in KSA, Qatar, and Bahrain record higher ROAA compared to their conventional counterparts during the study period. The case of UAE is an apparent anomaly to the bank rent explanation. The spread margin of Islamic banks is 3.29 per cent, whereas for conventional banks it is 3.62 per cent. As a result, ROAA is much lower for Islamic banks (1.23 per cent) than conventional banks (2.62 per cent), despite the fact that PLL for the former is less (3.86 per cent) than the latter (4.88 per cent). Among these five countries, it is obvious that the spread margin is the highest for Islamic banks in KSA (4.13 per cent) and lowest in Bahrain (2.53 per cent).

As mentioned in Chapter 4, Islamic banks require an extra spread over conventional banks for maintaining *Shari'ah* principles as a cushion to cover up the losses involved with PLS investment. Thus we can expect a minimum level of Islamic bank rent because they are complying with *Shari'ah* principles. The second element of Islamic bank rent which is 'premium for uncertainty involved with PLS financing' may vary depending on the degree of PLS financing activities by a particular bank. For instance, banks investing heavily on the pure PLS schemes should claim higher NIM than banks with lower investment in the PLS schemes. In this sense, a positive relation between NIM and the level of PLS investment is expected. We would like to mention in this regard that *murabaha* syndrome may lower NIM earned by Islamic banks. However, the lower NIM does not always equate with 'less desirable' for Islamic banks, so far as the risk-adjusted return from *murabaha* financing is still within a satisfactory level. When Islamic banks challenge to undertake the risk associated with *musharaka* and participatory financing, the risk-adjusted return (at least expected) from *musharaka* should be higher. Conventional banks can draw an 'indifference curve', showing the relationship between the associated risk and the expected return. However, it is intrinsically difficult for Islamic banks to estimate the expected return and associated risk in the participatory financing like *musharaka* under the PLS scheme. The estimation for the *musharaka* risk premium is based on their subjective assessment, which is more subject to fundamental uncertainty. Thus the challenge to *musharaka* may require a higher return (and also a higher risk-adjusted return upon subjective assessment) and additional α in the Islamic bank rent equation (see section 4.2 and 7.2) to cover the unexpected or unspecified risk and uncertainty peculiar to the participatory financing.

We have checked the investment pattern of Islamic banks in those countries. However, the reporting style and segregation of investment vary greatly from bank to bank across countries. Thus a concrete relationship between PLS investment and NIM cannot be drawn. However, we take example about the investment pattern of the largest Islamic bank of each country. The analysis shows that the pure *murabaha* mode of investment is the lowest for Al Rajhi Bank of Saudi Arabia (a point to note is that a portion of corporate *mutajara* and installment sales reported by the bank is also *murabaha* investment, but they are not reported separately). *Murabaha* accounted for 11.2 per cent in 2009 and declined to 6.9 per cent in 2013. This investment data postulates that the bank assumes higher credit risk involved with the PLS mode of investment. Moreover, the market penetration of the Islamic bank is the highest in KSA (Table 8.2) in the region. A combined effect of these helps Islamic banks in KSA to materialise the highest NIM. The behaviour of the NIM (Figure 8.4c) shows a declining trend of NIM for Islamic banks starting from 2007. However, this is clearly ahead of the NIM of conventional banks throughout the period. The existence of Islamic bank rent is therefore logically evident.

In contrast, Bahrain maintains a very low NIM for both Islamic and conventional banks among the reporting countries, and also the difference in spread between these two banking systems is the lowest. The logic for maintaining the lowest NIM for both classes of banks can be attributed to the lower inflation rate of the country. The inflation from 2005 to 2013 averaged 5.6 per cent, the lowest in the GCC countries. On the other hand, the narrow gap in NIM in favour of Islamic banks is due to the fact that Islamic banks have not yet been able to apprehend a good portion of banking market share (Table 8.2). Moreover, PLS participation of the sector is also very low. For instance, the *musharaka* and *mudaraba* mode of investment constituted merely 8 per cent in 2013 and 11.7 per cent in 2014 for Al Baraka Islamic Bank, the largest Islamic bank of Bahrain. It can be observed from the Figure 8.4d that until 2010, Islamic banks outperformed conventional banks in terms of NIM. Although a temporary decline was observed in 2011, pushing NIM below the level of conventional banks for the first time during the whole study period, the upward trend is again followed, converging to the level of conventional banks. While the Islamic banking market (domain) has been still protected (or developing) in KSA and Qatar, it has been relatively matured in Kuwait and Bahrain, where cut-throat competition between Islamic and conventional banks is pronounced. For instance, there is only one Islamic bank (Al Baraka Islamic Bank) in Bahrain among the top five banks. However, there are eleven Islamic banks among the top twenty banks in Bahrain. This implies that the conventional banks are dominating in a highly competitive market. Intense competition between and among Islamic and conventional banks on the one hand and reluctance of Islamic banks to accept uncertainty ensuing from PLS investment on the other hand justify a narrow difference in NIM between Islamic and conventional banks of the country.

The scenario is almost similar in Kuwait. The investment portfolio of the largest Islamic bank of the country, Kuwait Finance House (KFH), comprised about 79 per cent of the *murabaha* mode of investment in 2014. This means the investment behaviour of the bank is risk-averse and thus a higher level of rent should not be expected. We can further look at the behaviour of NIM depicted in Figure 8.4a. The spread margin of conventional banks remains neatly stable from 2007 onward. In contrast, the spread margin of Islamic banks experienced frequent fluctuations at the beginning of the study period. It seems that the spread margin of Islamic banks declined slightly during the worldwide financial crisis but remained above the conventional banks. This may be due to the dominance of a single Islamic bank (KFH), which has a huge international exposure. Of the five Islamic banks in Kuwait, KFH alone constitutes more than two-thirds (68 per cent) of the total Islamic banking assets. Moreover, the PLL for Islamic banks is the highest for Kuwait among the reporting countries. This may explain the fluctuation of NIM for Islamic banks.

The scenario of Qatar is also the same. Before 2009, data for only two Islamic banks were available, and both of these banks were enjoying much larger spread over conventional banks. These two banks (Qatar Islamic banks and Masraf Al Rayan) constitute more than two-thirds of the total Islamic banking assets in Qatar. With substantial market share, these banks have been able to maintain a premium for maintaining Islamic *Shari'ah* and participating PLS financing. The level of rent has been falling due to the erosion of monopolistic rent, as the number of Islamic banks has increased over the years. But they are still able to maintain Islamic bank rent, as shown by the positive gap.

The only anomaly to our Islamic bank rent explanation pertains to the case of UAE. If something is to be concluded from the graph (Figure 8.4e), it is that there is no difference between Islamic and conventional banks in terms of NIM. However, spread margin is slightly higher for the latter category of banks, especially starting from the year 2010. This is mainly due to the rise of NIM for the conventional banks rather than the decline of NIM for Islamic banks, as the spread for Islamic banks remains almost stable during the study period. The cause of increasing NIM for conventional banks can be explained by the fact that after the financial crisis, the government of the UAE maintained or even increased spending levels, despite a sharp decline in oil revenues. The government also introduced various other financial measures, which include capital and liquidity injections, lowering interest rates, easing liquidity through direct injections in the money market, reduction in reserve requirements, and relaxation of prudential loan-to-deposit ratios (Al-Hassan et al., 2010). Established financial institutions were able to reinstall the momentum of loan and deposit growth to the level of the pre-crisis period, capitalizing on these regulatory and financial measures. But Islamic banks could not materialize the benefits, partly due to their low penetration in the loan and deposit markets. For instance, among seven Islamic banks reported in our study (Dubai Bank is omitted from our sample because only initial three years data is available for this banks), comparatively three new banks (Ajman Banks, Noor Bank, and Hilal Bank) together constituted less than 20 per cent of the Islamic banking assets in 2014, and about 22 per cent in both loan and deposit markets. NIM of these three banks averaged 2.70 per cent, whereas for the remaining four banks the NIM accounted for 3.48 per cent, which was higher by 11 basis points than the average NIM of conventional banks. This proves that the inclusion of these three new Islamic banks in our data set, which were established in 2008 with major ownership by the government of respective emirates, tends to lower the average NIM for overall Islamic banking in the

Table 8.4 Country-wise data of PLL, ROAA, and NIM

| | | 2005 | 2006 | 2007 | 2008 | 2009 | 2010 | 2011 | 2012 | 2013 | 2014 | Average |
|---|---|---|---|---|---|---|---|---|---|---|---|---|
| **PLL** | | | | | | | | | | | | |
| KSA | Conventional | 2.83 | 2.63 | 2.43 | 1.90 | 3.06 | 3.45 | 3.34 | 2.39 | 1.99 | 1.73 | 2.57 |
| | Islamic | 4.08 | 3.11 | 2.51 | 2.36 | 2.98 | 3.39 | 3.50 | 3.39 | 2.24 | 2.46 | 3.00 |
| UAE | Conventional | 6.04 | 5.11 | 3.62 | 2.83 | 4.16 | 4.79 | 5.42 | 5.37 | 5.92 | 5.51 | 4.88 |
| | Islamic | 2.98 | 2.02 | 2.15 | 1.32 | 2.62 | 3.70 | 5.83 | 6.08 | 5.97 | 5.96 | 3.86 |
| Kuwait | Conventional | 6.07 | 5.55 | 4.17 | 5.71 | 5.63 | 5.76 | 5.07 | 5.09 | 4.94 | 5.59 | 5.36 |
| | Islamic | 5.57 | 3.97 | 2.86 | 4.26 | 5.50 | 4.50 | 3.88 | 3.46 | 3.49 | 3.25 | 4.07 |
| Qatar | Conventional | 3.55 | 1.42 | 1.16 | 0.96 | 1.77 | 2.25 | 1.73 | 1.76 | 1.87 | 1.93 | 1.84 |
| | Islamic | 3.54 | 3.71 | 2.36 | 1.23 | 0.67 | 2.81 | 1.13 | 0.96 | 0.80 | 0.54 | 1.77 |
| Bahrain | Conventional | 2.73 | 2.14 | 3.97 | 2.44 | 3.71 | 5.44 | 5.45 | 5.76 | 6.59 | 8.99 | 4.72 |
| | Islamic | 4.17 | 2.47 | 2.25 | 2.38 | 3.44 | 2.25 | 2.24 | 3.37 | 3.95 | 4.30 | 3.08 |
| **ROA** | | | | | | | | | | | | |
| KSA | Conventional | 3.45 | 3.87 | 2.65 | 2.01 | 1.64 | 1.69 | 1.96 | 1.98 | 1.98 | 2.00 | 2.32 |
| | Islamic | 3.52 | 7.48 | 3.48 | 2.63 | 1.25 | 1.11 | 1.80 | 2.31 | 1.96 | 2.33 | 2.79 |
| UAE | Conventional | 4.89 | 2.82 | 3.26 | 2.14 | 2.09 | 2.16 | 1.82 | 2.30 | 2.39 | 2.32 | 2.62 |
| | Islamic | 2.80 | 2.50 | 2.19 | 1.46 | -0.59 | 0.04 | 0.52 | 0.93 | 1.10 | 1.34 | 1.23 |
| Kuwait | Conventional | 3.63 | 3.27 | 2.89 | -0.01 | 0.68 | 1.21 | 1.19 | 0.98 | 0.87 | 1.09 | 1.58 |
| | Islamic | 2.51 | 2.92 | 3.32 | 1.48 | -1.56 | 0.70 | 0.61 | 0.99 | 1.01 | 1.01 | 1.30 |
| Qatar | Conventional | 3.63 | 3.17 | 3.02 | 2.32 | 1.95 | 2.40 | 2.50 | 2.24 | 1.95 | 1.83 | 2.50 |
| | Islamic | 6.31 | 8.43 | 6.58 | 6.51 | 2.78 | 2.65 | 2.57 | 2.12 | 2.15 | 2.32 | 4.24 |
| Bahrain | Conventional | 1.46 | 1.60 | 1.99 | 0.56 | 0.66 | 0.50 | 1.15 | 1.48 | 1.74 | 2.16 | 1.33 |
| | Islamic | 5.54 | 5.69 | 7.01 | 3.91 | 0.45 | -4.13 | 0.13 | 11.28 | 0.24 | 0.87 | 3.10 |

## NIM

| | | | | | | | | | | | | |
|---|---|---|---|---|---|---|---|---|---|---|---|---|
| **KSA** | Conventional | 3.37 | 3.53 | 3.38 | 3.09 | 2.92 | 2.86 | 2.78 | 2.66 | 2.59 | 2.55 | 2.97 |
| | Islamic | 4.26 | 5.27 | 5.29 | 4.61 | 4.12 | 3.81 | 3.81 | 3.58 | 3.41 | 3.18 | 4.13 |
| **UAE** | Conventional | 3.28 | 3.02 | 2.90 | 2.97 | 3.81 | 3.93 | 4.05 | 4.12 | 4.06 | 4.07 | 3.62 |
| | Islamic | 3.72 | 3.27 | 3.09 | 3.12 | 3.44 | 3.35 | 3.29 | 3.01 | 3.18 | 3.38 | 3.29 |
| **Kuwait** | Conventional | 3.94 | 3.78 | 2.99 | 2.98 | 2.93 | 2.89 | 2.95 | 2.87 | 2.95 | 2.69 | 3.10 |
| | Islamic | 2.62 | 3.17 | 3.79 | 3.80 | 3.49 | 3.06 | 2.82 | 3.05 | 3.27 | 2.98 | 3.20 |
| **Qatar** | Conventional | 3.09 | 3.17 | 2.86 | 2.98 | 2.65 | 3.22 | 3.25 | 2.70 | 2.70 | 2.52 | 2.91 |
| | Islamic | 5.77 | 5.91 | 3.96 | 4.79 | 4.03 | 4.36 | 3.77 | 3.00 | 2.86 | 2.59 | 4.10 |
| **Bahrain** | Conventional | 1.91 | 2.03 | 2.84 | 1.97 | 1.81 | 1.98 | 2.30 | 2.35 | 2.36 | 2.41 | 2.20 |
| | Islamic | 2.72 | 2.57 | 3.25 | 3.25 | 2.16 | 2.19 | 2.63 | 1.99 | 2.18 | 2.34 | 2.53 |

Source: Authors' calculation based on data from Bankscope.

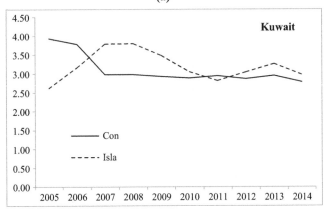

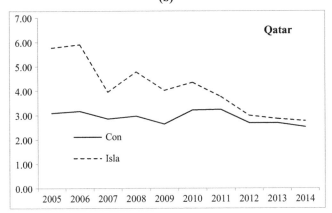

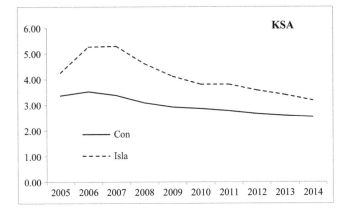

*Figure 8.4* NIM of five GCC countries

**(d)**

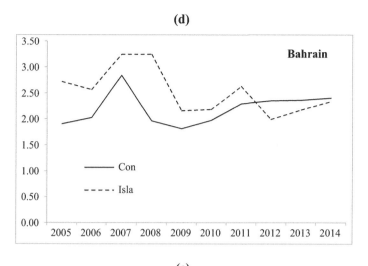

**(e)**

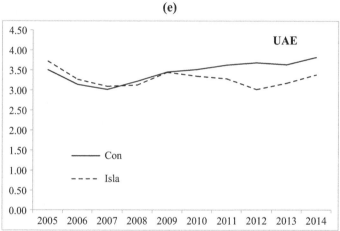

*Figure 8.4* (Continued)

UAE. (This means that the weighted average NIM would definitely be higher for Islamic banks than the conventional banks.)

Furthermore, the starting of these three banks amidst the worldwide financial crisis might cause them to be lagging behind in terms of market penetration and lower NIM than the matured Islamic banks of the country. Also, government ownership of these banks may imply that their activities aimed at taming the adverse effect of financial crisis rather than focusing on profit purpose. Furthermore, the banking sector in the UAE is utterly dominated by a conventional system, owing to the country's status as an international business hub. The size (in terms of assets) of the largest Islamic bank, Dubai Islamic Bank, is just one-third (33 per cent) of the largest conventional bank, National Bank of Abu Dhabi. Thus cut-throat competition with conventional banks may have fully squeezed the monopolistic rent from Islamic banks. It may make sense for some Islamic banks to seek for some governmental backups and to adopt a conservative credit policy. As a result, they put up with lower NIM, while they can save (and do not necessarily earn) α to cover the displacement risk and the unexpected risk and uncertainty. Theoretically, bank rent functions most as an incentive mechanism if the ownership of financial institutions is private. In this sense, the low NIM of newly established Islamic banks makes sense.

## 4. Conclusion

Financial sector rent has become an important tool to assess if financial institutions are provided with sufficient incentive for undertaking prudent monitoring as well as maintaining reputation. While this tool has been applied in various analyses for conventional banks, Islamic banks deserve special focus due to their unique and different institutional characteristics. In this pursuit, the current chapter has attempted to analyse the absence or presence of Islamic bank rent in five GCC countries. Aggregate data of the selected countries show the presence of Islamic bank rent, although they vary greatly from country to country. Islamic bank rent is evident in KSA, Bahrain, Qatar, and to some extent in Kuwait. Although no significant difference is observed between conventional and Islamic banks in terms of NIM for UAE until 2009, we see that the NIM of conventional banks surpassed the NIM of Islamic banks in the latter period. We have argued in explaining this anomaly that the newly established three Islamic banks have tended the average NIM curve lower for Islamic banks than the conventional banks. If we take this matter into account, Islamic banks capture 0.11 percentage points as Islamic bank rent.

While interpreting Islamic bank rent, we put a line of caution that a complete profit-and-loss sharing based financing is not observed from the experience of Islamic banking activities so far. We have argued already that they are suffering from the so-called *murabaha* syndrome – concentration of conservative credit portfolio on asset-backed transactions at mark-up pricing which is quite similar to conventional banking practice. Fundamental uncertainty is thus not associated with a *murabaha* contract to such an extent that would be involved with a pure profit-and-loss sharing agreement peculiar to *mudharaba* and *musharakah* investments. If so, we can expect Islamic bank rent only to cover up that cost of compliance to *Shari'ah* principles and premium for accepting uncertainty for the portion of *mudaraba* and *musharakha* financing only. In this context, it is logical to expect Islamic bank rent, but the magnitude should not be very high. That is what we see from the experience of Kuwait, Qatar, Bahrain, and for the UAE (until 2009). Also, it is not easy to get the information about the credit risk in banks' credit portfolio. There is the limitation of the method of simply comparing NIM earned by Islamic banks and conventional banks. (We cannot precisely compare the 'risk-adjusted' returns earned by them.) However, the theoretical framework using a concept of Islamic bank rent is expected to contribute to setting up various hypotheses for explaining the Islamic banking practice in each country.

## Note

1 A similar situation is observed in Malaysia. According to annual reports by Bank Negara Malaysia, in the asset portfolio of Malaysian Islamic banks, the share of *murabaha* and *murabaha*-related operation (*bai bithaman Ajil*) was 48.2 per cent in December 2008, 48.3 per cent in December 2010; the share of operating lease and lease-to-purchase financing (*ijarah* and *ijarah thumma al-bai*) was 33.1 per cent in December 2008, 29.8 per cent in December 2010. In parallel, it is worth noting that the share of *musharaka* in the Malaysian Islamic financial institutions was only 1.1 per cent in December 2008, 2.5 per cent in December 2010.

# 9 Japan's quantitative easing policy

## Implications for bank rents

*Yasushi Suzuki and Mohammad Dulal Miah*

## 1. Introduction

Monetary policy has multifaceted roles to play for an economy. During the time of economic depression, credit expansion through lowering interest can be warranted to stimulate private spending and investment, whereas the reversal is essential to tame a possible bubble during the period of economic boom. Lack of timely monetary policy intervention may result in destabilizing the economic and financial systems. Economists believe that the 2006–2007 worldwide financial meltdown was triggered by the huge influx of money resulting from the expansionary monetary policy. Stiglitz (2012) argues that the subprime mortgage crisis was not inevitable, but rather monetary and regulatory authority led the economy to the crisis. Similarly, Posner (2009) contends that the Fed (Federal Reserve System) did too much to push interest rates down and keep them down even as the bubble was forming. When the Fed started raising interest rates in 2005, they were raised very slowly, and therefore didn't have an impact on the house-buying frenzy and the mortgage lending until it was too late.

The current crisis is not an exception. History is replete with examples that most waves of financial crisis followed a wave of credit bubble (Kindleberger, 2005; Reinhart and Rogoff, 2009). In pursuit of explaining the great depression of 1929, Fisher (1933) forwarded a theory popularly known as 'debt-deflation theory of great depressions'. Fisher argues that in a general state of economy, equilibrium is disturbed if there is a huge influx of money which makes some sectors over indebted. Fisher's approach was further elaborated by Minsky (1977, 1982), introducing the concept of 'fragility' in an attempt to clarify the problem of over use of debt during an economic upswing. Kindleberger (2005) sketches a comprehensive historical analysis of financial crisis and shows that there have been four significant waves of financial crisis since the early 1970s (Latin America in the early 1980s, Japan in the 1990s, the Asian financial crisis in 1997, and the US subprime meltdown in 2006–2007), and all were preceded by rapid growth of loans from major international banks to government and government owned enterprises. This postulates that an untimed interference in the economy through monetary policy tools or inaction from the monetary authority at the time when such intervention is required may lead to an economic bubble and its eventual burst.

Once the economy is in shambles in the post-bubble period, interference from the monetary authority through various policy tools is critically required for stimulating the consumption and investment. Researchers argue that any solution to counteract the economic bubble or to neutralize an adverse effect in the post-bubble period should accompany the changes in monetary policy (Boivin, Kiley, and Mishkin, 2010; Mishkin, 2011). However, the conventional practices of lowering the interest rate by changing money supply in the market may prove ineffective during the time of financial instability. This can be attributed to the fact that the depth of recession in many circumstances requires negative nominal interest rates. But the market interest rates are effectively bounded by zero because agents can always hold non-interest bearing cash. Second, the solvency of financial intermediaries and borrowers in the post-crisis period may not be so strong that the banking system can effectively function as a monetary policy transmission mechanism. As a result, the usual reliable relationship between changes in official interest rates and market interest rates may collapse because banks may hold funds to improve their viability rather than lending to the private sector.

In this circumstance, an unconventional monetary policy stance such as quantitative easing (QE) from the central bank is urgently called for. QE refers to changes in the composition and/or size of a central bank's balance sheet that are designed to ease liquidity and/or credit conditions (Blinder, 2010). According to Bernanke and Reinhart (2004), when the size corresponds to expanding the balance sheet, while keeping its composition unchanged, the policy is narrowly defined as quantitative easing. On the other hand, when the composition corresponds to changing the composition of the balance sheet, while keeping its size unchanged by replacing conventional assets with unconventional assets, they narrowly define the policy as credit easing. In practice, given constraints on policy implementation, central banks have combined the two elements of their balance sheet – size and composition – to enhance the overall effects of unconventional policy. In this context, broadly defined quantitative easing, often used in a vague manner, better fits as a package of unconventional policy measures making use of both the asset and liability sides of the central bank balance sheet, designed to absorb the shocks hitting the economy (Shiratsuka, 2010).

Japan implemented a QE policy in 2001, following the period of zero interest rate policy (ZIRP) during 1999–2000. Under this policy, the Bank of Japan (BOJ) purchased Japanese Government Bonds (JGBs) as the main instrument to reach their operating target of current account balances (CAB) held by financial institutions at the BOJ as reserves. In addition, following the global financial crisis of 2006–2007, the BOJ increased the pace of its JGB purchases and adopted a number of unconventional measures to promote financial stability. In October 2010, the BOJ introduced its Comprehensive Monetary Easing (CME) policy to respond to the re-emergence of deflation and a slowing recovery (Berkmen, 2012). Furthermore, in a surprise move, the BOJ introduced the negative interest rate in January 2016 for the first time, proving that the ZIRP and QE policies adopted thus far were not successful to pave the way for economic recovery.

Several empirical studies have already suggested the limited effect of QE policy on raising aggregate demand and prices (see, for instance, Bernanke, Reinhart, and Sack, 2004; Kimura, Hiroshi, Jun, and Hiroshi, 2002; Okina and Shiratsuka, 2004; Shirakawa, 2002). However, the existing debate seems not to sufficiently explain the reason for the limited effect of QEP. In this chapter, we investigate the impact of QE policy on the bank rents in Japanese banks. As mentioned in Chapter 1, banks need sufficient spread margin called 'rent' as an incentive to undertake risk associated with borrowers. If QE creates a negative pressure on rents, banks will be prompt to look for alternative sources of income, particularly investing in government bonds because the ultra-low reference rate or base rate would encourage banks to be risk-averse, and they will find limited justification to absorb a given credit risk for a comparatively lower base rate. Hence they are likely to shy away from financing new borrowers at lower interest rates. If so, the objective of QE, which is to stimulate inflation by expanding credit for consumer spending, will not be achieved. From this vantage point, we raise a hypothesis that an increase in monetary supply which lowers the prospective yield of bonds and squeezes the bank rents may drain 'risk funds' in the financial market. By risk funds we mean the funds or capital that are provided by the investors who are willing to directly undertake and absorb the risk of borrowers (or issuers in the bond market), often appearing in the direct financing route. We argue that there is no clear-cut mechanism in the economic theory for underpinning the commonly accepted view upon which the QE policy is based. This theoretical analysis suggests that there may exist an appropriate level of market reference rate, which can encourage the investors to absorb the relatively wider range of credit risk in the bond market. An extremely higher market rate would discourage borrowers from raising funds. At the same time, a lower market rate may drain the risk funds in the bond market. In this context, the appropriate level of the market rate may stand on a narrow range of a 'knife's edge', although the level per se does not always guarantee the optimal allocation of financial resources.

The chapter is organized as follows: Section 2 briefly enumerates the quantitative easing policy (QEP) adopted by Japan to counteract the deflationary pressure. Section 3 suggests the limited instrumental rationality in the economic theory underpinning the QEP and argues that the appropriate level of the market rate may stand on a narrow range of a 'knife's edge'. Section 4 links the hypothesis to the empirical data with reference to the effect of Japan's QEP, whereas section 5 shows how the negative interest rate policy creates possible disincentive for banks toward lending activities. Section 6 finally concludes the chapter summarizing the major arguments and offering some policy implications.

## 2.   The quantitative easing in Japan

The traditional Keynesian view states that the scale of investment depends on the relation between the rate of interest and the schedule of the marginal efficiency of capital. In theory, a lower rate of interest would encourage borrowers (mainly enterprises) to make more investment, so far as their prospective yield of the investment remains unchanged. In contrast, a tighter monetary policy leads to the rise in real interest rate, which in turn raises the cost of capital, thereby causing a decline in investment, resulting in a fall in output and employment (Keynes, 1936; Mishkin, 1995). This view of monetary policy holds that money is exogenous, and any change in reserves aggregate is accompanied by the corresponding change in the supply of available money in the economy.

This conventional model, which is known as the 'money version' of the monetary system, considers the financial system essentially as a market for money in which the public's demand for money interacts with the supply of money (Belongia and Ireland, 2015; Bernanke, 1988). Since the central bank controls the supply of money, it reserves in theory the capacity to set the interest rate. The level of market interest rate in turn determines how much households and businesses decide to spend on new goods and services. People are considered in this model as having the following choices: how much of their portfolio to devote to money, with which they can make purchases, and how much to devote to the other, less liquid assets, which presumably offer a higher yield (Bernanke, 1988). The higher the volume of expenditures people intend to make, the greater their demand for money. The higher the interest rates on alternative financial assets, the less money they demand (Minsky, 1975).

On the other side of the model, banks supply money to those who need it, and they do so in two ways: by making loans and by buying marketable securities. When a bank makes a loan, it gives its collected deposit to the customers considered creditworthy. Also, banks can invest in the financial markets by buying treasury bills or other types of securities. In this model, banks are considered merely financial intermediaries that collect deposits and convert these deposits into credits. Thus they have a special role to play in transmitting money by changing the liability side of their balance sheet (Kashyap and Stein, 1994).

Financial markets settle at a certain level of interest rate that equates the demand for money to the supply of it. If banks can create more deposit than the public wants to hold at the current interest rate, they can clear the excess supply either by selling more credit to the public, or if banks prefer to hold more money-market securities, they can offer more prices for securities, resulting in slicing down the yield. Either way, banks' tendency to clear the excess supply of money creates a downward pressure on the interest rate. Conversely, if banks can mobilize less deposit than the demand for credit, a rise of interest rate will clear the excess demand for funds. Also, the money market securities banks hold in their portfolio can be sold at a lower price, bidding up the yields on these instruments. Now if the central bank wants to increase the supply of money, it can increase the reserves of commercial banks. This increase in reserves increases the bank's capacity to provide credit to businesses and households. The credit expansion *ceteris paribus* tends to lower the market clearing interest rate. The financial market responds quickly to this change in money reserves, whereas the market for goods and services adjusts rather slowly (Bernanke, 1988). Ultimately, the lower interest rate increases the spending. Consumers adjust their spending on durables including houses, cars, and other such goods, which in turn leads an economy to the expansionary mode.

This discussion implies that financial intermediaries function as transmission mechanisms of monetary policy which is affected through the change in interest rate. As we mentioned earlier, QE policy as an unconventional monetary policy is called for when conventional prescriptions are not so effective for the reasons mentioned previously. In Japan, such unconventional monetary policy was influenced by two critical factors. First, the banking system was fragile due to the accumulation of huge non-performing loan following the bubble burst in the early 1990s. As a result, the banking system was unable to work smoothly as a monetary policy transmission mechanism. Secondly, the BOJ faced zero lower bound constraint on nominal interest rates since 1999, which implies that boosting economic activities through further lowering interest rate was infeasible. In these circumstances, the BOJ has effected QE through (1) its commitment to maintain the zero interest rate until the annual inflation rate stabilizes at 2 per cent; (2) increasing in the current account balance at the BOJ; and (3) changing in the composition of banks' balance sheets.

The most important transmission channel of the commitment to maintain the zero interest rate is to foster the expectation among the private sector that short-term interest rates would be maintained at zero until the inflation rate fulfilled this condition in the future. In a situation when present short-term interest rates face a zero bound constraint, the commitment is essential to guide the private sector to expect that the zero interest rate would be maintained until the conditions of the commitment were satisfied, even if the economy picked up in the future. This expectation results in lowering the present short- to medium-term interest rates, because the market expects that the QE would only be lifted when the published core CPI reaches the target. In addition, the market considers that the CPI tends to respond to real economic indicators with a certain lag. Believing in this theory, the BOJ adopted the zero interest rate policy (ZIRP) in April 1999 (Figure 9.1). Ito (2009) points out that the actual decision was made in February to lower the policy rate to 0.15 per cent immediately. By mid-March, the rate was near zero (0.05 per cent). In April, the governor of the Bank of Japan stressed that ZIRP would continue until the inflation becomes stable at 2 per cent. But the BOJ did not wait for the stability of inflation rate. It exited the ZIRP in August 2000 while the inflation rate was still negative and declining (figure 9.2). As expected, the BOJ returned to ZIRP at the beginning of 2001. The inflation rate started increasing on a yearly basis since the mid-2002. Despite a zero interest rate, the economy in practice faced a situation in which monetary easing was lacking (Ugai, 2007). To compensate for this lacking, the central bank made a commitment that it would maintain monetary easing by not raising the policy rate, even when the economy and prices enter a recovery phase, a situation that warrants a raise in the policy rate under normal policy rules.

Although the inflation rate was rising on a yearly basis since the mid-2002 during the period of zero interest rate policy, the rate was not stable (Figure 9.2), which implies that the need for quantitative easing was not effectively compensated by

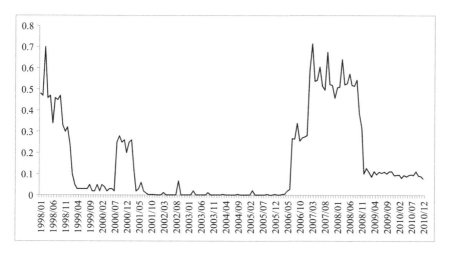

*Figure 9.1* Uncollateralized overnight rate (in percentage)
Source: Bankers' Association of Japan.

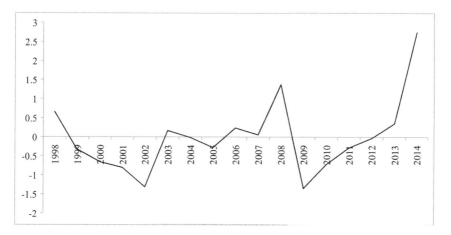

*Figure 9.2* Annual changes in CPI (in percentage)
Source: World Development Indicators (WDI).

the commitment to maintain the zero interest rate until the annual inflation rate is registered at 2 per cent. As a result, the BOJ initiated quantitative easing by increasing its current account balance (CAB). The initial target for the current account balance was set at 5 trillion yen, while the required reserve was about 4 trillion yen (Ito, 2009). Meanwhile, the postal bank became a part of the commercial banking system, and the required reserves increased to 5 trillion yen and

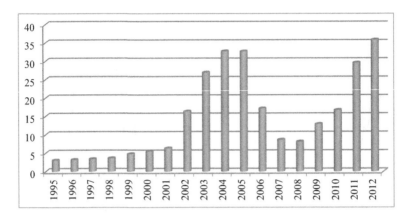

*Figure 9.3* Current account balance of BoJ (in trillion yen)
Source: BoJ.

the QE target was revised to 6 trillion yen. The current account balance target was increased from December 2001 to January 2004 in several steps. From January 2004 to March 2006, the target level was maintained at 30–35 trillion yen (Figure 9.3), while the required reserve was at around 6 trillion yen. The QE reserve targeting was ended in March 2006, and the policy target again became ZIRP.

When the interest rates were at their zero lower bound, the Bank of Japan purchased government securities from the banking sector and thereby boosted the level of cash reserves the banks held in the system. By purchasing assets, the central bank can expand its balance sheets. Asset purchases by central banks can either be of government bonds (or bills) or of assets issued by the private sector. Unlike traditional monetary policy, in which the interest rate is the primary target, asset purchases are explicitly about quantities. Here the central bank uses its ability to create an acceptable means of payment in an unlimited quantity to acquire assets. In doing so, the central bank expands its balance sheet and shifts the portfolio mix of assets held by the private sector, which come to hold more claims on the central bank ('money' – the liability side of the central bank's balance sheet) and fewer of the claims that the central bank has acquired (which now form the asset side of its balance sheet). As the central bank's balance sheet rises, its extra liabilities – most of which are likely to be in the form of greater reserves held by the banking system – are matched by greater assets. It is expected that by targeting a high enough level of reserves, lending into the broader economy will increase, which would eventually help drive asset prices up and overcome a deflationary problem.

As mentioned earlier, several empirical studies have offered limited explanations as to why the QE policy in Japan has failed to achieve its desired goals. In what follows we bring an unexplored dimension which encompasses the effects of interest rate on lenders' risk behavior driven by the ultra-low base rate.

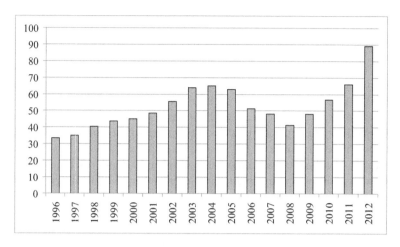

*Figure 9.4* Outright purchase of a Japanese government bond (in trillion yen)
Source: BoJ.

## 3. Knife-edge hypotheses on market reference rate

This section aims to critically assess the limited instrumental rationality in the economic theory underpinning the QEP. For the banks as financial intermediaries in the indirect financing route, their nominal net profit from the 'floating rate' lending is not affected by the change in market rate (the reference rate [or base rate] for the banks), so far as the spread margin as risk premium charged on borrowers remains unchanged and the loan exposure remains the same. In other words, the banks' net profit from the floating rate lending is affected only (1) if banks consider the borrowers' lowered funding cost to reasonably lower their probability of default (to increase their probability of success), and the banks are willing to increase the loan exposure toward the borrowers when higher risk-adjusted returns are expected, and (2) if the borrowers increase the demand of fund-raising for their investment. The former (1) is related to the banks' *subjective* judgment of screening and monitoring, while the latter (2) depends on the borrowers' *subjective* sentiment of investment.

Even though the market rate is lowered, borrowers do not necessarily increase the demand of fund-raising. Note that lower funding cost does not always ease the pessimistic sentiment of borrowers when the other factors (i.e., uncertainties about the product/technology obsolescence under the severe competition) are more significant. Using Keynes's term, a lowering of the rate of interest does not always stimulate investment if a lowering of the marginal efficiency of particular capital assets can offset the effect of stimulating investment. Even though borrowers increase the demand of fund-raising, banks do not necessarily respond sufficiently to the demand, because their credit policy is determined at each bank's discretion. Furthermore, even though the banks expect higher risk-adjusted returns and increase the loan exposure, they do not necessarily maintain the exposure when the spread margin is adjusted (diminished) with lower credit risk profile under the competitive credit market. There is no clear-cut or *a priori* mechanism in the relationship between the monetary policy and the loan exposure (consequently affecting the effective demand as a stimulus to the macro-economy). In short, how the monetary policy can affect the macro-economy depends on the lenders' subjective judgment of credit risk screening and the borrower's subjective sentiment of investment.

Furthermore, the increase in monetary supply may drain 'risk funds' provided by investors in financial markets. In a simple general equilibrium model of Arrow-Debreu as to the direct and indirect financial market, if we accept the unrealistic assumption that there were zero monitoring costs, the only possible general equilibrium would be one where all risk-adjusted interest rates are equal (Freixas and Rochet, 1997; see also Chapter 2). In this simplistic framework, the coupon rate on bonds (denoted by $r$) and the lending rate (denoted by $r_L$) for the firms should be perfect substitutes. If one of the two rates is lower than the other, firms would prefer to raise all the funds through those means, resulting in the potential disappearance of the other. In reality, each borrower has distinctive credit risks related to their type and the type of activity in which they engage. Therefore investors face significant and borrower-specific information and monitoring costs for screening and monitoring this credit risk. It is extremely difficult and costly for individual investors (particularly households) who are not professionals in monitoring to evaluate the credit risk of, in particular, small and middle-sized enterprises (SME), although it may be somewhat easier to do this for internationally reputable large firms.

Consider the floating rate notes (FRN) purchased by the investors in the corporate bond market to compare the floating rate lending by the banks in the credit market. FRN are bonds that have a variable coupon, equal to an interbank money market reference rate, like LIBOR (London Interbank Offered Rate) or the federal funds rate, plus a quoted spread (margin). The spread is a rate that remains constant. Almost all FRNs have quarterly coupons (i.e. they pay out interest every three months). At the beginning of each coupon period, the coupon is calculated by taking the fixing of the reference rate for that day and adding the spread. A typical coupon would look like 3 months USD LIBOR + 1.5 per cent (or 150 basis points or 150 bps).

The coupon rate (r) of the FRN is composed of the money market reference rate (denoted by $r_{IBOR}$) and the spread margin (denoted by *bps*). Basically the spread margin reflects the credit risk of each borrower.

$$r = r_{IBOR} + bps$$

We consider that each investor has its own benchmark, which makes them expect the satisfactory profit taking into account the associated risk, bringing the prospective yield (denoted by $r_Q$) of the investment. The prospective yield is based on the investor's subjective judgment of screening risk and return. In theory, if $r_Q > r$, the investor would not engage in the investment. On the contrary, if $r_Q < r$, it means that the coupon rate would be attractive for the investor. In other words, the minimum condition for engaging in the investment, $r_Q$, should be equal to $r$.

$$r_Q \leqq r$$

substituting $r = r_{IBOR} + bps$, we can obtain the following conditions:

$$r_Q - r_{IBOR} \leqq bps$$

or

$$r_Q - bps \leqq r_{IBOR}.$$

Assume that the spread (*bps*) as risk premium for each borrower remains unchanged, at least in the short-term period. When the market rate ($r_{IBOR}$) decreases, if the investors seek the fixed prospective yield, they may have less incentive to hold the bond in the same credit risk category. Some of them may have an incentive to engage in the other bond, offering a higher spread. However, the bond offering a higher spread is associated with a higher credit risk. Particularly for the *risk-averse* investors who are not professionals in monitoring to evaluate the credit risk of unknown or SME, $r_Q$ would be closer to ∞ for engaging in the high-yield junk bonds.

Rather, when the market rate ($r_{IBOR}$) decreases, some investors may have an incentive to leave for the other 'low-risk and low-return' type bond, which is on the same indifference curve as the risk-return preference. To illustrate this, assume that there are two bonds: one is the 'high-risk and high-return' type bond (Bond A, in which the spread is, for instance, 2 per cent), while the other is the 'low-risk and low-return' type bond (Bond B, in which the spread is 0.5 per cent). When the market rate stays at 5 per cent, the coupon rate (r) of Bond A becomes 7 per cent (5 + 2), while that of Bond B is 5.5 per cent (5 + 0.5). When the market rate decreases to 1 per cent, the coupon rate of Bond A would be 3 per cent (1 + 2), while that of Bond B would be 1.5 per cent (1 + 0.5). As the market rate ($r_{IBOR}$) decreases, the weight of $r_{IBOR}$ in the coupon rate would decrease (5/7 [71.4 per cent] to 1/3 [33.3 per cent] for Bond A, 5/5.5 [90.9 per cent] to 1/1.5 [66.7 per cent] for Bond B) if the spread remains unchanged. For the cash-rich investors who do not have to borrow the funds for purchasing the bond, the weight of $r_{IBOR}$ in the coupon rate functions as a buffer or cushion for absorbing the issuer's credit risk, which is reflected in the spread margin. In the previous case, the weight of the buffer in the coupon rate of Bond A would decrease if the market rate decreases. On the other hand, the weight of the spread in the coupon rate of Bond B would increase (from 9.1 per cent to 33.3 per cent), even though the associated credit risk remains unchanged. As a result, some risk-averse investors would leave for Bond B, because they feel that the weight of buffer attached to Bond A (1/3) is not enough to absorb the 200 bps risk and the weight of spread attached to Bond B (0.5/1.5 or 1/3) is attractive to absorb the 50 bps risk.

We hypothesize that as the market rate decreases, more investors would lose the incentive to absorb higher credit risk – in other words, lose the incentive to provide 'risk funds' because the market rate functions as a buffer for absorbing credit risk for the cash-rich and risk-averse investors. If this hypothesis is not rejected, it may explain a dimension of the cause of 'liquidity trap' argued in Krugman (1998), which is yet to be focused in the academic literature. For the banks being engaged in the floating rate lending, the lending rate ($r_L$) is determined by each bank's funding cost (the base rate covering the funding cost, denoted by $r_{BR}$) and the spread (*bps*) for each borrower. The funding cost is reflected in, for instance, the deposit rate (denoted by $r_D$); the money market reference rate ($r_{IBOD}$); the propensity to pay dividends (funding cost from equities, denoted by *div*), which is reflected in the policy for capital adequacy requirement; and the operating and administration cost (denoted by *op*):

$$r_L = r_{BR} + bps,$$

where

$$r_{BR} = f(r_D, r_{IBOD}, div, op).$$

As mentioned earlier, in a simple general equilibrium model of Arrow-Debreu as to the direct and indirect financial market, the coupon rate on securities ($r$) and the lending rate ($r_L$) for the firms should be perfect substitutes. If this condition is held,

$$r_{IBOD} + bps = r_{BR} + bps.$$

Therefore, we can reach to the following condition for the equilibrium:

$$r_{IBOD} = r_{BR}.$$

In reality, this condition is not held. This is because the other factors such as deposit rate ($r_D$) and propensity to pay dividends (*div*) in each bank may vary in the determination of the base rate ($r_{BR}$). One of the implications is that (1) if the bank relies only on the interbank money market for funding, (2) if the bank has no obligation to keep the capital adequacy requirement (or if the bank has the same liability composition and cost of deposit and equity as the reference bank), and also (3) if the operating cost is identical to that of the reference bank which offers the money market reference rate, then it is possible to hold the condition for a partial equilibrium in the financial market. In practice, we often observe that $r$ is lower than $r_L$, particularly for prominent borrowers. This implies that the funding cost in the average banks is higher than that in the reference bank. On the other hand, there are few capital/bond markets for SME because the risk-averse investors would not engage in the high yield junk bond, even though the high spread (*bps*) is offered, where the weight of base rate ($r_{BR}$) would become less meaningful for the investors. As a result, only the debt (bank loan) market is available for SME and marginally creditworthy borrowers.

As an alternative explanation leading to the situation where $r < r_L$ for prominent borrowers, we hypothesize that the risk preference of the investors (particularly households) may swing to a 'risk-neutral/loving' or 'euphoric' position toward the investment in prominent issuers. When the money market reference rate ($r_{IBOR}$) provides an adequate buffer for undertaking the associated risk, their subjective judgment of $r_Q < r$ will possibly lower the coupon rate through accepting the lower spread (*bps*) applied for the bond in the long run. On the contrary, when the money market reference rate decreases, the reduced credit risk buffer may lead the risk preference of the investors to swing back to a 'conservative' or 'risk-averse' strategy for the investment, consequently draining 'risk funds' in financial market. It is considered that the subjective prospective yield ($r_Q$) from the investment in a particular FRN is determined by the money market reference rate, the spread, and the risk preference (denoted by $\theta$). When the risk preference lies in the risk-neutral position, it is considered to be $\theta = 0$. The risk-loving preference would have an effect on accepting the lower yield, while the risk-averse preference would require higher risk premium or keep the investors completely away from the investment. It is worth noting that the risk preference or sentiment even in an individual may possibly swing all the times.

$$r_Q = f(r_{IBOR}, bps, \theta)$$

The coupon rate ($r$) and the floating lending rate ($r_L$) are considered to have a certain realistic upper limit. This is because a higher rate would discourage the issuers (or the borrowers) from raising funds. The spread margin (*bps*) is also considered to have a certain realistic upper limit. This is because the extremely high spread based upon less creditworthy non-rated firms would attract neither any investor nor any conservative bankers.

We hypothesize that the portion of the money market reference rate ($r_{IBOR}$) functions as a buffer for the investors to absorb the issuer's credit risk. An adequate level of buffer may shift the investor's risk preference to a risk-neutral or risk-loving direction, lowering the prospective yield ($r_Q$) and possibly providing more 'risk funds' in the bond market. Under this situation, it is likely that the coupon rate ($r$) would be lower than the floating lending rate ($r_L$) for the firms in the same and a certain range of prominent/acceptable credit risk category. When the market reference rate decreases, the reduced buffer may shift the investor's risk preference to a risk-neutral or risk-averse direction, requiring a relatively higher prospective yield against the coupon rate, resulting in the situation where $r_Q = r$ or $r_Q > r$. This situation would discourage the investors to engage in the bond, or encourage them to leave for the low-risk-low-return type bond, as mentioned earlier. From another perspective, as the market reference rate decreases, the convergence of debt and bond markets is accelerated in a sense that the banks would regain the comparative advantage in mediating funds, though the banks do not necessarily mediate funds.

## 4.   Changes in rent opportunity during the period of QE and ZIRP

In this section we analyze empirical data to test the hypothesis drawn in section 3. First, we would like to examine the changes in the balance sheet of the banking system in Japan. It is seen in Figure 9.5 that contrary to the expectation formed from the QEP that consumer spending will increase facilitated by banks' credit expansion, the overall level of credit from the banking system declined during the entire QE period. Total loans and bills discounted amounted to about JPY475 trillion in 2000, which declined to JPY414 trillion in 2005, an average annual decline of more than 2 per cent. Although the loans from the regional banks remained almost stable during the entire QE period, the city banks experienced an annual decline of about 3 per cent at the same period. Since this cluster of banks is the largest loan provider (about half of the total loans) to the economy, a change in their portfolio changes the overall scenario of the banking system. The declining share of the loan was offset mostly by the purchase of government bonds (Figure 9.5). Government bonds for investment purposes accounted for only 9 per cent (JPY43.3 trillion) of the total loans and bills discounted for the total banking system at the end of March 2000, which increased to 24 per cent (JPY99.57 trillion) at its peak at the end of March 2005.

As mentioned earlier, the BOJ increased the purchase of Japanese government bonds (Figure 9.4) as a mechanism to increase the current account balance, which put an upward pressure on their price, leading to a decline in their yields. In general, the yield on government bond is less than the rate charged on loans. Moreover, an increased demand for government bond will reduce its yield further. Thus it is expected that the overall level of interest income for banks will decline in commensuration with the decline of loan amount and yield on JGB. Indeed, this is obvious from Figures 9.6 and 9.7. Figure 9.6 presents the changes in interest income as percentage of total income. At the beginning of 2000, a temporary upshot of the share of interest income was observed, which was destined to fall sharply until the end of the QE policy in 2006. However, banks compensated their lost interest income by trading securities, mostly government bonds, in the secondary market (Figure 9.6). Trading income as percentage of total income

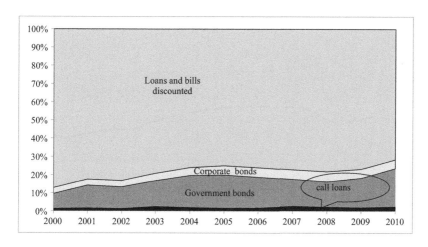

*Figure 9.5* Changes in the bank's asset
Source: BoJ.

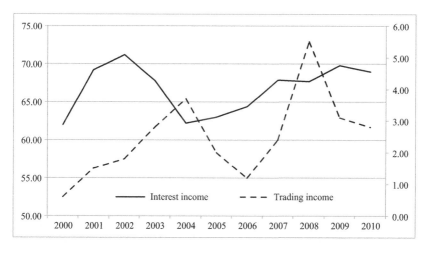

*Figure 9.6* Changes in interest income (left axis) and trading income from securities
(right axis) as a percentage of total income
Source: BoJ.

accounted for less than one per cent in March 2000, which rose to 3.7 per cent in 2004. After declining for a while, the share of trading income rose to 5.5 per cent in 2008. In addition, the gain from the sale of bonds alone amounted to JPY2.3 trillion in 2000, which declined afterward as the market was normalized gradually.

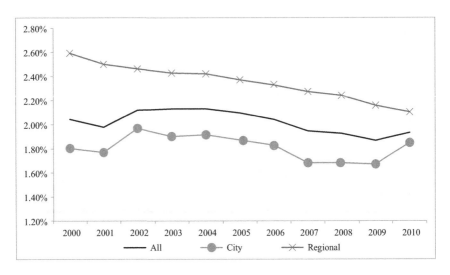

*Figure 9.7* Interest rate spread (as a percentage of total loans)
Source: BoJ.

Table 9.1 shows the changes in (a) interest revenue from lending, (b) revenue from marketable securities, and (c) revenue from selling (dealing) governmental bonds in the major 'Big 3' city banks – Mitsubishi Tokyo UFJ Bank, Mitsui Sumitomo Bank, and Mizuho Bank. Though each bank has its own strategy, it appears that the share of interest revenue from lending did not significantly increase during the period of FY2005 to FY2014. Rather, the share per se has been in a declining trend since the FY2010. On the other hand, it appears that they have been seeking profits by the non-lending activities, including revenue from marketable securities and revenue from selling governmental bonds (particularly observed for Mizuho Bank). We should note that the QEP did not clearly give even the Big 3 an incentive for expanding the profit-base from lending. Rather, the policy may have given them an incentive for seeking profit by the non-lending activities.

Similarly, interest rate spread as a percentage of total loans and bills discounted started declining from the year 2000 (Figure 9.7). IRS declined for both city banks and regional banks. However, the surprising fact is that the degree of decline is sharper for the regional banks than the city banks, despite the fact that the loan exposure of the former did not decline at all over the period. In addition, city banks charged less spread as risk premium than the regional banks, which means that the former cluster of banks serves comparatively less risky borrowers than the latter. In this sense, a convergence of IRS between these two clusters of banks, which was observed at the end of 2010, implies that their risk preference is getting similar.

Table 9.1 Composition of revenue of the three largest banks in Japan

| | FY2005 | | FY2010 | | FY2013 | | FY2014 | |
|---|---|---|---|---|---|---|---|---|
| **Mitsubishi Tokyo UFJ Bank** | | | | | | | | |
| (a) Interest revenue from lending | 787,546 | 35.5 | 996,944 | 37.0 | 977,439 | 33.5 | 986,729 | 34.5 |
| (b) Revenue from marketable securities | 405,407 | 18.3 | 433,249 | 16.1 | 415,873 | 14.2 | 472,622 | 16.5 |
| (c) Profits from selling TB | 44,516 | 2.0 | 268,098 | 10.0 | 268,196 | 9.2 | 207,481 | 7.3 |
| b + c | 449,923 | 20.3 | 701,347 | 26.1 | 684,069 | 23.4 | 680,103 | 23.8 |
| (Losses from selling TB) | 96,875 | 5.9 | 53,097 | 2.6 | 134,417 | 7.0 | 88,967 | 4.6 |
| **Mitsui Sumitomo Bank** | | | | | | | | |
| (a) Interest revenue from lending | 990,853 | 43.3 | 957,181 | 45.4 | 945,454 | 40.4 | 990,485 | 41.8 |
| (b) Revenue from marketable securities | 317,180 | 13.9 | 240,380 | 11.4 | 334,755 | 14.3 | 356,754 | 15.0 |
| (c) Profits from selling TB | 43,102 | 1.9 | 200,478 | 9.5 | 36,761 | 1.6 | 68,406 | 2.9 |
| b + c | 360,282 | 15.8 | 440,858 | 20.9 | 371,516 | 15.9 | 425,160 | 17.9 |
| (Losses from selling TB) | 53,317 | 3.4 | 46,164 | 3.1 | 22,441 | 1.6 | 20,179 | 1.4 |
| **Mizuho Bank** | | | | | | | | |
| (a) Interest revenue from lending | 499,195 | 42.7 | 476,273 | 46.0 | 711,695 | 37.9 | 807,368 | 36.1 |
| (b) Revenue from marketable securities | 95,170 | 8.1 | 116,182 | 11.2 | 274,925 | 14.6 | 327,025 | 14.6 |
| (c) Profits from selling TB | 9,998 | 0.9 | 61,358 | 5.9 | 85,648 | 4.6 | 161,203 | 7.2 |
| b + c | 105,168 | 9.0 | 177,540 | 17.1 | 360,573 | 19.2 | 488,228 | 21.8 |
| (Losses from selling TB) | 22,693 | 2.4 | 21,551 | 2.4 | 57,334 | 4.7 | 91,906 | 5.9 |

Source: Created by authors based on Japanese Bankers Association.

Note: The first and second columns under each year represent the amount in million Japanese yen and share in operating income (cost) respectively.

A declining IRS for the same level of loan exposure implies that the average interest rate fell conforming to the effectiveness of QE policy. However, we offer another explanation, as we mentioned in section 3, that when the base rate declines, lenders prefer low risk-profile borrowers. Thus when the low interest rate fails to increase loan exposure (for regional banks) and at worse leads to decline (for city banks), it can be inferred that financial institutions prefer to be risk-averse. Further evidence can be provided from the fact that the outstanding loans toward small and medium-sized enterprises (SME) dropped sharply – from JPY344.9 trillion in December 1998 to JPY260.3 trillion in December 2003, then to JPY253.1 trillion in December 2009, and finally to JPY247.2 trillion in December 2013 (SMEA, 2005, 2010, 2014; Suzuki, 2011, p. 5). Since loans to SMEs are considered comparatively riskier than the large and medium sized corporate loans, a decline in SME lending during the time of ultra-low interest rate indicates the risk-averse behavior of lenders and proves our hypothesis raised in section 3 that a decline in base rate might drain the risk funds.

We now turn to examine whether lower interest rate would entice investors to invest more. It is mentioned already that the lower interest rate might not stimulate investor's interest if their expected rate of return is not sufficiently realized, which is determined by their subjective sentiment of investment. For instance, an uncertainty over the business environment and future prospect of profitability might prohibit prospective investors to undertake new investment. Data on business confidence survey shows (Figure 9.8) that from 1998 to 2004 business confidence was almost negative over this period. Although the confidence rose for a short span of time, it again experienced a nosedive in 2009. Declining confidence about the business environment would likely have a depressing effect on investment. The data indeed show this effect. After the bubble burst in the early 1990s, manufacturing firms cut their investment substantially. The annual

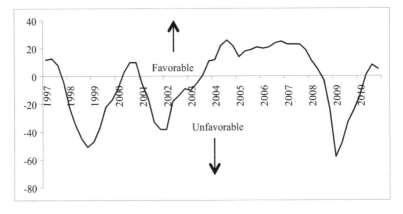

*Figure 9.8* Business condition survey (large enterprise/manufacturing)

Source: Tankan Survey, BoJ.

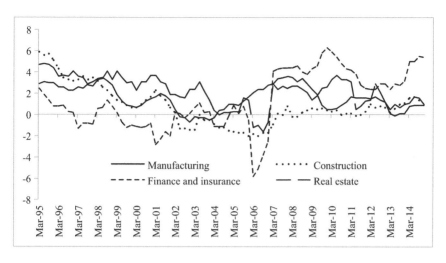

*Figure 9.9* Changes (year-on-year basis) in gross capital stock
Source: Cabinet office.

average decline of investment for the period of 1990 to 2000 was about 4 per cent a year, twice as large as that of non-manufacturing firms (Kang, 2014).

This declining trend of investment continued during the entire QE period. Figure 9.9 portrays the changes in capital stock of four vital sectors of the economy. It can be observed that the capital stock of all these four sectors declined from 1995 to 2006. After a short recovery, the declining trend has been continuing. Kang (2014) argues that because of this sluggish investment by manufacturing firms, the share of this sector in total investment declined to about 30 per cent in the early 2000s, from the peak of 45 per cent in early 1980s.

A lack of investment opportunity or investors' negative subjective judgment about the future business environment made them exceptionally cautions about the future exposure of risk. As a result, Japanese firms have deleveraged significantly over the past two decades (Figure 9.10). Both short-term and long-term borrowings by corporations from the banking system declined until 2005. Long-term borrowing made up more than 20 per cent of total assets for all types of firms in 1999, which declined to less than 15 per cent in 2005. Although the decline for long-term borrowing was halted for a short span of time, short-term borrowing kept declining throughout the study period. Overall, the leverage ratio, measured as total debt to asset ratio, has declined by more than 10 per cent in both manufacturing and non-manufacturing sectors over the last twenty-five years.

In a depressed economic condition, expansionary lending policy by the financial intermediaries is warranted. This was indeed the purpose of QE policy in Japan.

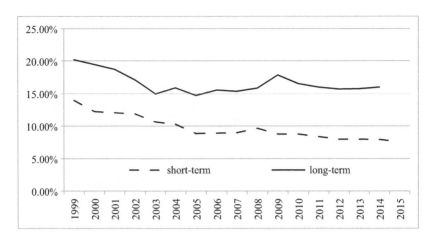

*Figure 9.10* Borrowing by corporations from the banking system (percentage of total assets)

Source: Financial Statement Statistics, Ministry of Finance.

However, as mentioned earlier, the ultra-low interest rate brought about by the ZIRP and QE failed to motivate financial institutions, particularly banks, toward expansionary lending because it was not worth for them to undertake the borrower's credit risk. But rather they diverted their funds toward safety assets, even if the attached yield on those assets was low. Banks considered that the monitoring activities of borrowers were not justified by the low base rate in an uncertain business environment.

## 5.   Rent in the negative interest rate regime

A number of major central banks in Europe have set key policy rates at negative levels in order to further encourage lending. The negative interest rate is believed to make it costly for banks to hold excess reserves at their central banks. Amid negative policy rates, nominal yields on some bonds of highly-rated European governments have also dropped below zero. Explanation for the phenomenon of negative yields includes very low inflation, further 'flight to safety' toward fixed income assets in Europe's core, and – perhaps the main proximate cause – the increased scarcity of highly-rated sovereign bonds eligible for the European Central Bank's asset purchase program (World Bank, 2015).

Negative rates may help boost exports by encouraging currency depreciation and may support lending and domestic demand by further easing credit conditions. On February 16, 2016, the Bank of Japan (BOJ) started the negative rate policy, seemingly to encourage JPY depreciation and easing credit conditions to stimulate Japan's stagnant economy. Just after the announcement of the policy on

January 19, 2016, the FOREX market reacted so that JPY currency was depreciated from the range of 118 JPY/USD to that of 121 JPY/USD. However, the rate was resumed back within just one week. Rather, the trend of JPY appreciation (hit at the range of 110 JPY/USD after around one year and three months interval, and then hit at the range of 106 JPY/USD on April 30, 2016) has been observed. Some market watchers refer to 'external shocks', seemingly in a bad timing for BOJ, including the sluggish crude oil price of giving ill-effects on the Shale Oil development in the United States as well as China's economic slowdown, which may have given the general investors the so-called risk-off sentiment with the risk-averse portfolio selection. According to their logic, the investors would prefer to hold JPY currency under the risk-off sentiment, because JPY currency is regarded as relatively 'safety asset' (Asakura, 2016; Shimizu, 2016). However, since September 2015, Standard & Poor's has cut Japan's long-term credit rating to single A⁺, the same rating for Slovakia and Ireland, saying it sees little chance of the Abe government's strategy turning around the poor outlook for economic growth over the next few years (according to Reuters September 16, 2015). Taking into consideration the negative outlook for Japan's sovereign risk, how can we make sense of the trend of yen appreciation under the risk-off sentiment? We point out that the QE policy may have created a new type of financial sector rent to be captured by US fund providers, which causes the higher volatility of yen currency.

Reiko Tokukatsu, a relative value analyst in BNP Paribas, sounds a note of warning that Japan's quantitative easing (QE) further implemented through the negative interest rate policy has widened the so-called Japan premium, which the Japanese banks have to additionally pay for raising the USD fund in the interbank market. This means that the USD funding cost for the Japanese banks has been increasing (consequently the cost of fund for their customers, mostly the Japanese firms, has also been increasing) in accordance with the downgrading of credit rating for Japan as well as the availability of ample JPY currency though the QE. For more Japanese internationally active firms and banks, the USD funding cost has been more concerned for their business. In fact, according to the survey by the Japan Bank for International Cooperation (JBIC), the overseas production ratio (overseas production/domestic + overseas production) by Japanese manufacturers has increased to 39.6 per cent in FY2015 from 24.6 per cent in FY2001 (JBIC, 2015). The overseas income ratio by Japanese mega-banks such as Sumitomo-Mitsui Banking Group has reached the level of 40 per cent (Tokukatsu, 2015). It makes sense that the Japanese internationally active firms and banks would take action to keep higher liquidity in the USD currency when they face external shocks or uncertainties.

Tokukatsu (2015) explains an instrument of raising fund in the interbank market – Foreign Exchange Swap, or FOREX Swap, by offering JPY currency to take USD currency. In comparison with the outright lending/borrowing, mutual lending/borrowing would facilitate the interbank deals because it can reduce the credit risk of the counter party, for whom the offered JPY currency is regarded

Day 1 (Spot transaction)

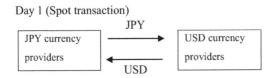

Day 2 (Forward transaction – for instance, 3 months or 6 months or 1 year later)

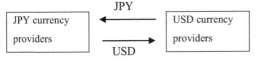

*Figure 9.11* Currency swap

as a kind of security or mortgage. Foreign exchange swap, or FOREX swap, is a simultaneous purchase and sale (the so-called buy-sell transaction) of identical amounts of one currency for another, with two different value dates (normally 'spot' to 'forward'; see Figure 9.11 for the illumination). Foreign exchange swap allows sums of a certain currency to be used to fund charges designated in another currency without acquiring foreign exchange risk.

What is the mechanism for determining the forward exchange rate? The relationship between spot and forward is known as the interest rate parity, which states that

$$F = s\left(\frac{1 + rdT}{1 + rfT}\right)$$

where

- F = forward rate
- S = spot rate
- $r_d$ = simple interest rate of the term currency
- $r_f$ = simple interest rate of the base currency
- T = tenor (calculated according to the appropriate day count convention)

Consider the following market circumstance: The USD interest rate is 2 per cent per annum, while the JPY interest rate is 0.5 per cent per annum. Spot foreign exchange rate is 100 JPY/USD. If we invest the money in US banks, we will get USD 1.02 [1 × (1 + 0.02)] one year later. If we invest the money in Japanese banks, we will get JPY 100.5 [100 × (1 + 0.005)] one year later. Upon the market mechanism as interest rate parity, the forward rate is to be calculated to 98.53 JPY/USD [100.5 / 1.02]. The currency with lower interest rate is to be appreciated in the forward transaction (see Figure 9.12 for the illumination).

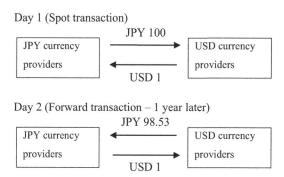

*Figure 9.12* Currency swap pricing upon the interest rate parity

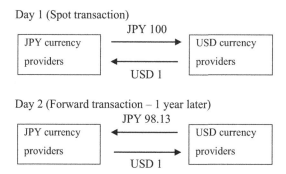

*Figure 9.13* Currency swap pricing upon the interest rate parity plus Japan premium

When the demand of raising USD fund is getting stronger (or the relative value of JPY currency is getting lower or the credit rating for Japanese banks is being downgraded), the USD currency providers would request 'premium' in the spot-forward swap. According to Tokukatsu (2015), the Japan premium for raising the USD fund has reached to the level of 20 bp (basis points) for one month transactions and 40 bp for one year transactions as of July 2015. This circumstance would bring further JPY appreciation in the real forward exchange transaction – in this sample case, 98.13 [98.53 – 0.40] JPY/USD (see Figure 9.13). JPY 0.40 is construed as 0.4 per cent or 40 bp as additional spread margin for JPY 100. This means that the Japanese banks pay the additional cost of 0.4 per cent (the so-called Japan premium) for raising a one year USD fund, while the US currency providers enjoy the additional premium of 40 bp (see Suzuki, 2009, pp. 157–162; Tokukatsu, 2015, pp. 182–185).

The forward points or swap points are quoted as the difference between forward and spot, $F - S$. The value of the swap points is basically proportional to the interest rate differential. The sudden change in the forward rate may influence the spot rate. Under the mechanism of interest rate parity, in the case of the occurrence of external shocks under conditions of uncertainty leading to widening Japan premium (more Japanese banks and firms wish to reserve the higher liquidity in USD fund), the real forward rate with further appreciation of JPY currency would possibly move the spot rate to the direction of JPY appreciation if the market interest rate differential remains unchanged.

For the USD fund providers who receive the premium (including the Japanese premium), the previously mentioned market circumstance gives them the opportunity to raise the JPY fund with substantially sub-Libor. They would prefer to invest in the Japanese government bond (JGB), even though the yield on JGB is negative, so far as the Japan premium can absorb the negative spread margin on JGB. According to Japan Bond Trading Co. Ltd., the yield curve estimated from the prices of JGB with the remaining period of 1 year is quoted as –0.225 per cent (22.5 bp) in the secondary market on April 28, 2016. If the US fund providers can enjoy the Japanese premium of 40 bp by offering the USD fund for one year (receiving a JPY fund during the period), they can enjoy the fixed margin of 17.5 bp (40 bp – 22.5 bp) additionally on the spot-forward premium by simply investing in JGB during the period with free of credit risk (only the sovereign risk[1]). This is the financial sector rent to be captured by USD fund providers under Japan's negative interest rate policy. Under this situation, ironically, the USD fund providers may also support the negative interest rate policy by BOJ.

Investors may hold instruments with negative returns for various reasons, such as for speculative and arbitrage reasons, institutional and regulatory requirements, or simply for a lack of alternative assets.

The World Bank (2015) points out that negative rates may erode bank profitability by narrowing banks' net interest margins (the gap between commercial banks' lending and deposit rates), since banks may be unwilling to pass through negative deposit rates to their customers to avoid the erosion of their customer base. On the other hand, banks can realize capital gains on the sale of their government bonds to central banks and, in doing so, bolster their capital position and therefore their capacity to extend loans. However, in the case of Japan's QE including the negative interest rate policy, we should not overlook that the policy may create a new type of financial sector rent opportunity to be captured by a USD fund provider, in exchange for making it costly for Japanese banks and firms to raise the USD fund. Also we should note that Japan's QE with the negative interest rate policy may lead the trend of JPY appreciation when the so-called Japanese premium is being widened under conditions of intensifying uncertainty.

## 6.   Conclusions

Keynes mentioned in the final chapter ("Concluding notes on the social philosophy towards which the General Theory might lead") of the General Theory, "thus it is to our best advantage to reduce the rate of interest to that point relatively to the schedule of the marginal efficiency of capital at which there is full employment" (Keynes, 1936, p. 375). Perhaps, in pursuit of this spirit, developed economies, including the United States, United Kingdom, and Japan have experimented heavily with the QE as an instrument to continuously stimulate their respective economies. However, this policy has failed more often than not to achieve the intended objectives. Although various explanations have been offered already by the burgeoning literature, the effects of QE on the bank rents and its eventual consequences on banking channel as transmission mechanism were not discussed. This chapter has attempted to fill this gap. This chapter has argued that the scale of investment is not always promoted by a low rate of interest as Keynes assumed in the General Theory. Keynes suggested that we aim in practice at "an increase in the volume of capital until it ceases to be scarce, so that the functionless investor will no longer receive a bonus" (Keynes, 1936, p. 376). While the spirit of this statement historically seems correct, there is no guarantee that the abundance of capital will ensure its effective utilization. Besides the availability of sufficient funds, screening and monitoring activities still matter because the failure of monitoring by (functional) lenders and investors would exacerbate the principal-agent problem or the general uncertainty from which lenders suffer, and thereby restrict the optimal allocation of risk funds. In our view, lenders and investors need a certain buffer or cushion for providing risk funds – in other words, for responding to the fundamental uncertainty.

Our analysis shows that banks' interest spread as a cushion to absorb the borrowers' credit risk squeezed since the inception of the ZIRP in 1999, and the declining trend continued throughout the entire QE regime. The narrower base rate has first de-motivated banks to absorb the risk and, second, diverted them away from the risky investment. As a result, banks persistently sought for diverse sources of income as compensation to their lost interest spread. The trading of government bond was one of such sources. Before the market completely adjusted with the QE effects, banks capitalized a huge amount simply from trading government bonds in the secondary market. Moreover, the cheaper deposit has enabled banks to materialize a positive return by investing in government bonds (carry trade), despite the fact that the central bank's purchase of JGB sliced the yield down. The combined effect was that banks, instead of expanding their loan exposure to new and existing borrowers, adopted risk-averse behavior which apparently acted as a hindrance toward achieving the objectives of QE policy. Based on these findings, we can offer some policy implications.

First, a wholesale reduction in interest rate will not necessarily accompany higher level of investment. From the lenders perspective, our analysis suggests that there may exist an appropriate level of market reference rate, which can encourage the investors to absorb the relatively wider range of credit risk in the bond market. An extremely higher market rate would discourage the borrowers from raising funds, while a lower market rate would drain 'risk funds' in the bond market. The appropriate level of market rate may stand on a narrow range of a 'knife's edge', although the level per se does not always guarantee the optimal allocation of financial resources.

Second, while it is to be recognized that the lower interest rate is likely to stimulate private investment, the investor's confidence is also a key determinant in this regard. Once confidence is restored, the availability of funds at a cheaper cost is likely to pay off. As such, the monetary authority should take more care of the side effects stemming from squeezing the interest rate alone. It is obvious that as the duration of quantitative easing is prolonged, its side effects get severer. Under the unprecedented QEP, it is suggested that the function of the rate of interest as an incentive for lenders and investors to provide risk funds to the future potentials should be carefully reviewed.

## Note

1  For the calculation of the required capital adequacy under the Basel accord, the risk weight for the A+ rated sovereign is 20 per cent. Therefore, the risk adjusted return of 17.5 bp is calculated to 87.5 bp [17.5 bp / 0.2]. If they place the JPY fund to Japanese banks with the credit rating of above A– on the condition of zero deposit rate, since the risk weight for the asset is 50 per cent, the risk-adjusted return in that case is calculated to 80 bp [40 bp / 0.5]. For some US fund providers, the investment in JGB would be more attractive.

# Conclusion

The importance of finance for economic development has long been recognized by the nascent financial literature. Two issues are at the center of the current debate – financial inclusion and financial stability. Evidences are presented in this book, showing the level of financial underdevelopment in many developing and underdeveloped countries. Furthermore, evidence has been drawn from various financial crises to illustrate that financial crunches are recurrent in nature and independent of a country's level of financial development. Policymakers and regulators have initiated various strategies to avoid a possible crisis and how to limit the macroeconomic damages of a crisis in case it happens. Furthermore, various forms of financial innovations have evolved to tap the financially unserved and stranded population under the umbrella of greater financial services. This book is an attempt to provide another dimension to the debate. It reinstates the role of rent on financial deepening and financial stability.

The debate on the role of financial sector rent has been advanced well theoretically. However, the theory needs to be updated, as some new economic realities have emerged which put the conventional theory into a test of empirical validity. Islamic banking is one of such cases, about which the concerned literature says nothing. Second, the conventional rent model has not been tested empirically against the reality to an extent that can help us draw reliable policy inferences. More specifically, enough cases are not studied by the existing literature. Echoing with the core of the financial restraint model which advocates for creating and maintaining financial sector rent, this book offers several contributions both theoretically and empirically to the concerned literature.

Rent 'as excess income' for a financial or banking sector is considered in the financial restraint model as an incentive for the proper screening and monitoring of borrowers. Consistent with this approach, this book analyzes and elaborates the concept of rent delving into the vast stock of existing literature. In so doing, it relates the concept of rent to the notion of profit portrayed in the classical and new classical scholarships. In view of the Marxian and classical economists, profit is considered as a surplus or residual income which remains as leftover after factors of production are paid off. Similarly, the new classical analysis of profit argues that residual income is required for agents to undertake necessary monitoring activities, without which there is a lack of social optimum level of monitoring. This book integrates these concepts and agrees on the idea that excess profit as rent is required for managerial incentive. Moreover, we disintegrate the typical concept of rent into different parts, such as operating rent, macroeconomic rent, and price rent. The rationale of disintegrating the notion of rent, as stated earlier, is believed to help policymakers and regulators formulate policies addressing a specific segment of rent. Besides theoretical underpinnings, the greater strength of this book lies on collecting and analyzing an assorted number of cases from developed, emerging, and developing economies. Moreover, this book has explored the applicability of the conventional rent-seeking model to previously unexplored branches of economics. It has investigated the effects of monetary policy, especially zero and negative interest rates, on banks' performance, considering rent as an incentive framework.

The rationale of rents for financial institutions is argued based on the assumption that financial markets are imperfect. Different schools of thoughts which shed light on the causes and remedies for financial market imperfections are analyzed. The New Keynesian or the mainstream economists' view is that the financial market fails to reach equilibrium due to the presence of market frictions, including asymmetry of information and transaction cost. Thus the school is concerned as to how asymmetry of information can be mitigated or how the associated transaction cost of information collection and monitoring can be reduced. If these conditions are better managed, our economy would get closer to an equilibrium where more financial resources are mediated for economic progress and perhaps for alleviation of poverty. While the previous arguments cannot be invoked, the New Keynesian view has failed to recognize the role of uncertainty hampering our economy from reaching equilibrium. Drawing upon the contribution of the post-Keynesian school, it is argued that the market failure particularly in credit/financial market is intrinsic due to fundamental uncertainty. Even if the asymmetry of information is attenuated and the magnitude of transaction cost is reduced, there is no guarantee that our economy will get closer to the equilibrium. Thus, while market frictions are necessarily the causes of market imperfection, the role of uncertainty is also to be emphasized for designing appropriate policy prescriptions.

The arguments of this book rely on both of these understandings. It explicitly focuses on how financial intermediation can cope with the given level of market frictions and uncertainty. Credible lending by financial intermediaries requires tighter screening and rigorous monitoring. Equivalently, they need an extra cushion to absorb the shocks stemming from fundamental uncertainty. In a competitive market, the profit margin between lending and deposit rate might not be large enough to help intermediaries economically deal with these issues. It is shown in various chapters that a lion's share of financial assets is owned by private financial institutions, and they will always attempt to maximize their profit within the existing legal framework. Screening and monitoring are costly, and private banks might fail to undertake these activities to such an extent that will ensure financial stability. As private entities, they tend to tradeoff between profit and transaction cost. The trading off may result in a limited amount of loan exposure of banks, only to those projects for which the cost of screening and monitoring is comparatively low. Or the effort of screening and monitoring will be less than required for prudential lending. If so, the chances of non-performing loan will be high, which can lead some banks to bankruptcy. It has been argued that a troubled bank can trigger a countrywide bank-run through its ripple effects. Thus incentive is to be provided for overall financial soundness.

From this vantage point, this book advances its analysis, arguing that bank rent opportunity, mainly created and maintained by the regulatory framework, should be given to banks as an incentive mainly for absorbing the transaction cost. Furthermore, the rent opportunity would function as a buffer or cushion to absorb the unexpected loss arising from uncertainty. In this sense, the bank-rent framework is a pragmatic approach to be applied in the financial markets.

Besides analyzing and explaining the previous logic on the concept of bank rent and its necessity for financial development, one of the salient contributions of this book is that it frames the concept of Islamic bank rent. Although the traditional bank rent model remains silent on the issue, this book argues that rent is essential for Islamic banks for various reasons. Specifically, Islamic banks are operating parallel to conventional banks in many Muslim and non-Muslim countries. Both clusters of banks compete each other in the same market. However, Islamic banks have to comply with Islamic principles (*Shari'ah*), an extra requirement beyond the conventional banking practices. A failure with this principle from the concerned bank might motivate depositors to withdraw their funds. This is termed as the 'displaced commercial risk'. *Shari'ah* compliance surely imposes extra cost compared to conventional banking practices. Moreover, the mode of financing in Islamic banks is involved with profit-and-loss sharing contracts, which are practically more risky than the conventional pre-determined interest rate financing. Thus Islamic banks need an extra cushion, termed in this book as $\alpha$ or Islamic bank rent.

Based on this theoretical framework, this book has accumulated a handful of cases to analyze the rent-effect on financial institutions. Both Islamic and conventional banks have been analyzed within and between classes. The additional major contributions of this book are summarized as follows.

First, the role of rent as incentive mechanism for financial institutions has been reaffirmed in this book. The Chinese banking system provides a strong support to the bank rent hypothesis. It has been found that in the post-1978 period, banks in China were repressed particularly by transferring rent from state-owned commercial banks to state-owned corporations. Until the formulation of the *Bo Gai Dai* policy in 1982, banks' interest margin was substantially negative, which resulted in huge accumulation of non-performing loans in the banking system. Commercial banks did not have a sufficient buffer to undertake prudential monitoring activities toward the borrowers. Despite these odds, the Chinese economy grew rapidly in the post-1978 reform era, which might construe that bank rent was irrelevant or a redundant policy option for the growing China. Explanation of this hypothesis is provided, showing that banks started emerging as profitable institutions, gradually recovering from financially submerged condition when directive and policy lending were replaced by commercial lending in the post-1982 period. Furthermore, they were able to substantially reduce the level of non-performing loans as well as increase profitability during the regime when positive interest rate spread. These reforms, however, accelerated the growth momentum of the Chinese economy, proving the validity of bank-rent effect. Moreover, creating rent for banks in the initial reform period could have accelerated economic growth more than China actually realized during the period.

Although the Sri Lankan case does not explicitly support the conventional notion of bank rent, a modification of the concept of rent indeed fits the case. It is shown in the context of Sri Lanka that although the interest rate spread of the banking system declined, the profitability did not decline; but rather increased consistently. To explain this anomaly, the conventional bank rent is disintegrated to price rent, operating rent, and macroeconomic rent. The decline of the interest rate spread was reflected in the price rent of Sri Lankan banks. In contrast, the operating rent and macroeconomic rent become more favorable due to improvements in operating conditions in the banking system, alongside the relative political stability of the country which emerged particularly after the ending of the prolonged civil war. These operating and macroeconomic rents actually boosted the profitability of banks despite the eroding price rent. Thus the effectiveness of rent as incentive mechanism remains valid.

Second, although various hypotheses have been put forth by the nascent Islamic banking literature to explain *murabaha* syndrome (the concentration of a particular mode of financing by Islamic banks), with the application of the bank rent approach this book has provided an additional dimension for understanding the problem properly and finding a suitable solution. It is natural that incentive will govern agents' behavior. Thus the preference of Islamic banks for this particular mode of financing can reasonably be explained by the bank rent approach. Two important dimensions of Islamic banks have been considered in this analysis. First, Islamic banks have to incur additional cost of compliance with the Islamic *Shari'ah*. Second, the Islamic mode of financing is based on PLS equity based partnership, which entails higher volatility in return. As a result, Islamic banks must earn sufficient rent to cover the extra cost of compliance and provide a cushion against the added uncertainty embedded with the pure equity based financing. Since this opportunity is absent at present, it is natural for Islamic banks to be biased to a particular mode of financing that involves with less uncertainty. *Murabaha* or markup pricing contract is therefore a logical response to the incentive provided by the existing institutional setup. This provides a credible explanation on '*murabaha* syndrome'. To check the validity of this claim, data are analyzed from some Asian countries such as Bangladesh, Pakistan, Malaysia, Indonesia, and the GCC countries.

No doubt, Islamic banks should challenge the participatory financing; otherwise their *raison d'être* cannot be justified. It has been argued that the current mode of profit-and-loss sharing provides, in practice, an idea of the difficulty in assuming the equity-based financing. Thus it is impractical to expect the acceleration of the participatory financing without preserving a much higher margin for security to cover further profit-and-loss sharing risk. This book also sheds light on how to accomplish this objective.

The Islamic mode of finance is a comparatively new innovation in many countries. Therefore this segment of the financial system is not as developed as the conventional one. If so, uniform baking regulations may unevenly hamper the growth of Islamic banks, given their higher cost of operations. Thus a dual approach of a financial system which creates rent opportunities for learning initially might be required. Once the Islamic segment of the financial system achieves a certain development threshold, regulators may choose to leave it to free competition. Thereafter, weak banks, whether Islamic or conventional, would be wiped out of the market.

Third, this book applies the bank-rent model to a new branch of economics, the monetary policy. It has been shown that due to various financial messes across the world, central banks of some advanced economies have attempted some unorthodox tools of monetary policy, including quantitative easing (QE) and zero interest rate policy (ZIRP). These tools also have failed to serve the intended purpose. As a result, the European Central Bank, Bank of Japan, and other smaller European economies have ventured for implementation of negative interest rate policy, once an uncharted territory for central banks. Our analysis on the experience of Japan during the recent QE as well as zero and negative interest rate regimes offers two important inferences relevant to bank-rent. First, the ultra-low interest rate (base or reference rate) adversely affects banks' rent. Lower spread or rent motivates banks to be more conservative in risk taking, because the base rate is so low that banks consider it unrealistic to prefer projects with a high risk-premium to projects with a low risk-premium. This tendency may drain the risk fund to safer assets; particularly, banks attempt to compensate their lost rent opportunity mainly by trading government bonds in the secondary markets. Second, it is predicted that the negative interest rate policy will follow the suit of QE and ZIRP because banks, during the negative interest rate regime, are forced to increase their lending. But due to the squeeze of rent opportunity, they would lose the incentive to challenge new risks and uncertainty. Thus banks' inability to pass the cost to their customers implies that new borrowers will be less attractive to them, and it will be difficult to increase lending among the existing borrowers in a saturated market.

The screening and monitoring of borrowers are critical for financial institutions in developing countries, particularly because borrowers in these economies are mostly firms that are small in size and without any credible credit rating. Financial institutions have to undertake rigorous screening and monitoring activities for successful lending. In the absence of sizable rent, these activities will be loosely performed, and credit will be unnecessarily rationed. As a result, rent as a policy option can be put into the priority list as far as the banking sector stability and deepening are concerned. Government can create rent for privately managed banks by setting the ceiling for deposit rate and the floor for lending rate (if required). At the same time, rents should be maintained by limiting excess competition because fierce competition among financial institutions in the developing stage of finance may create financial fragility and financial exclusion. Rent, thus created and maintained, should function as a managerial incentive toward monitoring borrowers and expansion of financial infrastructures. Even in an intervention-free economy, financial markets rarely reach the stage of perfect equilibrium. As a consequence, the welfare loss arising from restricted deposit and/or lending rates is expected not to be so high for the society. On the other hand, the lack of financial infrastructure may thwart the purpose of financial inclusion. In this sense, rent will have a welfare enhancing effect on society.

Of course, government should monitor the financial institutions because they may suffer from a moral hazard or free-riding problem in a less competitive environment. Monitoring from the part of the government may be costly, but if the restraint policy can be properly implemented, the positive effect of rent is likely to outweigh the cost. It will be fairly easy for the government to follow the 'carrot' (rent as incentive) and 'stick' (possible punishment in case of deviation from the principles) policy because financial institutions and the government rely heavily on each other for various purposes.

One critical challenge to the bank-rent argument is that rent should be dissipated once the financial system has reached the maturity stage. The mainstream literature of rent argues that phasing rent out would be difficult because incumbents, those who get the benefit from the rent, may resist the change. However, we recommend that other necessities of the economy should be carefully scrutinized before phasing rent out. Sustainable economic growth of frontier economies hinges critically on successful innovation, which in turn depends on investment in R&D. Given the intense competition in matured markets of developed economies, investors are increasingly exposed to fundamental uncertainty. From the perspective of banks, frontier economies make monitoring more difficult, but such activities are crucially important for the economy. Many advanced countries have attempted to increase investment through initiating QE and zero or negative interest rate policy. Such unconventional monetary policy is believed to make credit cheaper. Contrary to the expectation, some of these policies have already proved to be unsuccessful because they have failed to produce enough rent (given the low base rate or reference rate) to incentivize banks toward financing innovative projects. Thus before phasing rent out, once a country has achieved the target level of financial deepening, other necessity of rents should be carefully studied.

It is time to conclude our argument. Financial markets are complex in nature. Moreover, the dimensions of their complexities have further increased by the unprecedented level of financial liberalization in the twenty-first century. There is no scope to deny that financial markets are more integrated today than ever before. Therefore a cohesive analysis of a particular financial problem is essential to draw any valid inferences. Keeping this in mind, this book has analyzed relevant cases in a comparative and dialectic way. Although most cases in this volume are consisted of countries in Asia, conclusions drawn here are general and can be applied to similar cases. Of course, further research exploring more countries from other parts of the world could contribute to develop a general theory of financial sector rent. Toward this direction, the current volume is the first step.

# References

Abdul-Rahman, A., Abdul Latif, R., Muda, R., and Abdullah, M. A. (2014) 'Failure and Potential of Profit-loss Sharing Contracts: A Perspective of New Institutional, Economic (NIE) Theory', *Pacific-Basin Finance Journal, 28*, pp. 136–151.

Ahmad, E., and Malik, A. (2009) 'Financial Sector Development and Economic Growth: An Empirical Analysis of Developing Countries', *Journal of Economic Cooperation and Development, 30*(1), pp. 17–40.

Ahumada, L. A., and Fuentes, J. R. (2004) 'Banking Industry and Monetary Policy: An Overview', in L. A. Ahumada and J. R. Fuentes (Eds.) *Banking Market Structure and Monetary Policy* (Vol. 7). Santiago, Chile: Central Bank of Chile, pp. 1–26.

Alchian, A. A., and H. Demsetz (1972) 'Production, Information Costs, and Economic Organization', *American Economic Review, 62*(5), pp. 777–795.

Al-Hassan, A., Khamis, M., and Oulidi, N. (2010) 'The GCC Banking Sector: Topography and Analysis', *IMF Working Paper No. 10/87*. Retrieved from: www.imf.org/external/pubs/ft/wp/2010/wp1087.pdf (last accessed on September 2015).

Allen, F., and Gale, D. (1995) 'A Welfare Comparison of Intermediaries and Financial Markets in Germany and the US', *European Economic Review, 39*(2), pp. 179–209. http://dx.doi.org/10.1016/0014-2921(94)00095-H

Allen, F., and Gale, D. (1997) 'Financial Markets, Intermediaries, and Intertemporal Smoothing', *Journal of Political Economy, 105*(3), pp. 523–546.

Altunbas, Y., Evans, L., and Molyneux, P. (2001) 'Bank Ownership and Efficiency', *Journal of Money, Credit and Banking, 33*(4), pp. 926–954.

Amirzadeh, R., and Shoorvarzy, R. (2013) 'Prioritizing Service Quality Factors in Iranian Islamic Banking Using a Fuzzy Approach', *International Journal of Islamic and Middle Eastern Finance and Management, 6*(1), pp. 64–78.

Amor-Tapia, B., Fanjul, J. L., and Tascón, M. T. (2010) 'Country Creditor Rights, Information Sharing, and Commercial Banks' Profitability', *Czech Journal of Economics and Finance, 60*(4), pp. 336–354.

Aoki, M. (1994) 'Monitoring Characteristics of the Main Bank System: An Analytical and Developmental View', in M. Aoki and H. Patrick (Eds.) *The Japanese Main Bank System: Its Relevance for Developing and Transforming Economies*. Oxford: Oxford University Press, pp. 109–141.

Aoki, M., and Saxonhouse, G. (2000) *Finance, Governance, and Competitiveness in Japan*, Oxford: Oxford University Press.

Ariff, M. (2014) 'Whither Islamic Banking?' *The World Economy, 37*(6), pp. 733–746.

Arrow, K. J. (1974) *The Limits of Organization*. New York: W. W. Norton and Co.

Asakura, K. (2016) *Sekai Keizai no Trend ga Kawatta* (in Japanese). Tokyo: Gento sha.

Asian Development Bank. (2005) *Sri Lanka: Financial Sector Assessment.* Manila: Asian Development Bank.

Auty, R. M. (1993) *Sustaining Development in Mineral Economies: The Resource Curse Thesis.* London and New York: Routledge.

Avkiran, N. K. (1999) 'The Evidence on Efficiency Gains: The Role of Mergers and the Benefits to the Public', *Journal of Banking and Finance, 23*(7), pp. 991–1013.

Avkiran, N. K. (2006) 'Developing Foreign Bank Efficiency Models for DEA Grounded in Finance Theory', *Socio-Economic Planning Sciences, 40*(4), pp. 275–296.

Ayub, M. (2007) *Understanding Islamic Finance.* Chichester: Wiley & Sons.

Azariadis, C., and Smith, B. D. (1996) 'Private Information, Money, and Growth: Indeterminacy, Fluctuations, and the Mundell-Tobin Effect', *Journal of Economic Growth, 1*(3), pp. 309–332.

Baddeley, M. C. (December 2008) 'Poverty, Armed Conflict and Financial Instability', *Cambridge Working Papers in Economics No. 0857.*

Bagehot, W. (1873) *Lombard Street* (1962 ed.). Homewood, IL: Richard D. Irwin.

Balasooriya, A. F., Alam, Q., and Coghill, K. (2008) 'Market-Based Reforms and Privatization in Sri Lanka', *International Journal of Public Sector Management, 21*(1), pp. 58–73.

Bangladesh Bank. (2012) *Annual Report 2011–2012.* Dhaka, Bangladesh: Bangladesh Bank. Retrieved from: www.bb.org.bd/pub/annual/anreport/ar1112/index1112.php

Bank Negara Malaysia (BNM). (2011) *Financial Sector Blueprint 2011–2020: Strengthening Our Future.* Kuala Lumpur: Bank Negara Malaysia.

Bank Negara Malaysia (BNM). (2014) *Financial Stability and Payment Systems Report 2014.* Kuala Lumpur: Bank Negara Malaysia.

Barajas, A., Steiner, R., and Salazar, N. (1999) 'Interest Spreads in Banking in Colombia, 1974–1996', *International Monetary Fund Staff Papers, 46*, pp. 196–224.

Barro, R. J. (1995) 'Inflation and Economic Growth', *NBER Working Paper No. 5326.* Retrieved from: www.nber.org/papers/w5326.pdf

Beck, T. (2011) 'The Role of Finance in Economic Development: Benefits, Risks, and Politics', *European Banking Center Discussion Paper No. 2011–038.* Retrieved from: https://papers.ssrn.com/sol3/papers.cfm?abstract_id=1974471 (last accessed on January 2016).

Beck, T., Demirguc-Kunt, A., and Levine, R. (2001) 'Law, Politics, and Finance', *World Bank Policy Research Working Paper No. 2585.*

Beck, T., Demirguc-Kunt, A., and Peria, M. S. (2007) 'Reaching Out: Access to and Use of Banking Services across Countries', *Journal of Financial Economics, 85*(1), pp. 234–266.

Belongia, M. T., and Ireland, P. N. (2015) 'Interest Rates and Money in the Measurement of Monetary Policy', *Journal of Business & Economic Statistics, 33*(2), pp. 255–269.

Bencivenga, V. R., and B. D. Smith (1991) 'Financial Intermediation and Endogenous Growth', *Review of Economic Studies* 58(2): 195–209.

Berger, A. N., and Mester, L. J. (1997) 'Inside the Black Box: What Explains Differences in the Efficiencies of Financial Institutions?', *Journal of Banking & Finance, 21*(7), pp. 895–947.

Berger, A. N., and Mester, L. J. (2003) 'Explaining the Dramatic Changes in Performance of US Banks: Technological Change, Deregulation, and Dynamic Changes in Competition', *Journal of Financial Intermediation*, 12(1), pp. 57–95.

Berglof, E., and Bolton, P. (2005) 'The Great Divide and beyond: Financial Architecture in Transition', in C. A. E. Goodhart (Ed.) *Financial Development and Economic Growth: Explaining the Links*. Basingstoke: Palgrave Macmillan, pp. 106–134.

Berkmen, P. S. (2012) 'Bank of Japan's Quantitative and Credit Easing: Are They Now More Effective', *International Monetary Fund Working Paper # 12/2*.

Bernanke, B. (1988) 'Monetary Policy Transmission: Through Money or Credit?', *Business Review* (November/December), *11*, pp. 3–11.

Bernanke, B., and Reinhart, V. R. (2004) 'Conducting Monetary Policy at Very Low Short-Term Interest Rates', *American Economic Review*, 94(2), pp. 5–90.

Bernanke, B., Reinhart, V., and Sack, B. (2004) 'Monetary Policy Alternatives at the Zero Bound: An Empirical Assessment', *Brookings Papers on Economic Activity*, 2, pp. 1–100.

Bhambra, H. (2007) 'Supervisory Implications of Islamic Finance in the Current Regulatory Environment', in S. Archer and R. A. Karim (Eds.) *Islamic Finance: The New Regulatory Challenge*. Singapore: John Wiley and Sons, pp. 198–212.

Bhattacharya, S., and Thakor, A. V. (1993) 'Contemporary Banking Theory', *Journal of Financial Intermediation*, 3(1), pp. 2–50. doi:10.1006/jfin.1993.1001

Bhattacharyya, A., Lovell, C. A. K., and Sahay, P. (1997) 'The Impact of Liberalization on the Productive Efficiency of Indian Commercial Banks', *European Journal of Operational Research*, 98(2), pp. 332–345.

Binhadi. (1995) *Financial System Deregulation, Banking Development, and Monetary Policy*. Jakarta: Institut Bankir Indonesia.

Blattman, C., and Miguel, E. (2010) 'Civil War', *Journal of Economic Literature*, 48(1), pp. 3–57.

Blinder, A. S. (2010) 'Quantitative Easing: Entrance and Exit Strategies', *Federal Reserve Bank of St. Louis Review*, 92(6), pp. 465–479.

Bloch, H., and Tang, S. H. K. (2003) 'The Role of Financial Development in Economic Growth', *Progress in Development Studies*, 3(3), pp. 243–251.

Boivin, J., Kiley, M. T., and Mishkin, F. S. (2010) 'How Has the Monetary Transmission Mechanism Evolved Over Time?', *NBER, Working Paper # 15879*. Retrieved from: www.nber.org/papers/w15879 (last accessed on October 2015).

Botric, V., and Slijepcevic, S. (2008) 'Economic Growth in South-Eastern Europe: The Role of the Banking Sector', *Post-Communist Economies*, 20(2), pp. 253–262.

Bouffard, S., and Carment, D. (2006) 'The Sri Lanka Peace Process', *Journal of South Asian Development*, 1(2), pp. 151–177.

Calderón, C., and Liu, L. (2003) 'The Direction of Causality between Financial Development and Economic Growth', *Journal of Development Economics*, 72(1), pp. 321–334.

Calomiris, C. W., and Haber, S. H. (2014) *Fragile by Design: The Political Origins of Banking Crises and Scarce Credit*. Princeton: Princeton University Press.

Campbell, T. S., and Kracaw, W. A. (1980) 'Information Production, Market Signalling, and the Theory of Financial Intermediation', *Journal of Finance*, 35(4), pp. 863–882. doi:10.2307/2327206

Caprio, G., and Klingebiel, D. (2002) 'Episodes of Systemic and Borderline Banking Crises', in D. Klingebiel and L. Laeven (Eds.) *Managing the Real and Fiscal Effects of Banking Crises*. World Bank Discussion Paper # 428, pp. 31–49.

CBSL. (1998) *Central Bank of Sri Lanka Annual Report*. Central Bank of Sri Lanka.

CBSL. (2001) *Central Bank of Sri Lanka Annual Report*. Central Bank of Sri Lanka.

CBSL. (2002) *Central Bank of Sri Lanka Annual Report*. Central Bank of Sri Lanka.

CBSL (2010) *Central Bank of Sri Lanka Annual Report 2010*. Colombo: Central Bank of Sri Lanka. Retrieved from: www.cbsl.gov.lk/pics_n_docs/10_pub/_docs/efr/annual_report/AR2010/English/content.htm

Chang, C. E., Hasan, I., and Hunter, W. C. (1998) 'Efficiency of Multinational Banks: An Empirical Investigation', *Applied Financial Economics*, 8(6), pp. 689–696.

Chong, B., and Liu, M. (2009) 'Islamic Banking: Interest-Free or Interest-Based?' *Pacific-Basin Finance Journal*, 17(1), pp. 125–144.

Çizakça, M. (2011) *Islamic Capitalism and Finance: Origins, Evolution and the Future*. Cheltenham: Edward Elgar Publishing.

Claessens, S., and Laeven, L. (2005) 'Financial Dependence, Banking Sector Competition, and Economic Growth', *Journal of the European Economic Association*, 3(1), pp. 179–207.

Clarke, G., Cull, R., Martinez Peria, M. S., and Sanchez, S. M. (2002) 'Foreign Bank Entry – Experience, Implications for Developing Countries, and Agenda for Further Research', *World Bank Policy Research Working Paper No. 2698*. Retrieved from: https://papers.ssrn.com/sol3/Papers.cfm?abstract_id=285769

Coelli, T. (1996) 'A Guide to DEAP Version 2.1: A Data Envelopment Analysis (Computer) Program', *CEPA Working Paper 96/08*.

Cohen, B. C., and Kaufman, G. G. (1965) 'Factors Determining Bank Deposit Growth by State: An Empirical Analysis', *Journal of Finance*, 20(1), pp. 59–70.

Collier, P. (2007) *The Bottom Billion: Why the Poorest Countries Are Failing and What Can Be Done About*. Oxford: Oxford University Press.

Colwell, R. J., and Davis, E. P. (1992) 'Output and Productivity in Banking', *Scandinavian Journal of Economics*, 94, pp. 111–129.

Crisis Group Asia. (2006) *Sri Lanka: The Failure of the Peace Process*. Retrieved from: www.proasyl.de/fileadmin/proasyl/fm_redakteure/Newsletter_Anhaenge/118/sri_lanka_the_failure_of_the_peace_process.pdf

Crotty, J. (2009) 'Structural Causes of the Global Financial Crisis: A Critical Assessment of the "New Financial Architecture"', *Cambridge Journal of Economics*, 33(4), pp. 563–580.

Cull, R., and Xu, L. C. (2000) 'Bureaucrats, State Banks, and the Efficiency of Credit Allocation: The Experience of Chinese State-Owned Enterprises', *Journal of Comparative Economics*, 28(1), pp. 1–31.

Daily News. (July 29, 2008) 'Clues for Achieving a Strong Savings Culture', *Daily News Online*. Retrieved from: www.dailynews.lk/2008/07/29/bus11.asp

Dawson, P. J. (2008) 'Financial Development and Economic Growth in Developing Countries', *Progress in Development Studies*, 8(4), pp. 325–331.

Deepak, M. (2016) 'GCC Sovereign Bond Issuance on the Rise', *The Gulf News*, September 25, 2016.

Demetriades, P. O., and Hussein, K. A. (1996) 'Does Financial Development Cause Economic Growth? Time-Series Evidence from 16 Countries', *Journal of Development Economics*, 51(2), pp. 387–411.

Demetriades, P. O., and Luintel, K. B. (1997) 'The Direct Costs of Financial Repression: Evidence from India', *Review of Economics and Statistics*, 79(2), pp. 311–320.

Demirgüç-Kunt, A., and Huizinga, H. (1999) 'Determinants of Commercial Bank Interest Margins and Profitability: Some International Evidence', *World Bank Economic Review*, *13*(2), pp. 379–408.

Demirgüç-Kunt, A., and Levine, R. (1996) 'Stock Market Development and Financial Intermediaries: Stylized Facts', *World Bank Economic Review*, *10*(2), pp. 291–321. doi:10.1093/wber/10.2.291

De-Young, R., and Nolle, D. E. (1996) 'Foreign-Owned Banks in the United States: Earning Market Share or Buying It?' *Journal of Money, Credit, and Banking*, *28*(4), pp. 622–636.

Diamond, D. W. (1984) 'Financial Intermediation and Delegated Monitoring', *Review of Economic Studies*, *51*(3), pp. 393–414.

Dore, R. (2000) *Stock Market Capitalism, Welfare Capitalism: Japan and Germany versus the Anglo-Saxons*. Oxford: Oxford University Press.

Drake, L., Hall, M. J., and Simper, R. (2009) 'Bank Modelling Methodologies: A Comparative Non-Parametric Analysis of Efficiency in the Japanese Banking Sector', *Journal of International Financial Markets, Institutions and Money*, *19*(1), pp. 1–15.

Dullien, S. (2009) 'Central Banking, Financial Institutions and Credit Creation in Developing Countries', *United Nations Conference on Trade and Development Discussion Paper No. 193*.

Dymski, G. (1993) 'Keynesian Uncertainty and Asymmetric Information: Complementary or Contradictory?', *Journal of Post Keynesian Economics*, *16*(1), pp. 49–54.

Edirisuriya, P. (2007) 'Effects of Financial Sector Reforms in Sri Lanka: Evidence from the Banking Sector', *Asia Pacific Journal of Finance and Banking Research*, *1*(1), pp. 45–63.

El-Gamal, M. A. (2006) *Islamic Finance: Law, Economics, and Practice*. Cambridge: Cambridge University Press.

El-Gamal, M. A. (2007) 'Mutuality as an Antidote to Rent-Seeking Shari'ah Arbitrage in Islamic Finance', *Thunderbird International Business Review*, *49*(2), pp. 187–202. doi:10.1002/tie.20139

El-Hawary, D., Grais, W., and Iqbal, Z. (2007) 'Diversity in the Regulation of Islamic Financial Institutions', *Quarterly Review of Economics and Finance*, *46*(5), pp. 778–800.

El Tiby, A. (2011) *Islamic Banking: How to Manage Risk and Improve Profitability*. New York: John Wiley and Sons.

Emran, M. S., and Stiglitz, J. E. (2009) 'Financial Liberalization, Financial Restraint and Entrepreneurial Development', *Institute for International Economic Policy Working Paper No. 2009-2*. George Washington University

Fair, C. (2006) 'Faltering Sri Lankan Peace Process: Sri Lanka's Drift Back into War', *Journal of International Peace Operations*, *2*(3), pp. 1–3.

Fama, E. F. (1980) 'Banking in the Theory of Finance', *Journal of Monetary Economics*, *6*(1), pp. 39–57. doi:http://dx.doi.org/10.1016/0304-3932(80)90017-3

Farook, S., and Farooq, M. (2011) 'Incentive-Based Regulation for Islamic Banks', *Journal of Islamic Accounting and Business Research*, *2*(1), pp. 8–21.

Figueira, C., Nellis, J., and Parker, D. (2009) 'The Effects of Ownership on Bank Efficiency in Latin America', *Applied Economics*, *41*(18), pp. 2353–2368.

Financial Services Authority (FSA). (December 2014) *Indonesian Banking Statistics*. Jakarta: Financial Services Authority, Republic of Indonesia.

Fink, G., Haiss, P., and Mantler, H. C. (2005) 'The Finance-Growth Nexus: Market Economies vs. Transition Countries', *EI Working Paper No. 64*. Retrieved from: http://dx.doi.org/10.2139/ssrn.863424

Fisher, I. (1933) 'The Debt-Deflation Theory of Great Depressions', *Econometrica*, *1*(4), pp. 337–357.

Freixas, X., and Rochet, J. C. (2008) *Microeconomics of Banking* (2nd ed.). Cambridge, MA: The MIT Press.

Garcia-Herrero, A., and Santabarbara, D. (2004) 'Where Is the Chinese Banking System Going with the Ongoing Reform?', *Occasional Paper, Banco De Espana*. Retrieved from: http://ideas.repec.org/p/wpa/wuwpma/0408001.html (last accessed on October 12, 2007).

Gerschenkron, A. (1962) *Economic Backwardness in Historical Perspective: A Book of Essays*. Cambridge, MA: Belknap Press of Harvard University Press.

Gokkent, G. (2014) 'GCC: Strong Diversified Growth, Limited Risk', *IIF Regional Overview*, Institute of International Finance.

Goldsmith, R. W. (1969) *Financial Structure and Development*. New Haven: Yale University Press.

Greenwood, J., and Jovanovic, B. (1990) 'Financial Development, Growth, and the Distribution of Income', *Journal of Political Economy*, *98*(1), pp. 1076–1107.

Gurley, J. G., and Shaw, E. S. (1960) *Money in a Theory of Finance*. Washington: Brookings Institution.

Guzman, M. G. (2000) 'Bank Structure, Capital Accumulation and Growth: A Simple Macroeconomic Model', *Economic Theory*, *16*(2), pp. 421–455.

Hadad, M. D., Hall, M. J. B., Kenjegalieva, K., Santoso, W., Satria, R., and Simper, R. (2008) 'Banking Efficiency and Stock Market Performance: An Analysis of Listed Indonesian Banks', *Departmental Working Paper*, Department of Economics, Loughborough University.

Hanazaki, M., and Horiuchi, A. (2001) 'Can the Financial Restraint Hypothesis Explain Japan's Postwar Experience?', *Center for Economic Institutions, Institute of Economic Research*, Hitotsubashi University.

Harrison, P., Sussman, O., and Zeira, J. (1999) 'Finance and Growth: Theory and New Evidence', *FEDS Working Paper No. 99*. Federal Reserve Board.

He, L. (2005) 'Evolution of Financial Institutions in Post-1978 China: Interaction between the State and Market', *China and World Economy*, *13*(6), pp. 10–26.

Hellmann, T., and Murdock, K. (1998) 'Financial Sector Development Policy: The Importance of Reputational Capital and Governance', in R. Sabot and I. Székely (Eds.) *Development Strategy and Management of the Market Economy* (Vol. 2). Oxford: Oxford University Press, pp. 269–324.

Hellmann, T., Murdock, K., and Stiglitz, J. (1997) 'Financial Restraint: Toward a New Paradigm', in M. Aoki, H.-K. Kim and M. Okuno-Fujiwara (Eds.) *The Role of Government in East Asian Economic Development: Comparative Institutional Analysis*. Oxford: Clarendon Press, pp. 163–207.

Hemachandra, W. M. (2003) 'Financial Deepening and Its Implications on Savings and Investments in Sri Lanka', *CBSL Staff Studies*, *33*(1 and 2), pp. 15–32.

Hofman, B. (1998) 'Fiscal Decline and Quasi-Fiscal Response: China's Fiscal Policy and System 1978–94', in O. Bouin, F. Coricelli and F. Lemoine (Eds.) *Different Paths to a Market Economy: China and European Economies in Transition*. Paris: OECD, pp. 17–41.

Honohan, P. (2005) 'Financial Development, Growth and Poverty: How Close Are the Links?', in C. A. E. Goodhart (Ed.) *Financial Development and Economic Growth*. Basingstoke: Palgrave Macmillan, pp. 1–37.

Hoshi, T., Kashyap, A. K., and Sharfstein, D. S. (1990) 'Bank Monitoring and Investment: Evidence from the Changing Structure of Japanese Corporate Banking Relationship', in R. G. Hubbard (Ed.) *Asymmetric Information, Corporate Finance, and Investment*. Chicago: University of Chicago Press, pp. 105–126.

Huybens, E., and Smith, B. D. (1999) 'Inflation, Financial Markets and Long-Run Real Activity', *Journal of Monetary Economics*, 43(2), pp. 283–315.

Imai, H. (1985) 'China's New Banking System: Changes in the Monetary Policy', *Pacific Affairs*, 58(3), pp. 451–472.

Imai, K., and Watanabe, M. (2006) *Kigyo no Seicho to Kinyuu Seido (Corporate Growth and Financial System)* (in Japanese). Nagoya: Nagoya University Press.

Institute for Conflict Management. (2011) *South Asia Terrorism Portal*. Retrieved 22 April 2011, from: http://satp.org/satporgtp/countries/shrila-nka/database/annual_casualties.htm

Ito, T. (2009) 'Zero Interest Rate Policy (ZIRP) and Quantitative Easing (QE)', in M. Dewatripont, X. Freixas and R. Portes (Eds.) *Macroeconomic Stability and Financial Regulation: Key Issues for the G20*. London: CEPR, pp. 67–78.

Japan Bank for International Cooperation (JBIC). (2015) *FY2015 Survey (the 27th) Report on Overseas Business Operations by Japanese Manufacturing Companies*. JBIC. Retrieved from: www.jbic.go.jp/en/information/press/press-2015/1203-44407

Jappelli, T., and Pagano, M. (1994) 'Saving, Growth, and Liquidity Constraints', *Quarterly Journal of Economics*, 109(1), pp. 83–109.

Jayaratne, J., and Strahan, P. E. (1996) 'The Finance-Growth Nexus: Evidence from Bank Branch Deregulation', *Quarterly Journal of Economics*, 111(3), pp. 639–670.

Johnes, J., Izzeldin, M., and Pappas, V. (2013) 'A Comparison of Performance of Islamic and Conventional Banks 2004–2009', *Journal of Economic Behavior & Organization*, 103, pp. S93–S107. doi: 10.1016/j.jebo.2013.07.016

Kang, J. S. (2014) 'Balance Sheet Repair and Corporate Investment in Japan', *IMF Working Paper No. 14/141*. Retrieved from: www.imf.org/external/pubs/ft/wp/2014/wp14141.pdf

Kang, S. J., and Sawada, Y. (2000) 'Financial Repression and External Openness in an Endogenous Growth Model', *Journal of International Trade & Economic Development*, 9(4), pp. 427–443.

Kashyap, A. K., and Stein, J. C. (1994) 'Monetary Policy and Bank Lending', in Gregory N. Mankiw (Ed.) *Monetary Policy*. Chicago: The University of Chicago Press, pp. 221–261.

Kern, S. (2012) 'GCC Financial Markets: Long-Term Prospects for Finance in the Gulf', *Deutsche Bank Research*. Retrieved from: www.dbresearch.com

Keynes, J. M. (1936) *The General Theory of Employment, Interest and Money* (7th ed.). Cambridge: Macmillan and Cambridge University Press.

Khan, M. (2000) 'Rents, Efficiency and Growth', in M. Khan and J. K. Sundaram (Eds.) *Rents, Rent-Seeking and Economic Development: Theory and Evidence in Asia*. Cambridge: Cambridge University Press, pp. 21–69.

Khandelwal, P., Miyajima, M. K., and Santos, M. A. O. (2016) 'The Impact of Oil Prices on the Banking System in the GCC. International Monetary Fund', working paper #16/161. Retrieved from: www.imf.org/external/pubs/ft/wp/2016/wp16161.pdf (last accessed on June 19, 2016)

Khrawish, H., Al-Abadi, M., and Hejazi, M. (2008) 'Determinants of Commercial Bank Interest Rate Margins: Evidence from Jordan', *Jordan Journal of Business Administration*, 4(4), pp. 485–502.

Kimura, T., Hiroshi, K., Jun, M., and Hiroshi, U. (2002) 'The Effect of the Increase in Monetary Base on Japan's Economy at Zero Interest Rates: An Empirical Analysis', in *Monetary Policy in a Changing Environment*. Basle: Bank for International Settlements, pp. 276–312.

Kindleberger, C. P. (2005) *Manias, Panics, and Crashes: A History of Financial Crises* (5th ed.). Hoboken, NJ: John Wiley and Sons, Inc.

King, R. G., and Levine, R. (1993) 'Finance and Growth: Schumpeter Might Be Right', *Quarterly Journal of Economics*, 108(3), pp. 717–737.

Knight, F. (2009) 'From Risk, Uncertainty and Profit.' In Kroszner, R., and Putterman, L. (eds.), *The Economic Nature of the Firm: A Reader* (3rd edition). Cambridge: Cambridge University Press, pp. 52–57.

Korosteleva, J., and Lawson, C. (2010) 'The Belarusian Case of Transition: Whither Financial Repression?', *Post-Communist Economies*, 22(1), pp. 33–53.

Krasa, S., and Villamil, A. P. (1992) 'Monitoring the Monitor: An Incentive Structure for a Financial Intermediary', *Journal of Economic Theory*, 57(1), pp. 197–221. doi:http://dx.doi.org/10.1016/S0022-0531(05)80048-1

Krugman, P. (1998) 'It's Back: Japan's Slump and the Return of the Liquidity Trap', *Brookings Papers on Economic Activity*, 29(2), pp. 137–205.

Kumbhakar, S. C., and Sarkar, S. (2003) 'Deregulation, Ownership, and Productivity Growth in the Banking Industry: Evidence from India', *Journal of Money, Credit and Banking*, 35(3), pp. 403–424.

Lal, D. (2006) 'A Proposal to Privatize Chinese Enterprises and End Financial Repression', *Cato Journal*, 26(2), pp. 275–286.

Lanzillotti, R. F., and Saving, T. R. (1969) 'State Branching Restrictions and the Availability of Branching Services: Comment', *Journal of Money, Credit and Banking*, 1(4), pp. 778–788.

Lardy, N. R. (1998) *China's Unfinished Economic Revolution*. Washington, DC: Brookings Institution Press.

Lardy, N. R. (1999) 'The Challenge of Bank Restructuring in China', *BIS Policy Paper No. 7*. Basel, Switzerland: Bank for International Settlements (BIS).

Lau, L. J. (1999) 'The Macro Economy and the Reform of the Banking Sector in China', *BIS Policy Paper No. 7*. Basel, Switzerland: Bank for International Settlements (BIS).

Law, S. H., Azman-Saini, W. N. W., and Ibrahim, M. H. (2013) 'Institutional Quality Thresholds and the Finance-Growth Nexus', *Journal of Banking & Finance*, 37(12), pp. 5373–5381. doi:http://dx.doi.org/10.1016/j.jbankfin.2013.03.011

Law, S. H., and Singh, N. (2014) 'Does Too Much Finance Harm Economic Growth?', *Journal of Banking & Finance*, 41, pp. 36–44. doi:http://dx.doi.org/10.1016/j.jbankfin.2013.12.020

Leland, H. E., and Pyle, D. H. (1977) 'Informational Asymmetries, Financial Structure, and Financial Intermediation', *Journal of Finance*, 32(2), pp. 371–387. doi:10.2307/2326770

Lensink, R., and Naaborg, I. (2007) 'Does Foreign Ownership Foster Bank Performance?', *Applied Financial Economics*, 17(11), pp. 881–885.

Levine, R. (1997) 'Financial Development and Economic Growth: Views and Agenda', *Journal of Economic Literature*, 35(2), pp. 688–726.

Levine, R. (July-August 2003) 'More on Finance and Growth, More Finance, More Growth?', *Federal Reserve Bank of St. Louis Review*, 85, pp. 31–46.

Li, D. D. (2001) 'Beating the Trap of Financial Repression in China', *Cato Journal*, 21(1), pp. 77–90.

Lucas, R. E. (1988) 'On the Mechanics of Economic Development', *Journal of Monetary Economics*, 22(1), pp. 3–42.

Ma, G. (2006) 'Sharing China's Bank Restructuring Bill', *China and World Economy*, 14(3), pp. 19–37.

Ma, G., and Fung, B. (2002) 'China's Asset Management Corporations', *BIS Working Paper No. 115*. Basel, Switzerland: Bank for International Settlements (BIS).

Mayer, C. (1988) 'New Issues in Corporate Finance', *European Economic Review*, 32(5), pp. 1167–1189. http://dx.doi.org/10.1016/0014-2921(88)90077-3

McKinnon, R. I. (1973) *Money and Capital in Economic Development*. Washington, DC: Brookings Institute.

Ministry of Defense. (2011) *Humanitarian Operation Factual Analysis: July 2006 – May 2009*. Sri Lanka: Ministry of Defense.

Minsky, H. P. (1975) *John Maynard Keynes*. New York: Columbia University Press.

Minsky, H. P. (1977) 'A Theory of Systemic Fragility', in E. D. Altman and A. W. Sametz (Eds.) *Financial Crises: Institutions and Markets in a Fragile Environment*. New York: John Wiley and Sons, pp. 138–152.

Minsky, H. P. (1982) *Can "It" Happen again? Essays on Instability and Finance*. Armonk, NY: M.E. Sharpe Inc.

Mishkin, F. S. (1995) 'Symposium on the Monetary Transmission Mechanism', *Journal of Economic Perspectives*, 9(4), pp. 3–10.

Mishkin, F. S. (2011) 'Over the Cliff: From the Subprime to the Global Financial Crisis', *Journal of Economic Perspectives*, 25(1), pp. 49–70.

Mittal, M., and Dhade, A. (2007) 'Profitability and Productivity in Indian Banks: A Comparative Study', *AIMS International Journal of Management*, 1(2), pp. 137–152.

Muda, M. (1996) 'Financial Positioning of Commercial Banks and Its Implications to Bank Management', *Asian Academy of Management Journal*, 1(2), pp. 99–108.

Mujeri, M. K., and Younus, S. (2009) 'An Analysis of Interest Rate Spread in the Banking Sector in Bangladesh', *Bangladesh Development Studies*, 32(4), pp. 1–33.

Murphy, K. R., and Myors, B. (2004) *Statistical Power Analysis: A Simple and General Model for Traditional and Modern Hypothesis Tests* (2nd ed.). London: L. Erlbaum Associates, Publishers.

Nagarajan, G. (1997) 'Developing Micro-Finance Institutions in Conflict-Affected Countries: Emerging Issues, First Lessons Learnt and Challenges Ahead', *International Labour Organization*. Retrieved from: www.ilo.int/wcmsp5/groups/public/---ed_emp/---emp_ent/---ifp_crisis/documents/publication/wcms_116728.pdf

National Bureau of Statistics (NBS). (2006) *China Statistical Year Book 2006*. Beijing, China: NBS. Retrieved from: www.stats.gov.cn/tjsj/ndsj/2006/indexeh.htm

NORAD. (2011) *Pawns of Peace: Evaluation of Norwegian Peace Efforts in Sri Lanka, 1997–2009*. Chr. Michelsen Institute/School of Oriental and African Studies, University of London.

North, D., and Weingast, B. (1989) 'Constitutions and Commitment: The Evolution of Institutions Governing Public Choice in Seventeenth-Century England', *Journal of Economic History*, XLIX(4), pp. 803–832.

Okina, K., and Shiratsuka, S. (2004) 'Policy Commitment and Expectation Formation: Japan's Experience under Zero Interest Rates', *North American Journal of Economics and Finance*, 15(1), pp. 75–100.

Organization for Economic Cooperation and Development (OECD). (2005) *Economic Surveys: China*. Paris: OECD Publishing.

Papava, V. (2006) 'The Political Economy of Georgia's Rose Revolution', *Orbis*, 50(4), pp. 657–667.

Patrick, H. T. (1966) 'Financial Development and Economic Growth in Underdeveloped Countries', *Economic Development and Cultural Change*, 14(2), pp. 174–189.

People's Bank of China (PBC). (2006) *Quarterly Statistical Bulletin*. Beijing: People's Bank of China.

Podder, S. (2006) 'Challenges to Peace Negotiations: The Sri Lankan Experience', *Strategic Analysis, Institute for Defence Studies and Analyses*, 30(3), pp. 576–598.

Posner, R. A. (2009) *A Failure of Capitalism: The Crisis of '08 and the Descent into Depression*. Cambridge, MA: Harvard University Press.

Prahalad, C. K., and Hart, S. L. (2004) *The Fortune at the Bottom of the Pyramid: Eradicating Poverty through Profit*. Upper Saddle River, NJ: Prentice Hall.

Pyle, D. H. (1971) 'On the Theory of Financial Intermediation', *Journal of Finance*, 26(3), pp. 737–747. doi:10.2307/2325957

Radelet, S., and Sachs, J. (1998) 'The East Asian Financial Crisis: Diagnosis, Remedies, Prospects', *Brookings Papers on Economic Activity*, 1, pp. 1–90.

Rajan, R. G., and Zingales, L. (2004) *Saving Capitalism from the Capitalists: Unleashing the Power of Financial Markets to Create Wealth and Spread Opportunity*. Princeton: Princeton University Press.

Randall, R. (1998) 'Interest Rate Spreads in the Eastern Carribean', *IMF Working Paper, WP/98/59*.

Reinhart, C. M., and Rogoff, K. S. (2009) *This Time Is Different: Eight Centuries of Financial Folly*. Princeton: Princeton University Press.

Reinhart, C. M., and Rogoff, K. S. (2013) 'Banking Crises: An Equal Opportunity Menace', *Journal of Banking & Finance*, 37(11), pp. 4557–4573.

Robinson, J. (1952) 'The Generalization of the General Theory', in J. Robinson (Ed.) *The Rate of Interest and Other Essays*. London: MacMillan, pp. 67–146.

Rochet, J. C. (2009) *Why Are There So Many Banking Crises? The Politics and Policy of Bank Regulation*. Princeton: Princeton University Press.

Rodrik, D. (1999) 'Where Did All the Growth Go? External Shocks, Social Conflict, and Growth Collapses', *Journal of Economic Growth*, 4(4), pp. 385–412.

Reinhart, C. M., and Rogoff, K. S. (2009) *This Time Is Different: Eight Centuries of Financial Folly*. Princeton: Princeton University Press.

Rousseau, P. L., and Wachtel, P. (2002) 'Inflation Thresholds and the Finance-Growth Nexus', *Journal of International Money and Finance*, 21(6), pp. 777–793. doi:http://dx.doi.org/10.1016/S0261-5606(02)00022-0

Sabot, R., and Székely, I. (1998) 'Introduction', in R. Sabot and I. Székely (Eds.) *Development Strategy and Management of the Market Economy* (Vol. 2). Oxford: Oxford University Press, pp. 1–8.

Sairally, B. S. (2002) 'Murrbabah Financing: Some Controversial Issues', *Review of Islamic Economics*, 12, pp. 73–86.

Sambanis, N. (2004) 'What Is Civil War? Conceptual and Empirical Complexities of an Operational Definition', *Journal of Conflict Resolution*, 48(6), pp. 814–858.

Sastrosuwito, S. (2010) 'The Indonesian Financial Crisis of 1997/98: Unsound Banking System Problem', *Research Journal of International Studies*, *16*, pp. 104–118.

Sathye, M. (2003) 'Efficiency of Banks in a Developing Economy: The Case of India', *European Journal of Operational Research*, *148*(3), pp. 662–671.

Schenone, C. (2009) 'Lending Relationships and Information Rents: Do Banks Exploit Their Information Advantages?', *Review of Financial Studies*, *23*(3), pp. 1149–1199.

Schumpeter, J. A. (1934) *The Theory of Economic Development*. Cambridge, MA: Harvard University Press.

Sharpe, S. A. (1990) 'Asymmetric Information, Bank Lending and Implicit Contracts: A Stylized Model of Customer Relationships', *Journal of Finance*, *45*(4), pp. 1069–1087.

Shaw, E. S. (1973) *Financial Deepening in Economic Development*. New York: Oxford University Press.

Shiller, R. J. (2000) *Irrational Exuberance*. Princeton: Princeton University Press.

Shimizu, I. (2016) *Kinkyu Kaisetsu Minus Kinri* (in Japanese). Tokyo: Nihon Keizai Shimbun Shuppan sha.

Shirakawa, M. (2002) 'One Year under "Quantitative Easing"', *IMES Discussion Paper Series, No. 2002-E-3*, Bank of Japan.

Shiratsuka, S. (2010) 'Size and Composition of the Central Bank Balance Sheet: Revisiting Japan's Experience of the Quantitative Easing Policy', *Monetary and Economic Studies*, *28*(3), pp. 79–105.

SMEA (Small and Medium Enterprise Agency). (2005) *Nendo Chusho Kigyo Hakusho* (White Paper).

SMEA. (2010) *Nendo Chusho Kigyo Hakusho* (White Paper).

SMEA. (2014) *Nendo Chusho Kigyo Hakusho* (White Paper).

Smith, A. (1776) *The Wealth of Nations*. New York: The Modern Library.

Soylu, A., and Durmaz, N. (2013) 'Profitability of Interest-free versus Interest-based Banks in Turkey', *Australian Economic Review*, *46*(2), pp. 176–188.

Spellman, L. J. (1980) 'Deposit Ceilings and the Efficiency of Financial Intermediation', *Journal of Finance*, *35*(1), pp. 129–136.

Stark, W. (1944) *The History of Economics in Relation to Its Social Development*. London: Routledge and Kegan Paul.

Starr, P. (1988) 'The Meaning of Privatization', *Yale Law and Policy Review*, *6*(1), pp. 6–41.

Stiglitz, J. E. (1993) 'The Role of the State in Financial Markets', in M. Bruno and B. Pleskovic (Eds.) *The World Bank Annual Bank Conference on Development Economics*. Washington, DC: World Bank, pp. 19–52.

Stiglitz, J. E. (1994) *Whither Socialism*. Cambridge, MA: The MIT Press.

Stiglitz, J. E. (2012) 'Macroeconomics, Monetary Policy, and the Crisis', in Olivier J. Blanchard, David Romer, Michael Spence and J. E. Stiglitz (Eds.) *The Wake of the Crisis: Leading Economists Reassess Economic Policy*. Cambridge, MA: The MIT Press, pp. 31–45.

Stiglitz, J. E., and Weiss, A. (1981) 'Credit Rationing in Markets with Imperfect Information', *American Economic Review*, *71*(3), pp. 393–410.

Sundararajan, V., and Errico, L. (2002) 'Islamic Financial Institutions and Products in the Global Financial System: Key Issues in Risk Management and Challenges Ahead', *International Monetary Fund Working Paper #192*.

Suzuki, Y. (2005) *Financial Market, Institutions and Credit Monitoring*. Tokyo: Yuigaku Shobo.

Suzuki, Y. (2009) *The Essence of Financial Management*. Tokyo: Yuigaku Shobo.

Suzuki, Y. (2011) *Japan's Financial Slump: Collapse of the Monitoring System under Institutional and Transition Failures*. Basingstoke: Palgrave Macmillan.

Suzuki, Y., Miah, M. D., and Wanniarachchige, M. K. (2010) 'Civil War and Financial Underdevelopment: The Case of Georgia with Special Reference to Sri Lanka', *Ritsumeikan International Affairs*, 8, pp. 31–56.

Suzuki, Y., and Sastrosuwito, S. (2011) 'The Determinants of Post-Crisis Indonesian Banking System Profitability', *Journal Economics and Finance Review*, 1(11), pp. 48–57.

Suzuki, Y., and Sastrosuwito, S. (2012) 'The Impact of Competition on Bank Efficiency: The Evidence from Indonesia', *Journal of Business and Management Review*, 2(6), pp. 1–9.

Suzuki, Y., and Uddin, S. M. S. (2014) 'Islamic Bank Rent: A Case Study of Islamic Banking in Bangladesh', *International Journal of Islamic and Middle Eastern Finance and Management*, 7(2), pp. 170–181.

Tamaki, T., and Yamazawa, K. (2005) *Chugoku no Kinyuu wa korekara dou narunoka* (in Japanese). Tokyo: Toyo Keizai.

Tang, D. (2006) 'The Effect of Financial Development on Economic Growth: Evidence from the APEC Countries, 1981–2000', *Applied Economics*, 38(16), pp. 1889–1904.

Tian, X., and Zhou, M. (2008) 'Banking System Efficiency and Chinese Regional Economic Growth: An Empirical Analysis Based on Banks' Micro-Efficiency', *International Journal of Business and Finance Research*, 2(1), pp. 41–51.

Tokukatsu, R. (2015) *Minus Kinri (Minus Interest)* (in Japanese). Tokyo: Toyo Keizai Shimpo Sha.

Tone, K. (2001) 'A Slacks-Based Measure of Efficiency in Data Envelopment Analysis', *European Journal of Operational Research*, 130(3), pp. 498–509.

Tsai, K. S. (2002) *Back-Alley Banking: Private Entrepreneurs in China*. New York: Cornell University Press.

Tuuli, K. (2002) 'Do Efficient Banking Sectors Accelerate Economic Growth in Transition Countries?', *BOFIT Discussion Papers 14/2002*.

Uddin, S. M. S., and Suzuki, Y. (2015) 'The Dynamics of Concentration and Competition in the Banking Sector of Bangladesh: An Empirical Investigation', *South Asian Journal of Management*, 22(1), pp. 114–136.

Ugai, H. (2007) 'Effects of the Quantitative Easing Policy: A Survey of Empirical Analyses', *Bank of Japan Working Paper Series # 06-E-10*. Retrieved from: http://edwesterhout.nl/wp-content/uploads/2016/03/wp06e10.pdf

Van Damme, E. (1994) 'Banking: A Survey of Recent Microeconomic Theory', *Oxford Review of Economic Policy*, 10(4), pp. 14–33. doi:10.1093/oxrep/10.4.14

Visser, H. (2009) *Islamic Finance: Principles and Practice*. London: Edward Elgar.

Wanniarachchige, M. K., and Suzuki, Y. (2010) 'Bank Competition and Efficiency: The Case of Sri Lanka', *Asia Pacific World*, 1(1), pp. 117–131.

Wanniarachchige, M. K., and Suzuki, Y. (2011) 'How Does Ownership Affect Bank Performance? The Case of Indian Commercial Banks', *International Business & Economics Research Journal*, 10(3), pp. 71–82.

Wanniarachchige, M. K., Suzuki, Y., and Kjærland, F. (2011) 'Does Bank Ownership Matter in Performance? Experience and Lessons from Sri Lanka', in B. W.

Åmo (Ed.) *Conditions for Entrepreneurship in Sri Lanka: A Handbook*. Aachen, Germany: Shaker Verlag, pp. 235–254.

White, L. J. (1976) 'Price Regulation and Quality Rivalry in a Profit-Maximizing Model: The Case of Bank Branching', *Journal of Money, Credit and Banking*, *8*(1), pp. 97–106.

Williamson, O. E. (1985) *The Economic Institutions of Capitalism: Firms, Markets, Relational Contracting*. New York: The Free Press.

Williamson, S. D. (1986) 'Costly Monitoring, Financial Intermediation, and Equilibrium Credit Rationing', *Journal of Monetary Economics*, *18*(2), pp. 159–179. doi:http://dx.doi.org/10.1016/0304-3932(86)90074-7

Wolf, M. (2014) *The Shifts and the Shocks: What We've Learned-and Have Still to Learn-from the Financial Crisis*. New York: Penguin.

World Bank. (2000a) *Sri Lanka: Recapturing Missed Opportunities*. Retrieved from: http://siteresources.worldbank.org/SRILANKAEXTN/Resources/Missed-opportunities/full_report.pdf (last accessed on 22 April, 2011).

World Bank. (2000b) *The World Business Environment Survey (WBES) 2000*. Washington, DC: World Bank Group.

World Bank. (2015) *Global Economic Prospects: The Global Economy in Transition, June 2015*. Retrieved from: www.worldbank.org/content/dam/Worldbank/GEP/GEP2015b/Global-Economic-Prospects-June-2015-Global-economy-in-transition.pdf

World Development Indicator, online version. Retrieved from: http://databank.worldbank.org/data/home.aspx

Worthington, A. C. (2000) 'Cost Efficiency in Australian Non-Bank Financial Institutions: A Non-Parametric Approach', *Accounting and Finance*, *40*(1), pp. 75–97.

Wu, S. (2005) 'Productivity and Efficiency Analysis of Australia Banking Sector under Derregulation', *Proceedings of the Australian Conference of Economists 2005*. Melbourne: University of Melbourne/Conference Maker, pp. 1–43.

Yilmazkuday, H. (2011) 'Thresholds in the Finance-Growth Nexus: A Cross-Country Analysis', *World Bank Economic Review*, *25*(2), pp. 278–295. doi:10.1093/wber/lhr011

Younis, M., Lin, X. X., Sharahili, Y., and Selvarathinam, S. (2008) 'Political Stability and Economic Growth in Asia', *American Journal of Applied Sciences*, *5*(3), pp. 203–208.

Zaher, T., and Hassan, M. (2001) 'A Comparative Literature Survey of Islamic Finance and Banking', *Financial Markets, Institutions & Instruments*, *10*(4), pp. 155–199.

# Index

adverse selection 40–1, 51
Agricultural Bank of China (ABC) 72
Alchian, A. A. 17, 19
Al Rajhi Bank 148
Amor-Tapia, B. 95
Arrow-Debreu general equilibrium
  model 27
asset substitution effect 24
asset transformation and liquidity
  insurance 36
Azman-Saini, W.N.W. 28

Bagehot, W. 27
Bahrain *see* Gulf Cooperative Council
  (GCC) countries
bai'salam 139
Bangladesh 7, 58, 107; illustration of
  Islamic bank rent from 62–6; Islamic
  banking overview in 124–7; Islamic
  bank rent in 127–34, *135–6*; non-
  performing loans (NPLs) in 63–4, 129
bank-centered system, Chinese 71–3
Bank Negara Malaysia (BNM) 126–7
Bank of China (BOC) 72–3
Bank of Japan (BOJ) 157, 160–2,
  174, 185
banks: absorbing general uncertainty
  35; asset transformation and liquidity
  insurance 36; crises 1–2; dealing with
  borrowers' credit risk 2; definition
  of 31; economizing on transaction
  cost 33–5; facilitating information
  collection 32–3; as financial
  intermediaries 31–6; financial restraint
  policy and 20–5, 42–6; franchise
  value 21, 40, 58; moral hazard in 22;
  ownership in Sri Lanka 100–5; risk
  taking by 2, 22–3; state-owned, in
  China 71–3; sunk costs 17

Basel Committee on Banking
  Supervision (BCBS) 39, 54, 76, 86
Beck, T. 27, 94
Berger, A. N. 102
Bhattacharya, S. 36
Bhattacharyya, A. 104
Bloch, H. 27
borrowers: creditable 14, 41–2; default
  risk 19, 41; heterogeneity of 41
Botric, V. 27–8

Calomiris, C. W. 2
Campbell, T. S. 33–4
capitalism 16; inclusive 26; Japanese
  77–8; search for profit and labor
  process 19
capital market, Gulf Cooperative
  Council (GCC) countries 143–4
Caprio, G. 1
China 6, 84–5, 183–4; bank-centered
  system 71–3; Banking Regulatory
  Commission 72; economic realities in
  73–7; extremely high ratio of NPLs
  in big four banks of 75–6; financial
  deepening in the post-reform era
  74–5; financial restraint model and
  rent creation in 77–8; four state-
  owned banks of 72, 75; limited role
  of state-owned commercial banks in
  81–4; negative and zero interest rate
  regimes 80–1; policy burden of the
  big four banks in 76–7; removing
  distortions in banking system of
  79–81
China Construction Bank (CCB) 72–3
city commercial banks (CCBs) 83–4
Claessens, S. 28
competition, excessive 23
creditable borrowers 14, 41–2

credit bubbles 156–7
credit markets 2, 38–9; expansion in
   Sri Lanka 99–100
credit rationing 39, 42
cube, bank rent 54–5
Cull, R. 75

data envelopment analysis (DEA) 101–4
Dawson, P. J. 28
default risk of borrowers 19
deflation 28
Demirguc-Kunt, A. 27, 94
Demsetz, H. 17, 19
Dore, R. 77
Drake, L. 102–3
Dubai Islamic Bank 154
Durbin-Watson (DW) test 96
Durmaz, N. 63

economic development 37, 181–6;
   banks as financial intermediaries
   and 31–6; financial inclusion for 26;
   financial markets effects on 26–7;
   limited role of SOCB's in China and
   81–4; overview of finance-growth
   nexus in 27–9
El-Gamal, M. A. 58
equity and bond markets 30
European Central Bank 185
excess income 13, 16, 40, 181
excessive competition 23
expected default frequency (EDF) 19

Farook, S. 59
Farooq, M. 59
financial crises 1–2, 156–7
financial intermediaries, banks
   as 31–6
financial repression 20–1, 45–6
financial restraint 20–5, 42–3, 73; in
   China 77–8; critique of 44–6
financial systems: anatomy of 29–31;
   components 26–7; finance-growth
   nexus and 27–9
Fink, G. 29
firms: input performance of members
   of 18–19; profitability through
   specialization 17–18, 27; risk taking
   in financing of 22–3, 32–3; surplus
   16–17
fisher 156
floating rate notes (FRN) 164
franchise value 21, 40; Islamic banks
   and 58

free market competition 22
free riding problem 34, 45

Goldsmith, R. W. 27
Greenwood, J. 28
gross domestic product (GDP) 1, 6,
   74–5, 141
Gulf Cooperative Council (GCC)
   countries 7–8, 138–9, 154–5;
   analysis of Islamic bank rents in
   144–54; banking systems 141–3;
   capital market 143–4; financial
   profile of 139–44; macroeconomic
   outlook 139–40; *see also* Islamic
   banking
Gurley, J. G. 34

Haber, S. H. 2
Hadad, M. D. 102–3
Haiss, P. 29
Hall, M. J. 102–3
Harrison, P. 28
Hart, S. L. 26
Hassan, M. 62, 65
He, L. 83
Hellmann, T. 14; critique of 44–6;
   financial restraint model 20–2, 38,
   42, 73, 77; on safety and deposit
   rate 48–9
Hemachandra, W. M. 99
household savings 22, 49

Ibrahim, M. H. 28
Imai, H. 73
imperfect information 48
inclusive capitalism 26
income, excess 13, 16, 40, 181
India 87, 90–1, 107, 109
Indonesia 7, 58; Islamic banking
   overview in 124–7; Islamic bank rent
   in 127–34, *135–6*; non-performing
   loans (NPLs) in 129
Indonesian Banking Restructuring
   Agency (IBRA) 125
Industrial and Commercial Bank of
   China (ICBC) 72
inflation 44; in Sri Lanka 106–8
information collection, bank facilitation
   of 32–3
Institute for Conflict Management 111
interest rates 15; banking system
   structure influence on 50; and
   branch network expansion in Sri
   Lanka 92–100; ceilings and financial

deepening 24; expected return versus nominal lending rate 19; franchise value and 21; LIBOR (London Interbank Offered Rate) 164; negative and zero interest rate regimes in China 80–1; positive interest rate spread regime in China 81; price rent opportunities 47–9; rent and negative 174–8; risky borrowers and 32–3; savings rate and 22; spreads 47–9, 81
International Monetary Fund (IMF) 13, 87, 125
Islamic banking 3–4, 6, 66–7, 121–2, 136–9, 183–5; conceptualization of rent in 59–62, 122–4; introduction to 58–9; *murabaha* 58–61, 63–4, 66–7, 121, 138–9, 184; *musharakha* 133–4, 154; non-performing loans (NPL) 63–4; overview in Bangladesh, Indonesia, Malaysia, and Pakistan 124–7; profit-and-loss sharing (PLS) contracts 3–4, 7–8; rent in Bangladesh 62–6, 127–34, *135–6*; rent in Indonesia 127–34, *135–6*; rent in Malaysia 127–34, *135–6*; rent in Pakistan 127–34, *135–6*; rent in the GCC 144–54; return on assets (ROA) 63; riba-free and riba-based 64–6, 131, *132–3*, *135–6*; rise of 121
Izzeldin, M. 63

Janatha Vimukti Peramuna (JVP) 106, 109
Japan 8, 9n2, 72–3, 81, 157–8; capitalism in 77–8; changes in rent opportunity during period of QE and ZIRP 168–74; household savings rate 49; knife-edge hypotheses on market reference rate and 163–8; quantitative easing in 157–62, *163*, 185; rent in negative interest rate regime in 174–8; transition failure from bank rent-based financial mode to other alternative 22; zero interest rate policy (ZIRP) 157, 160–2, 168–74, 185
Japan Bank for International Cooperation (JBIC) 175
Jappelli, T. 28
Jayaratne, J. 28
Johnes, J. 63
joint-stock commercial banks (JSCBs) 83–4
Jovanovic, B. 28

Keynes, John M. 35, 60, 163, 178–9
Keynesian uncertainty 35
Khan, M. 40
Kindleberger, C. P. 156
King, R. G. 27
Kingdom of Saudi Arabia *see* Gulf Cooperative Council (GCC) countries
Klingebiel, D. 1
knight 35
Kracaw, W. A. 33–4
Krasa, S. 35
Kuwait *see* Gulf Cooperative Council (GCC) countries
Kuwait Finance House (KFH) 148

Laeven, L. 28
laissez-faire policy 22
Lardy, N. R. 75
Lau, L. J. 76
Law, S. H. 28
least developed countries (LDCs) 1
Leland, H. E. 33–4
Levine, R. 27–8, 94
Liberation Tigers of Tamil Elam (LTTE) 109–12
LIBOR (London Interbank Offered Rate) 164
liquidity risk management 36
losses, macroeconomic 52–3
Lovell, C.A.K. 104
Lucas, R. E. 28

macroeconomic rent opportunities 52–3
Malaysia 7, 58; Islamic banking overview in 124–7; Islamic bank rent in 127–34, *135–6*; non-performing loans (NPLs) in 129
management, firm 18–19
Mantler, H. C. 29
market friction 31
Marxian economics 16, 181; capitalist search for profit and labor process in 19
McKinnon 27, 46, 77, 94, 96
measurable uncertainty 35
Mester, L. J. 102
Minsky, H. P. 156
moral hazard effect 19–20, 22, 34; banking system infrastructure and 50–1; screening and monitoring systems for reducing 40–1
*mudaraba* 133–4

*murabaha* 58–61, 63–4, 66–7, 121, 138–9, 154, 184
*musharakha* 133–4, 154

National Bank of Dubai 154
New Institutional Economics (NIE) 2–3
New Keynesian economics 182
non-performing loans (NPL): in Bangladesh 63–4, 129; in China 71–85; in Sri Lanka 88

Oman *see* Gulf Cooperative Council (GCC) countries
operating rent opportunities 49–51

Pagano, M. 28
Pakistan 7, 59; Islamic banking overview in 124–7; Islamic bank rent in 127–34, *135–6*; non-performing loans (NPLs) in 129
Pappas, V. 63
Patrick 1966 28
People's Bank of China 71, 78
political instability 52
political rent seeking 45
poor institutional structure 45
Posner, R. A. 156
Prahalad, C. K. 26
price rent opportunities 47–9
producer's surplus 16–17
profitability and specialization 17–18, 27
profit-and-loss sharing (PLS) contracts 3–4, 7–8
Pyle, D. H. 33–4

Qatar *see* Gulf Cooperative Council (GCC) countries
quantitative easing (QE) 8, 156–7, 178–9, 185; changes in rent opportunity during period of 168–74; in Japan 157–62, *163*; knife-edge hypotheses on market reference rate 163–8; negative interest rate regime and rents with 174–8; zero interest rate policy (ZIRP) and 157, 160–2, 168–74

rent, bank 3–7, 53–5; changes during period of QE and ZIRP 157, 160–2, 168–74; concept and its roles 14–19; conceptualization in Islamic banking 59–62, 122–4; creating franchise value 21, 40; creation in China 77–9; creation of 41–3; critical challenges

186; cube 54–5; default risk of borrowers and 19; defined as excess income 13, 16, 40, 181; effects of 39–41; extended model 46–53, 55–7; financial deepening and 21–4; financial restraint policy and 20–4; implications of new model of 55–7; macroeconomic rent opportunities 52–3; in negative interest rate regime 174–8; net benefit to society 16; operating rent opportunities 49–51; political rent seeking 45; price rent opportunities 47–9; types of 4
residual income 14
riba-based banking 64–6, 131, *132–3*, *135–6*
riba-free banking 64–6, 131, *132–3*
risk-taking 2, 22–3, 32–3, 41; imperfect information and 48
Robinson, J. 28
Rousseau, P. L. 28

Sahay, P. 104
Sambanis, N. 110
savings rate 22, 24, 30–1, 48–9; deposit collections in Sri Lanka 96–9; inflation and 44
Schumpeter, J. A. 27
Shari'ah compliant banking *see* Islamic banking
Shaw, E. S. 27, 34, 77
Simper, R. 102–3
Singh, N. 28
slack based model (SBM) 102–3
Slijepcevic, S. 27–8
socio-political instability and civil war in Sri Lanka 109–17
Soylu, A. 63
specialization 17–18, 27
Sri Lanka 7, 86, 118–19, 184; banking system stagnation in 89–92; bank ownership in 100–5; credit expansion in 99–100; deposit collection in 96–9; high and volatile inflation in 106–8; interest rates and branch network expansion in 92–100; macroeconomic context and banking system 86–8, *89*; socio-political instability associated with civil war in 109–17
State Bank of Pakistan (SBP) 127
Stiglitz, J. E. 2, 14, 39, 45–6, 77, 156
Strahan, P. E. 28
sunk costs 17

Sussman, O. 28
Suzuki, Y. 22, 117, 122

Tang, D. 28
Tang, S.H.K. 27
taxation and financial repression 20–1
Thailand 107
Thakor, A. V. 36
Tone, K. 102
transaction costs, banks
    economizing on 33–5
Tsai, K. S. 83

Uddin, S. 122
uncertainty absorbed by banks 35
United Arab Emirates *see* Gulf
    Cooperative Council (GCC) countries
United Kingdom 109, 179
United States 179

Villamil, A. P. 35

Wachtel, P. 28
Wakalah 60
Weiss, A. 14, 39, 77
Wholesale Price Index
    (WPI) 96
World Bank 9n1, 75, 178
World Development Indicators (WDI)
    1, 9n1

Xu, L. C. 75

Yilmazkuday, H. 28

Zaher, T. 62, 65
Zeira, J. 28
zero interest rate policy (ZIRP)
    157, 160–2, 168–74, 185

For Product Safety Concerns and Information please contact our EU
representative GPSR@taylorandfrancis.com Taylor & Francis Verlag GmbH,
Kaufingerstraße 24, 80331 München, Germany


Printed and bound by CPI Group (UK) Ltd, Croydon, CR0 4YY

01/05/2025

01858353-0001